AS Media Studies

John Price
Joe Nicholas

Published in 2003 by:
Nelson Thornes Ltd
Delta Place
27 Bath Road
CHELTENHAM
GL53 7TH
United Kingdom

03 04 05 06 07 / 10 9 8 7 6 5 4 3 2 1

A catalogue record for this book is available from the British Library

ISBN 0 7487 6840 8

Illustrations by IFA Design Ltd, Plymouth, Devon
Page make-up by IFA Design Ltd, Plymouth, Devon

Printed and bound in Great Britain by Scotprint

Introduction

This textbook is organised so that it is relevant to three exam board AS syllabuses – WJEC, AQA and OCR.

The organisation of the book is based on the WJEC format:

> Section A Analysing media forms (advertising, newspapers, magazines, films and television)
> Section B Representation and reception (including ethnicity/nationhood and gender)
> Section C Making media texts

Within that format the AQA topics of film and broadcast fiction, documentaries, advertising and marketing and British newspapers are covered.

The OCR topics for comparative textual study of consumerism in lifestyle magazines, celebrity in the tabloid press and gender in TV sitcoms are covered, as is the OCR topic for textual analysis in 2003/4 – action/adventure films.

The key concepts of narrative, genre, audience and institutions are explained and there are many activities designed to help students develop their understanding of these.

Acknowledgements

The authors and publishers would like to thank the copyright holders for permission to reproduce material.

Every effort has been made to contact copyright holders and we apologise if any have been overlooked. Should copyright have been unwittingly infringed in this book, the owners should contact the publishers who will make corrections at reprint.

Picture credits

p2 Pierce Brosnan: Kobal Collection/Tri-Star/Phoenix Pictures; p3 Nicole Kidman, Julia Roberts: Kobal Collection; p3 Denzel Washington: Kobal Collection/Bedford Falls/20th Century Fox; p3 *Psycho*: Kobal Collection/Paramount; p7 Rover Ad: Tim Bret Day; p8 Emirates Pic: Associated Press/Kamran Jebreili; p10 Amish boy: Kobal Collection/Paramount; p11 ©*Daily Mirror*: p16 *Roger Rabbit*: Kobal Collection/ Touchstone/Amblin; p29 all: BBC Picture Library; p32 *Stagecoach*: Kobal Collection/ United Artists; p33 *Unforgiven*: Kobal Collection/Warner Bros; p37 *Raiders of the Lost Ark*: Kobal Collection; p40 *French Connection*: Kobal Collection/20th Century Fox; p40 *French Connection*: Vinmag archive/20th Century Fox; p44 *Mask of Zorro*: Kobal Collection/Tristar/Amblin; p47 *Spinal Tap*: Kobal Collection/Spinal Tap Production; p52 *Cathy Come Home*: BBC Picture Library; p65 *Top Gun*: Kobal Collection/Paramount; p72 NI Syndication ©*The Times*; p73, 74 NI Syndication ©*Sun*; p80 Atlantic Syndication Mahood: *Daily Mail*/Atlantic Syndication; p80 Mac cartoon: *Daily Mail*/Atlantic Syndication; p81 Royal Family: Hulton Archive; p94 NI Syndication ©*News of the World*; p97 *The Patriot*: Kobal Collection/Columbia Tristar; p98 *Rules of Engagement*: Vinmag Archive; p103 top Protest: PA Photos/Stefan Rousseau; middle Protest: Guardian Syndication; bottom Protest: Getty Images/ Scott Barbour; p114 Jean Harlow: Kobal Collection; p110 Olivia De Havilland: Kobal Collection, Naomi Campbell: Rex Features Limited/CROLLALANZA, Ellen Macarthur: Rex Features Limited/Sipa, Mrs Thatcher: Rex Features Limited/David Cole, Princess Diana: Rex Features Limited/Tim Rooke, Kate Adie: Rex Features Limited/Sipa, Bodybuilding: Rex Features, Limited/Rex USA, Ab Fab: Rex Features Limited/Everett Collection, Charlie Dymock: Rex Features Limited/NILS JORGENSEN; p116 Vinnie Jones: Topham Picturepoint/Universal Pictorial Press, Soldier: Topham Picturepoint/Photri, Julian Clary: Rex Features Limited/Ken McKay, Man and Baby: Rex Features/Phanie Agency, Bin Laden: Rex Features/Sipa, Tyson: Rex Features/Mark Campbell; p117 Dennis the Menace and Walter the Softy: Vin Mag Archive/DC Thomson; p133 *American Beauty*: Vin Mag Archive/ Dreamworks/ Jinks/Cohen; p134 – 6 *American Beauty*: Kobal Collection/Dreamworks/Jinks/ Cohen; p138 *Titanic*: Kobal Collection/20th Century Fox/ Paramount; p142 *Small Time Crooks*: Kobal Collection/Dreamworks LLC; p153 NI Syndication ©*News of the World*; p156 ©*Daily Star*; p159 NI Syndication ©*Sun*; p166 *Livingetc*: IPC Media; p168 *Red* magazine: Hachette Filipacchi UK Ltd; p174 *Harpers and Queen*: National Magazine Company; p179 *Natural Born Killers*: Kobal Collection/Warner Bros; p180 Beavis & Butt-Head: Kobal Collection/Touchstone; p181 *Indiana Jones*: Vin Mag Archive; p186 Rupert Murdoch: Rex Features/Sipa; p188 Greg Dyke: Press Association/Fiona Hanson; p210 *Arlington Road*: Kobal Collection/Polygram/ Lakeshore; p223, 224 NI Syndication ©*News of the World*; p226, p227 NI Syndication ©*Sun*, p229 *Empire*: EMAP and *CD:uk*: Hachette Filipacchi UK Ltd.

Picture Research by Sue Sharp

Contents

Image analysis

INTRODUCTION

This chapter explains some of the technical terms you need to use in analysing media texts. It concentrates on how to analyse television and film. It shows you how to recognise different sorts of camerawork and different editing techniques. It helps you to be more aware of sound effects, casting decisions, use of make-up and costume, use of colour and the importance of settings. It explains technical terms such as mise en scène, metonymy, denotation and connotation and broadcast and narrowcast codes.

(a)

(b)

(c)

(d)

(e)

(a) Extreme long shot (ELS); (b) long shot (LS); (c) medium shot; (d) close-up (CU); (e) extreme close-up (ECU).

Moving images

When you analyse moving images in film and television you should consider the following:

- Camerawork
  Shot distance is the simplest variable. Normal shots include long shot, medium shot and close-ups. Less frequently used are extreme close-ups and extreme long shots. All these labels are defined by the amount of subject viewed. They are not definitive and when a medium shot becomes a long shot is debatable.
  Shot distance is used to ***influence the viewer's sympathies***. The normal distance is medium shot to close-up; which gives a comfortable relationship with the person on the screen. Extreme close-ups are used to make the viewer feel uncomfortable, with an evil character for instance, or to emphasise the tension felt by a person being interviewed.
  There is an implication here that ***seeing closely means seeing better***. Sometimes a camera person will zoom in on a face if there is some suggestion in an interview of lying or guilt.
  If an interviewee is placed in ***partial shade*** this can increase drama because it suggests that the viewer is being privileged to hear some significant, secret information.
  What to put in the ***frame*** can depend on the ***size of the frame***. The invention of widescreen formats like Cinemascope, for instance, led to an increase in landscape shots in Westerns.
  Film-makers can also decide whether to keep subjects in the frame, by letting the camera follow them when they move, for instance, or they can let the subject leave the frame and return. The former is called 'closed form', the latter 'open form'.
  The camera can ***move*** or be ***static***. Movement tends to draw attention to the film-making process, while the static camera does not distract the

The sleeping medicine is given prominence in this shot from *Citizen Kane*

viewer. However, moving, hand-held cameras are often used in documentaries to give the viewer the impression of having by chance come across something 'real'.

Proximity or ***nearness*** is important. Subjects close to the camera have greater importance. In the above picture a bottle of sleeping medicine is in the foreground, a woman is in bed in medium shot and in the background Kane enters the room. Reverse the order and the sleeping medicine becomes insignificant.

Soft focus, where parts of the image are slightly fuzzy, is usually associated with romantic moods. ***Shallow focus*** which has either the foreground, middle ground or background of the image in focus gives control to the film-maker who directs the viewer's attention. ***Deep focus***, which keeps everything in the image in focus, gives more power to the viewer who can select what to concentrate on. Deep focus is often used where realism is required.

- Editing

  The practice of beginning with an ***establishing shot*** to indicate place and perhaps time and atmosphere and then narrowing down from that generalisation is a convention common to film and television.

  Traditional Hollywood ***dialogue editing*** has come to seem natural to viewers, though in fact in reality we never experience a conversation in that manner, where we look alternately over each speaker's shoulder.

  Accelerated editing is a characteristic of chase scenes where the pace of the cutting from one shot to the next increases as the chase progresses, giving the viewer a sense of growing excitement.

  Parallel editing allows the viewer to see two simultaneous actions separately – this is a technique used in action films, particularly in chase sequences.

- Music and sound effects

  Music is often used to arouse ***emotions***, in effect encouraging the viewer to respond in a particular way to a scene. It can also indicate a ***locale***, so that for instance a calypso will indicate a West Indian setting.

  Early film sound systems were not sophisticated enough to allow for equal separation of voice, noise and music. Digital surround sound, introduced in

Casting: well-known actors have 'residues of meaning'.

Pierce Brosnan

Nicole Kidman

Denzel Washington

Julia Roberts

the 1990s, allowed a much greater flexibility. Whereas previously voice was privileged over music and noise, modern sound systems allow complex layers of all three to co-exist on the same ***soundtrack***. The result is a heightened realism.

- Casting
  The use of stars makes a film or TV programme have links with everything else that actor has appeared in. Well-known actors bring with them '***residues of meaning***' from other roles they have played and also from information about them in magazines, showbiz columns and other publicity. Conventionally, in fictional TV programmes involving violence, characters who are white, male, middle class or classless and in the prime of life are almost certain to be alive at the end of a programme. Conversely characters who deviate from the norm are likely to be killed, with the chances increasing the more 'deviant' they are.
- Body language
  Some stars have characteristic body language, trademarks by which they are recognised. Impressionists often rely on imitating body language as well as voice.
  Touch conveys messages about relationships. There is the fleeting, surreptitious touch that indicates a secret liaison, a tender touch that indicates affection, the grabbing of someone round the neck that indicates hostility, and so on. Touch is one of the most culturally variable of codes.
  Proximity carries messages which differ from culture to culture. Within a metre is regarded as 'intimate' by middle-class British and two metres as 'personal'. The distances are shorter for working class people and even more so for Arabs. Intimate proximity can be either loving or threatening.
  Gestures can be insulting, as with the V sign, or friendly, such as a wave, though again this varies between cultures. Frequent arm and hand movements can indicate emotional arousal or specific emotional states.
- Posture
  Our ways of standing, sitting or lying can carry meaning, such as hostility, friendliness, superiority or inferiority. Exaggerated emotional body language often indicates melodrama.
- Facial expression
  This shows less cross-cultural variation than other body language. It is mainly to do with the eyes. Staring can be threatening, though making eyes at someone can show a desire for more closeness. Facing each other can make some forms of communication difficult

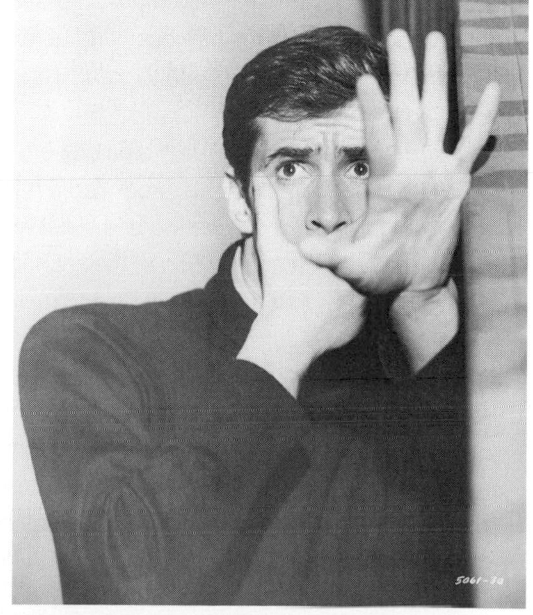
Anthony Perkins in *Psycho*

Activity

Discuss what 'residues of meaning' are attached to the actors in the figures on the previous pages. Write a treatment for a new film featuring any two of them. Describe briefly the kind of film it would be and the characters the actors would play.

A treatment is an outline of an idea for a film or TV programme. It should in this case say what genre of film you have in mind, what sort of story there is and who it is aimed at. Describe briefly the roles the actors would play and why you think the film would be commercially viable.

and it is noticeable that serious, confrontational or 'dangerous' conversations often take place while characters are travelling in cars and facing front, not looking at each other.

- Make-up and costume

  Appearance is used to send messages about ***social status***, ***personality*** and ***conformity***. In the second ***Blackadder*** series, social status was indicated by extravagant and decorative clothes of the most elevated (queens and generals) the good quality but less extravagant clothes and accessories of the upper class (Blackadder) and the dirty, tattered and dishevelled appearance and dress of the lower classes, such as servants (Baldric). Change in status is often signalled by change of dress, as in the films *Trading Places* (USA 1983) or ***Pretty Woman*** (USA 1990).

  Teenagers are particularly adept at dressing in a way that shows their defiance of adult values but emphasises their conformity to their peer group. Some genres such as science fiction, Westerns, war films and costume dramas depend to a large extent on costume.

- Colour

  Colours create different ***moods***. Bright colours are generally associated with happiness, for instance. Red and black are often linked to the dramatic, the deadly and the sexual.

  Sometimes colour is used for very specific effects, however. For example, Hitchcock's ***Marnie*** (USA 1964) begins with a close shot of the heroine's bright yellow pocketbook. The other colours are subdued. It seems as if the pocketbook is carrying the woman. This is the effect the director wants because, in fact, it is full of money and an example of how her life is dominated by her compulsion to steal. (See also 'metonymy' below.)

- Lighting

  Lighting can be used to create a natural effect. The Hollywood style of using key lights and fill lights produced a natural effect and is much used in television because it is flattering and suitable for glamour shots. Lighting from below can create a mood of melancholy, backlighting can either dominate or emphasise a subject, and highlighting can focus on a detail.

- *Mise en scène*

  Mise en scène refers to a film-maker's choice of what to shoot and how to shoot it. How a shot is to be framed or ***what will be placed in the frame*** is something that involves balance, shape, form, space, light, colour, movement, set design, properties, costume and so on. The ***mise en scène*** can be rich, as in the opening sequence of the film ***The Piano*** (Australia 1993), or it can be sparse, as in many of the warehouse shots in ***Reservoir Dogs*** (USA 1991).

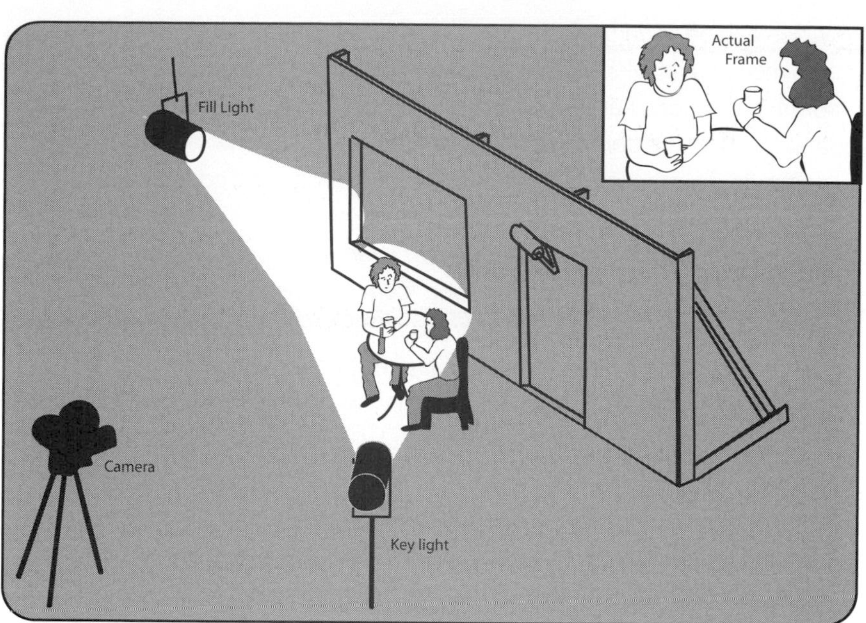

Hollywood style lighting

- Settings
  A setting involves both *time* and *space*. Is the setting in the contemporary world, in the past, e.g. most war films like ***Schindler's List*** (USA 1993) or ***Braveheart*** (USA 1995), in a hypothetical future, e.g. ***Minority Report*** (USA 2002) or ***Blade Runner*** (USA 1992), or in some unspecified time, as in fantasy films such as ***Lord of the Rings*** (USA 2001, 2002)?
  What is the ***location***? In what country, which town, which building? Is the location vast, or confined, urban or rural, glamorous or seedy?
- Metonymy
  A metonym is a figure of speech in which an associated detail is used to invoke an idea or represent an object.
  In films it is a kind of ***cinematic shorthand***. The falling pages of a calendar indicate the passage of time, a close up of the moving wheels of a train indicates a journey. A man's face seen in a cracked mirror is a metonym for schizophrenia (split personality).
  In his book ***How to Read a Film*** (Oxford University Press 2000) James Monaco describes director Michelangelo Antonioni's use of the 'metonymics of colour' in ***Red Desert*** (Italy/France 1964):
  'Throughout most of the film, Guiliana is oppressed psychologically and politically by a grey and deathly urban industrial environment. When she manages to break away from its grip on several occasions, Antonioni signals her temporary independence (and possible return to health) with bright colours, which is a detail associated with health and happiness not only in this film but in general culture as well.'
- Broadcast and narrowcast codes
  A broadcast code is one that is ***shared by members of a mass audience***. It has to recognise the common values of the audience. A narrowcast code is one which is aimed at a ***specialised audience*** which is able to understand it because it is familiar with the terms or reference being used. So, a performance by Westlife uses broadcast codes, in terms of movements, dress, appearance, gestures, lyrics, song structure, backing music, etc.,

which can be understood by many people. An operatic aria, however, which is aimed at a smaller, more specialised audience, uses narrowcast codes. Broadcast codes have to be easily understood, and have immediate appeal. They are ***community oriented***, appealing to what people have in common. They have to be in tune with the feelings and concerns of society at large. The success of the Pop Idol TV formula was due to its ability to be ***in tune with some viewers' values and interests***. It dealt with competition, entertainment, success and rejection, comradeship and individuality, courage, stress and humour. This was all done with the participation, in a minor way, of the audience through the telephone voting procedure as contestants were eliminated. Millions of viewers were involved in the final decision, with almost half the adult population declaring for Gareth or Will, the two finalists.

Narrowcast codes are aimed at a defined, limited audience. They do not depend on conformity, on shared communal experience, but on common educational or intellectual experiences. They are individualist and person-orientated. The audience expects to be ***enriched*** or ***changed*** by the communication, whereas broadcast audiences expect to be reassured.

Denotation and connotation

Words, sounds and images have layers of meanings which depend on the culture of the person interpreting them.

To illustrate, a dog is a dog is a dog. However, in Britain most of us consider ***dogs*** as pets, yet British farmers regard sheep dogs as ***workers***, pet shop owners probably regard them as ***commodities*** and vets see them as ***patients***.

Meanwhile in the mythical country of Oskaa they are regarded as ***gods***. Oskaavites revere and worship them, whereas in the neighbouring mythical country of Gutsi, dogs are eaten with relish and regarded as a ***culinary delicacy***.

Analysis of images, words and sounds needs to be on two levels – that of the ***literal meaning*** and then at the level of the ***associated*** or ***deeper meaning***, which depends on the culture of the reader. These two levels are labelled as denotation and connotation.

Case study

CASE STUDY CASE STUDY CASE STU

Here, as an example, is a brief analysis of a still image for the print advertisement shown on the next page. (Denotation and connotation analysis applies equally to still or moving images.)

THE SURFACE MEANING (DENOTATION)

The scene is a modern looking, quiet section of an airport. A private jet is being unloaded. An attractive and expensively dressed woman is moving away from the plane from which it seems she has emerged. She has two jaguars on leads. She is looking in surprise over her shoulder at a young man who is carrying luggage and which he seems about to place in the

'Just one of life's little luxuries', Rover advert in *Sunday Times* magazine 13/1/02

CASE STUDY CASE STUDY CASE STUDY CASE STUDY CASE STUDY CASE STUDY

boot of a Rover car which is parked next to the plane. Behind the woman is another young man who is stepping down from the plane and carrying more luggage.

THE ASSOCIATED MEANINGS OR CONNOTATIONS

The purpose of the images is to impress the reader with the Rover car. It is trying to attract, among others, people who would like to buy a Jaguar car but can't afford one.

The images suggest that the car is linked with expensive lifestyles, sex and youthfulness. The private jet suggests lavish living and huge private wealth. The youth of the woman, her expensive clothes, carefully cultivated looks, exotic pets and copious luggage suggest the lifestyle of a film star.

The young men who are her attendants could have any kind of relationship with her, but the slightly challenging, flirtatious look of the young man near the car suggests a certain familiarity. It could be her partner, as indeed could the young man standing obediently behind her.

There is an ambiguity here which is deliberate and hints at an unconventional liaison. There is a tension in the image. The beautiful, rich young woman is about to make a decision. Will she go into the car, will it hold all her luggage, who will comfort the jaguars? Perhaps she will discard the jaguars (and indirectly Jaguar cars) and settle for the Rover and her young partner(s).

SE STUDY

So, if we assume that this advert is aimed mainly at middle-aged men, the car promises associations with wealth and beautiful women who will become 'tamed' and give up their interest in both jaguars and Jaguars. And the two young men can follow on with the luggage in a taxi.

Activity

Analyse the image below in terms of its denotations and connotations.

SECTION A **Chapter 2**

Narrative

Introduction

Narrative is a more technical word for story or stories. All media products can be analysed as texts with narrative aspects that include storyline, character, narration, point of view, etc.

The purpose of this kind of analysis is to help you become aware of common patterns that you may not otherwise notice. Narrative theory is concerned not with the content of individual stories but with *what stories have in common*.

This chapter helps you to understand the concept of narrative codes, showing how the cultural experiences of the 'readers' of the texts affect both their interpretation and enjoyment. In other words it is about understanding how media audiences come to interpret and gain pleasure from stories.

The chapter will help you to answer the following questions:

- What is a story?
- What makes a good story?
- How do stories work?
- How are stories structured?
- How can you analyse narrative aspects of media products?
- How can you improve your own storytelling?

Activity

Examine how pervasive storytelling is in your life. List three stories you hear during the course of a day. Say who told the story and how far your response to it was affected by the storyteller. Write a report of your findings.

These are some of the sorts of story you might come across:

- accounts of sporting fixtures, including accounts that seem to differ according to the allegiance of the teller;
- accounts of break-ups in relationships with allocation of blame and explanation of causes;
- excuses from friends who have forgotten our birthdays or failed to turn up at a social gathering;
- media stories in fiction, e.g. dramas and soap operas;
- media stories in news broadcasts, wildlife programmes, documentaries and even quiz shows.

Narrative structures

Todorov

The story analyst Tzvetan Todorov suggested that all stories are based on a change from *equilibrium* to *disequilibrium*. This can also be described as stability versus instability or stasis versus change.

The Amish boy in *Witness*

For example, in ***Witness*** (USA 1985) the film begins with a portrayal of the equilibrium of the Amish community living in the countryside of the United States. The community comes from a German ethnic background and shares a stable religious lifestyle which has not changed in hundreds of years.

The instability that is to come from a collision between this age-old community and the modern world is hinted at in the opening sequence where a long shot of an Amish horse and carriage is juxtaposed with a huge lorry in the background of the frame.

An incident upsets the equilibrium. Such an incident is called an '***inciting incident***' or '***an agent of change***'. An Amish boy, who has come to the city with his mother to visit a relative, witnesses a man being murdered in a public toilet. The boy is hidden in the toilet and evades discovery. Once he is identified as a potential witness, the narrative of disequilibrium begins.

Activity

Analyse the following news stories as two-part narrative structures by summarising briefly the states of equilibrium and disequilibrium.

Story A

Jim, a shop assistant in a general store in Birmingham, had already been held up in another job when he was attacked by a man with a pistol.

> "I was cashing up at about 9.15 a.m. A girl came in wanting to know if there were any jobs.
> While I was talking to her – I realised later she was part of the gang – her accomplice came into the shop.
> He came up behind me and held a gun to my head. He told me to hand over the cash and some other goods."
> The gunman locked Jim in a meat freezer and escaped.
> The attack left Jim in a state of shock. "I'd left my previous job in an off-licence after I got held up with a knife.
> When it happened a second time it just tipped me over the edge. My manager told me to buy a bottle of whisky and take some time off."

Jim had to have counselling but has not been able to return to his job.

Suggest an ending to this story which would provide a new equilibrium.

Story B

BACK ON BOOZE

Ozzy drinking again over his wife's cancer

HELLRAISER: Ozzy's wild days

ILLNESS: Sharon, who is fighting cancer of the colon, with husband Ozzy

ROCK wildman Ozzy Osbourne is back on the booze as he struggles to cope with his wife's cancer, it was revealed yesterday.

By MARK ELLIS, Foreign Editor

Sharon Osbourne, who has cancer of the colon, let slip that the former Black Sabbath star had started drinking again. Ozzy, 53, became a household name in America with the fly-on-the-wall MTV show The Osbournes. But Sharon told a US chat show the family would not be inviting the cameras into their Beverly Hills home again.

She said: "This is definitely the last year. We can't do it anymore. We agreed to do the show and so the cameras are here all the time.

"It's a little bit invasive right now and we have no privacy. You know when you're sick, you want to be on your own. I can't throw up on my own and Ozzy can't get drunk on his own."

The series made the lives of Ozzy, Sharon and their children, Kelly and Jack, cult viewing as TV's most dysfunctional family and a new 10-part series starts on MTV later this month.

Sharon, 50, revealed the show, which drew record ratings, had changed their lives.

Apart from Ozzy drinking, she said Kelly and Jack now had their own lawyers and business managers.

She added: "Because it's a moment in time when we were innocent to it all, we went in feet first and you can't re-create that. In this series people will see what the first series has done to our lives and it will take people to the next stage. But after that, it's over."

The decision will shock American audiences who this week tuned into an MTV special, Catching Up With The Osbournes.

The family will be back in the spotlight in January when they present the American Music Awards.

But MTV boss Van Toffler said he still expected the family to do another series, which would be screened next year. He said: "Sharon was probably having a difficult time and she was venting it at that moment.

"I've developed a sort of iron stomach because of Sharon Osbourne's volatility. I'm accustomed to this and perhaps the rest of the country isn't."

The first series of The Osbournes starts this Friday on Channel 4.

m.ellis@mgn.co.uk

(*Daily Mirror* 6/11/02)

BACK ON BOOZE

Rock wild man Ozzy Osbourne is back on the booze as he struggles to cope with his wife's cancer, it was revealed yesterday.

Sharon Osbourne, who has cancer of the colon, let slip that the former Black Sabbath star had started drinking again. Ozzy, 53, became a household name in America with the fly-on-the-wall MTV show The Osbournes. But Sharon told a US chat show the family would not be inviting the cameras into their Beverly Hills home again.

She said: "This is definitely the last year. We can't do it any more. We agreed to do the show and so the cameras are here all the time. It's a little bit invasive and we have no privacy. You know, when you're sick you want to be on your own. I can't throw up on my own and Ozzy can't get drunk on his own."

The series made the lives of Ozzy, Sharon and their children, Kelly and Jack, cult viewing as TV's most dysfunctional family and a new 10-part series starts on MTV later this month.

Sharon, 50, revealed how the show, which drew record ratings, had changed their lives. "Because it's a moment in time when we were innocent to it all, we went in feet first and you can't recreate that. In this series people will see what the first series has done to our lives."

Three-part narrative structures

There is an argument that a story must have a minimum of three elements in its structure. For example, take the biblical story of Adam and Eve.

'Eve persuaded Adam to eat the apple of the knowledge of good and evil' is one element. Add 'Adam blamed Eve' and arguably the story is still incomplete. The argument is that no story exists until there are at least three elements:

1 God told Adam and Eve not to eat from the tree of knowledge.
2 Eve persuaded Adam to eat an apple from the tree.
3 God expelled them from paradise.

This is sometimes called the '***rule of three***'. You will already have come across the much repeated reminder that every story must have a beginning, a middle and an end.

Todorov's theory of narrative structure develops into three parts. He argues that narratives work by overturning a pre-existing stability. The narrative then proceeds through instability and its ***resolution***, which is a new stability.

Thus in the film ***Witness***, the middle of the film consists of the instabilities of the pursuit of the Amish boy by the 'bad guys' and a love story involving the 'good guy' and the boy's mother.

The new stability is established, not only by the defeat of the bad guys, but also by the departure of the good guy and the return of the mother to a suitor from her community.

The three-part narrative structure can be seen as:

1 Beginning
Setting, character and a starting point for the narrative are established.
Conflict is established and equilibrium is threatened.

2 Middle
   Relationships between characters become complicated. Conflict increases. Instability is moved towards a point of crisis.

3 End
   The crisis reaches a climax. Some things are resolved, some unresolved. A new stability is indicated or established.

This structure is a useful starting point from which to move on and analyse ***ideology***.

Ideology refers to views of the world such as those put forward as personal beliefs, ethical values or political allegiance. The selection and treatment of story content inevitably results in some degree of ideological bias, which narrative structure analysis can reveal. It all depends on what is seen as equilibrium (the norm) and what as disequilibrium.

This becomes especially apparent in three-part narrative structures where, after disequilibrium, a ***new equilibrium*** is established. The question then is whether order returned because of the power of force, resistance, violence, punishment, revenge, forgiveness, repentance, reward or whatever. There is always an ideological element in the survival or transformation of a particular order. Some possibilities are:

- the power of love,
- the toughness and ruthlessness of law enforcement,
- the value of forgiveness,
- a new self-awareness,
- a religious conversion.

Four-part structure

This theory looks at these topics:

- What problem does the story examine?
- What solution does it offer?
- What is the background to the story?. That is, what do we need to know in order to understand the problem?
- How should the solution be evaluated?

This is referred to as the BPSE structure: Background – Problem – Solution – Evaluation. An important point to remember is that these elements are often *repeated* within a story and they can crop up *in any order*.

Activity

Analyse this newspaper story as a four-part narrative identifying background, problem, solution and evaluation.

THUGS FORCE WONDERBOY WAYNE OUT OF HIS HOME

Football wonderkid Wayne Rooney and his family are moving house – after hate mobs vandalised their car.

Thugs used nails to puncture tyres on the Rooneys' people carrier in two separate attacks outside their council semi.

Wayne senior uses the blue Ford Galaxy to drive his 17-year-old son to Everton training sessions and matches at Goodison Park.

Now club bosses are moving the Rooneys into a plush £250,000 pad.

Wayne hit the news with stunning strikes against Arsenal and Leeds and is about to sign a contract that will make him the highest paid youngster in English football.

Last night one neighbour said: "He's making the headlines and that gets up some people's noses. The kids round here love him but others are probably jealous. The trouble is that they will probably do the same wherever he moves to."

(Adapted from the *Sun* 9/11/02, with permission)

Six-part narrative structure

Here is a six-part narrative structure. It is similar to the BPSE pattern. It was evolved mainly by William Labov in order to analyse spoken, face-to-face communication. It consists of these terms: abstract, orientation, complicating action, evaluation, resolution and coda.

- Abstract – what is it all about and why is it being told?
- Orientation – who is who, when and where did it happen and how did it begin?
- Complicating action – what happened then? This is the central part of the story.
- Evaluation – so what? What was the impact of these events? Why are these events worth recounting?
- Resolution – what happened in the end?
- Coda – this wraps up the story by returning to reality. For example, news bulletins end up with a signing off such as 'From me for now, that's all'.

Here is a news story adapted from the ***Guardian*** of 17 December 2002. The story is of the 'hard news' genre: it concerns crime, is packed with realistic detail and contains quotations from a police officer. It follows the 'upside-down pyramid' structure of hard news reporting, that is to say that the most important information is at the top of the story, with the least important at the end. The Labov structure seems to apply as follows:

- The headline and opening paragraph provide an abstract or summary of the story.

  Headline: Hunt for robber as missing student flies home.

  Paragraph 1

  Police are searching for a homeless man in Manchester who is alleged to have robbed student Vicky Stephenson whose four-day disappearance sparked a national search.

- The next paragraph seems to perform the function of ***resolution***. The story seems to set up the ending before going back to the previous action. It answers the question 'What happened in the end?'

  Paragraph 2

  Detectives in the city interviewed the 19-year-old yesterday after her return from Dublin where she walked into a police station on Saturday saying she had been traumatised by the attack.

- The story then goes back to an ***orientation*** which explains how it all began.

  Paragraph 3

  The teenager, who comes from Norwood, south London, started a community studies and sociology course at Manchester Metropolitan University this year. She disappeared after going to interview the homeless man as part of her course.

- The ***complicating*** action is recounted in the next two and a half paragraphs.

  Paragraphs 4, 5 and 6

  She told police she had arranged to meet him in Cheadle, on the southern edge of Manchester, but he had forced her to hand over her credit cards and mobile phone.

  Officers had combed waste ground and scrub along the three mile route to her meeting place with the homeless man from her student flat.

  Detective Superintendent Peter Minshall said:

  > "Traumatised by the robbery, Vicky subsequently made her way to Dublin where she has family."

- The rest of paragraph 6 arguably moves on to an ***evaluation*** of the story in terms of the feelings of the student and her family.

  Paragraph 6 continued

  > "She is extremely upset about the whole situation – not least because her friends and family have been terribly worried about her. She would now like to put this behind her and get on with her life."

- The final paragraph is more open to interpretation. It could be seen to fit the ***coda*** category or it could be argued that it is part of the ***resolution*** of the story.

  Paragraph 7

  Ms Stephenson, who flew back from Dublin with two Greater Manchester police officers, has been reunited with her parents and the family of her best friend, with whom she has lived since she was 16.

  Note that the coda in a newspaper story could be seen to be typographical – a line, border, or another headline indicating that the story is finished.

Classical structure

Robert McKee in his study of cinema screenwriting identifies a *classical structure* of narrative which he says is 'the meat, potatoes, pasta, rice and couscous of world cinema. For the past one hundred years it has informed the vast majority of films that have found an international audience.'

He cites a wide variety of film stories as examples of the structure, including:

The Great Train Robbery (USA 1904)
The Battleship Potemkin (USSR 1925)

Citizen Kane (USA 1941)
Brief Encounter (UK 1945)
The Seven Samurai (Japan 1954)
The Seventh Seal (Sweden 1957)
2001: A Space Odyssey (USA 1968)
A Fish Called Wanda (UK 1988)
Thelma and Louise (USA 1991)
Four Weddings and a Funeral (UK 1994)
Shine (Australia 1996)

The characteristics of the structure are:

1 Closed ending
All questions raised by the story are answered. Emotions stirred are satisfied and the audience leaves feeling they have had a rounded, closed experience.
A story climax of absolute, irreversible change that answers questions raised by the telling and satisfies all audience emotion is called a ***closed ending***.
A story climax that leaves some questions unanswered and some emotion unfulfilled is an ***open ending***.
2 External rather than internal conflict
Characters may have inner struggles but the emphasis is on their struggles with personal relationships, social institutions or forces in the physical world.
3 Single rather than multiple protagonist
One main character is at the heart of the telling of the story.
4 Active rather than passive protagonist
The main character tends to be active and dynamic, wilfully pursuing his/her goals through increasing conflict and change.
5 Linear rather than non-linear time
Linear time is where the story is told in a chronological order. There may be use of flashbacks but the audience can follow what happened and when. Non-linear stories blur continuity so that the audience cannot sort out what happens before and after what. The film ***Memento*** (USA 2000) is a good example of non-linear time.

What's real in *Who Framed Roger Rabbit?*

6 Causality rather than coincidence
The story is driven by actions which cause effects which lead to more actions which cause more effects, and so on, rather than things happening by accident.

7 Consistent realities
In a fictional reality the rules must not be changed. McKee gives the example of ***Who Framed Roger Rabbit?*** (USA 1988). A human chases a cartoon character (Roger) towards a closed door. Roger suddenly flattens into two dimensions and slides under the door. The human crashes into the door. This is now a story rule that has to be followed if the 'reality' of the fiction is to be upheld. No human can catch Roger because he can switch to two dimensions and escape.

Propp's spheres of action

Some narrative study focuses not on what characters are but *what they do*.

Vladimir Propp analysed one hundred Russian folk tales and found an identical narrative structure in each of them. He identified '***spheres of action***' where he was more concerned with what characters did than what they were. So the villain fighting or pursuing the hero is a sphere of action which could be performed by different characters at different times: 'The functions of characters are stable constant elements in a tale, independent of how and by whom they are fulfilled.'

The eight character roles and their spheres of action are:

- the villain – villainy, fighting, action;
- the donor or provider – giving, magical agent or helper;
- the helper – moves the hero, makes good a lack, rescues from a pursuit, solves difficult tasks, transforms the hero;
- the princess and her father – a sought-for person who assigns difficult tasks, brands, exposes, recognises, punishes;
- the dispatcher – sends the hero on quest or mission;
- the hero – departs on search, reacts to donor, attempts difficult tasks, marries;
- the false hero – unfounded claims to hero's sphere of action.

Activity

Referring to any soap opera, situation comedy or individual film that you know well, identify and describe as many of Propp's character roles as you can. How close a fit can you find?

Note Sarah Kozloff's warning in *Narrative Theory and Television in Channels of Discourse Reassembled*: '...followers of Propp are overly casual in their application of his schema, using it piecemeal, constantly stretching points, making exceptions, and forcing things to fit.'

Compare Propp's list of character functions with Carl Jung's ***archetypes***.

Archetypes

Psychologist Carl Jung developed theories about a collective unconscious, that is a kind of knowledge that we are all born with which influences our behaviour and experiences without our being aware of it. Examples of this are love at first sight, déjà vu or the feeling that we have been here before, and the similar recollections which are reported by people from different cultures after near-death experiences.

Jung studied the traditional stories of different cultures and different periods of history and traced ***patterns of storytelling*** and images which kept cropping up. If he was right then there are a limited number of ***character types and themes***, a basic unwritten formula for stories, understood intuitively by both producers of texts and the audience. The characteristics of the people in the story will vary, in terms of appearance and personality, but the ***basic types*** are constant. Certain ***themes***, such as good versus evil, the need for life to have some purpose or direction and the problem of the misfit or outsider in society, will ***recur***.

Here are some of the archetypes he identified.

The mother figure. We are born with the need to be mothered; we have an in-built ability to recognise a certain relationship which can be called 'mothering'. We project the archetype onto a particular person, usually our own mother, but we can also turn it into a story-book character.

In mythology this is the earth mother persona, in western tradition it is Eve or Mary, but it can also be ***symbolised impersonally*** by the church or the nation or the forest or the ocean.

According to Jung, someone whose own mother had failed to satisfy the demands of the archetype may well spend his or her life seeking comfort in the church or meditating on the figure of Mary or spending a life at sea.

The shadow. The shadow is derived from our pre-human, animal past. It is the dark side of our being and is amoral, neither good nor bad. When we were animals we could be tender (e.g. when caring for offspring) or vicious (e.g. when killing for food). But as humans we have learned to abhor brutality and we are ashamed of those aspects of our thoughts and behaviour which seem animal. The shadow is the repository of those aspects which we do not want to admit to. We deny it in ourselves and project it onto others who are seen as enemies, outsiders or exotic presences. So we are fascinated by the great shadow image Satan, by outlaws like Robin Hood, by strange powerful figures like the Terminator or Batman. Symbols of this shadow can be snakes, monsters and demons.

The persona. This is the mask that we put on in public. It is the self which we want others to recognise. It can be used to create a false impression and it can delude ourselves. For example, see the transformations in the film ***The Mask*** (USA 1994) and Johnny Depp believing he is Don Juan in the film ***Don Juan De Marco*** (USA 1995).

Anima and animus. Jung believed that we are all bisexual to a certain extent. We learn our gender roles through socialisation. That is, society teaches us to behave and think in different ways. A strong socialising tendency in many societies is for women to be caring and less aggressive and for men to be strong and less emotional.

Jung felt that by living up to such expectations people were, in effect, developing only part of their full potential. He called the female aspect present in the collective unconscious of men the 'anima' and the male aspect present in the collective unconscious of women the 'animus'. This archetype is seen as being responsible for love life, the theory being that we are always looking for our other half in members of the opposite sex.

The anima may appear as an exotic dancing girl or a weathered old hag, the form reflecting whatever our present needs are. The animus may appear as an exotic, sensual young man or as an old grouch like the Wizard of Oz. Lois Lane has no interest in Clark Kent, but she is infatuated with her animus, Superman.

The father. Any authority figure.

The child. This represents the future, becoming, rebirth, the promise of new beginnings.

Mana or spiritual power. Sometimes symbolised as the hero figure, e.g. Luke Skywalker in the Star Wars films.

The maiden. Representing purity or innocence and naiveté, e.g. Princess Leia, who later becomes the animus.

The wise old man. He guides the hero and often has magical powers, e.g. Merlin, Gandalf or Obi Wan Kenobi.

The trickster. Always causing trouble for the hero. In Norse mythology many of the gods' adventures are originated by the tricks played by the half-god Loki.

Activity

Watch the film *The Pianist* (Poland/France/UK 2002) and then analyse the narrative structure using one of the theories outlined above.

Divide the class into groups. Each group is given or chooses a narrative structure theory – equilibrium, BPSE, six-part structure, classical or spheres of action.

Individuals work at home trying to apply the theory to the film.

Exchange ideas and responses in group discussion, trying to find reasons for difficulties rather than aiming at a consensus.

Each group reports its findings to the rest of the class.

Narrative codes

There are always *intended meanings* from the people who produce the media text and *interpreted meanings* from the people who read/see/hear it. These will differ unless the *mode of expression* is understood by both the sender and the receiver. For this to happen there need to be codes which are learned through experience. In other words, meanings will be encoded by the narrator and decoded by the person seeing, hearing or reading the story.

Programme-specific codes

Sometimes in television and film these codes can be *programme-specific*. When Clark Kent goes into a phone box, experienced viewers have learned that he will turn into Superman and that a heroic rescue will ensue. Similarly Popeye fans know that when he eats his spinach he gains extraordinary strength and some remarkable physical feat is about to take place.

Roland Barthes' codes

The French critic Roland Barthes put forward a scheme of five types of narrative coding useful for analysing stories.

1 The action code
Actions have a logical relationship to the real world. For example, a journey involves preparation, departure, travel and arrival.
We know from our viewing experience that certain actions will lead to other actions. The gunslinger draws his gun on his adversary and we know there will be an exchange of shots, but we want to find out what the result will be. We wait to see if he kills his opponent or is wounded himself. Suspense is created by action rather than by a wish to have a mystery explained.

Another example would be the packing of a suitcase, which tells us (because we have seen this action in other films or television drama) that there is a confrontation or an escape in the offing.
A nun in ***The Magdelene Sisters*** (UK 2002) reprimands a girl for talking to someone outside the convent walls and then picks up a leather strap and the audience expects the girl to be beaten.

2 The semic code
This code includes all signs and meanings in the text which depict character.
For example, in traditional horror films characters are linked to the supernatural through typical signifiers, e.g. fear of light/the day, rapid increase of body hair, stiff, mechanical limb movements, monotone voices and so on.

3 Mystery code
There are mystery or enigma codes for puzzling the audience and increasing suspense. These codes raise questions on the part of viewers which we want answering. We are not satisfied by a narrative unless all the loose ends are tied up. The opening sequence in ***Memento*** (USA 2000), for

instance, has reverse action with a Polaroid photo fading and sliding back into a camera, a corpse reviving, a gun pulled from the head, a bullet sucked back into the barrel. Not only do we want answers to who has been killed by whom and why, but why everything happens backwards.

Another example would be the 'love triangle' where protagonist C is pulled in two directions by a desire for character A on the one hand and character B on the other. This generates questions such as should C choose A or B? Whom will C choose? Which was the right choice?

The participation of the audience in the mystery code involves trying to second-guess and having hunches confirmed or contradicted by the turns in the story.

4 The cultural code

Stories make sense and possess realism by making reference to information which is part of the real world. For example, James Bond has tastes for products such as Martini which are part of the real world. Likewise advertisers often construct stories around their products which encourage the reader to want to participate – by buying and using the product. Note that it can be difficult to separate out the semic and the cultural codes.

5 Code of oppositions

These are binary opposites such as nature v civilisation, life v death, childishness v maturity, etc. It is useful when looking at oppositions to consider which 'side' the narrative favours.

Activity

Here are some examples of the narrative codes outlined above, taken from *My Big Fat Greek Wedding* (USA 2002). Which code would you match them with?

a) There are many references to the Greek language. The Greek father, Gus, believes that most words in the English language derive from Greek and his son keeps prompting his sister's boyfriend/fiancé to make comments in Greek, which are in reality somewhat rude.

b) There is a long shot of the New York skyline from the sea.

c) The film seems to be built around an in-group (Greeks) versus an out-group (white Anglo-Saxon types.)

d) The main character, Toula, has been concealing something torn from a newspaper. She reads it but the contents are still hidden from the viewing audience.

e) An important set of key signs indicate 'Greek civilisation' – such as porticoes, columns and copies of classical statues.

f) At one point the main character goes through a makeover: she exchanges her unstylish glasses for contact lenses, uses make-up to enhance her appearance and transforms herself from 'frump' to a more conventionally attractive person.

g) The Greek father of the main character is chauvinist and xenophobic. That is, he believes Greek culture is superior to all others and foreigners are only OK as long as they don't try to do things like marry his daughter.

Note that it is possible to apply more than one code in some cases.

Case study

Here is an analysis of a story using Barthes' theories about codes.

THINGS MY GIRLFRIEND AND I ARGUE ABOUT

by Mil Millington (*Guardian* 31/1/03, reproduced with permission)

Music. I'd like to say that Our Tune is the Sex Pistols' Anarchy in the UK, but that's just because I'm a tremendous wag and much-in-demand after-dinner speaker.

We have no Our Tune. We also listen to music in different rooms, and in the car there's a constant low-level scuffle as Margret uses her other hand (i.e. the one she's not using to operate the indicator while I'm driving) to war with me over the radio station.

Just as she does when I'm watching a Nastassja Kinski or Angelina Jolie movie, if she ever walks in and I'm listening to Kate Bush or Alanis Morissette or Bjork, Margret will tut, "Chhk – one of your Mad Women, eh?". (Which, you know – Stones? Glass houses?) She appreciates neither White Zombie nor Clawfinger, nor even Black Grape. And yet she can put on a Moby CD without any hint of irony. Moby. Jesus – how close have you got to be to not caring whether you're alive or dead to listen to Moby?

But music itself doesn't generally cause any arguments. What does start warming things up is this habit she has, this reflex, of turning down the volume of whatever I'm listening to as she passes. It doesn't matter that she's not going to be in the room – she might just have popped in to collect something immediately before leaving for a month in Egypt.

Neither does it matter how loud it is – quite possibly, I could be listening with headphones on – she will always pause as she moves by and reduce the volume by a third.

The only civilised response to this, of course, is for me to rise and pointedly turn it back up, to a third louder than it was originally. I think you can save me time by predicting for yourselves how events progress from this point.

Analysis

The story explains how the narrator and his girlfriend come to argue about things such as their taste in music and movies, and the appropriate volume to listen to audio.

Character

The character code is relatively straightforward and on the surface. There is the writer who appears to be writing about himself, and his girlfriend Margret. The column is humorous and thus he (Mil) has a distinctive sense of humour, whereas he hints that his girlfriend is perhaps more serious.

> 'Yet she can put on a Moby CD without a hint of irony. Moby. Jesus – how close have you got to be to not caring whether you're alive or dead to listen to Moby?'

In this particular story, respective characters are revealed partly through their taste in music. Perhaps she likes Moby; he certainly doesn't. This could lead on to the cultural reference code and the action code.

The cultural reference code

The story is very much about taste in popular culture, music in particular. The music and artists we recognise enhance the realism of the narrative and place it in the context of a cultural world we recognise and share – The Sex Pistols, Natassja Kinski, Kate Bush, etc. There is also a reference to a well known proverb about stones and glass houses.

The mystery code

This code seems less apparent in the story. However, the narrative does end with a lack of closure and an implied question.

> 'I think you can save me time by predicting for yourselves how events progress from this point.'

This shows how the mystery code is engaged with the participation of the audience. We may be left wondering whether our own expectations of what will happen subsequently is what the author anticipated.

Binary oppositions

The oppositions include the following:

male v female; alive v dead; war v peace; high v low; civilised v uncivilised; sanity v insanity.

In some cases the opposites are actually words used in the text, e.g. alive or dead. Other oppositions are less clear, as only one side is explicitly used in the text. For example, war is used, peace is not, which shows the bias of the piece towards the male point of view.

Activity

Working on your own or in pairs, examine the use of everyday actions in the narrative above. How do the actions increase suspense for the reader?

Activity

Prepare a storyboard for a film version of the following incident from Fleming's novel *Diamonds Are Forever*. Then explain which of Barthes' narrative codes you have used.

'Bond had walked for only a few minutes when it suddenly occurred to him that he was being followed. There was no evidence for it except a slight tingling of the scalp and an extra awareness of the people near him, but he had faith in his sixth sense and he at once stopped in front of the shop window he was passing and looked casually back along 46th Street. Nothing but a lot of miscellaneous people moving slowly along the sidewalks, mostly on the same side as himself, the side that was sheltered from the sun. There was no sudden movement into a doorway, nobody casually wiping his face with a handkerchief to avoid recognition, nobody bending down to tie a shoelace.

Bond examined the Swiss watches in his shop window and then turned and sauntered on. After a few steps he stopped again. Still nothing. He went on and turned right into the Avenue of the Americas, stopping in the first doorway, the entrance to a women's underwear store where a man in a tan suit with his back to him was examining the black lace pants on a particularly realistic dummy. Bond turned and leant against a pillar and gazed lazily but watchfully out into the street.

And then something gripped his pistol arm and a voice snarled: "All right, Limey. Take it easy unless you want lead for lunch," and he felt something press into his back just above the kidneys.

What was there familiar about that voice? The Law? The Gang? Bond glanced down to see what was holding his right arm. It was a steel hook. Well, if the man had only one arm! Like lightning he swivelled, bending sideways and bringing his left fist round in a flailing blow, low down.

There was a smack as his fist was caught in the other man's left hand, and at the same time as the contact telegraphed to Bond's mind that there could have been no gun, there came the well remembered laugh and a lazy voice saying: "No good, James. The angels have got you."

Bond straightened himself slowly and for a moment he could only gaze into the grinning hawk-like face of Felix Leitter with blank disbelief, his built up tension slowly relaxing.

"So you were doing a front tail, you lousy bastard," he finally said.'

(from *Diamonds are Forever*, Ian Fleming)

The storyteller

It is possible to distinguish between ***external*** and ***internal*** storytellers. The external storyteller stands outside the story and purports to be the 'true' source of the story in the external world, e.g. the scriptwriter. Internal storytellers are persons with roles in the story.

This leads to the question of how much the storyteller knows. An external storyteller will know the story's outcome, be able to see into the minds of all the characters and have the ability to move in time and space. Where the storyteller knows everything like this he/she is known as an ***omniscient*** narrator.

Whoever tells the story has an influence on how the story is received and trusted by the audience. Omniscient and ***anonymous narrators*** (e.g. in documentaries or other factual programmes) often carry great authority, seeming to guarantee truth. The 'factual' voiceover unifies the subject matter and tends to limit controversy and other points of view.

With ***character storytellers*** there is more of a question of reliability. There may be a problem over a distance in space and time. In the Western ***Little Big Man*** (USA 1970), which tells a very tall story of a white man who was captured by Indians and learned their values and ways of life, we discover near the end of the film that the story is being related by an extremely old man recounting his own experiences and we realise that we must take his words with a large pinch of salt.

In the film ***The Green Mile*** (USA 1999) the story seems very realistic for most of the time, but then becomes surreal when a prisoner starts to work miracles, bringing things back to life, curing chronic illnesses. Then we remember that the story is being told again by an extremely old man living in an institution and we realise that this is a fairy tale. We have to question the ***reliability*** of the storyteller, the ***distance in space and time*** the storyteller is from the events being related and what ***motives*** there might be for telling the story. Narrators with subjective points of view within the story carry less credibility. ***Fictional characters*** carry less authority because we know they are presenting a partial view of events.

Named experts and reporters in news programmes will carry some authority but this may depend on the knowledge, experience and prejudices of the recipient of the story. Viewers form perceptions about reporters and newsreaders, for instance, which can be based on nothing more substantial than the way they dress or their accent. Or it could be about the way they report certain stories or certain attitudes they express. After Angela Rippon appeared as a scantily clad dancer on the ***Morecambe and Wise Show***, many viewers later found it difficult, apparently, to accept her authority as a newsreader. Similarly, some politicians and political commentators towards the end of 2002 criticised the Liberal Democrat party leader Charles Kennedy after he appeared as the anchor person or host on the satirical BBC news quiz, *Have I Got News For You?*

Activity

Conduct research among friends and family to find out which newsreaders/reporters are the most trustworthy.

Make a list of current newsreaders /reporters with their photos. Ask people to rate them from 1 to 5:

1 completely trustworthy

2 very trustworthy

3 trustworthy

4 not sure about him/her

5 wouldn't trust him/her.

Present your findings as a chart.

The role of storyteller can be complicated in factual narratives. For example, newspaper and magazine stories often carry quotations. These sometimes draw in important or significant persons in the narrative and place them as narrators within the story.

The distinction between external and internal storytellers may not be clear in factual media narrative. For instance, in investigative journalism especially the journalist both authors and appears in the narrative.

Time in narratives

Stories do not have to be told in chronological order, i.e. the order in which events happened. It is quite common, for instance, for narratives to start 'at the end' and flashback to preceding events.

Crime stories often show a series of ***flashbacks***, each adding more details to a story of the significant past events in the life of a protagonist. The flashbacks 'explain' why the protagonist has ended up in the situation they are now in. In the classic *film noir* ***Double Indemnity*** (USA 1944) the insurance agent and protagonist Walter Neff staggers wounded into his office and begins to record a taped confession of his involvement in an insurance scam. The film then flashes back to his first encounter with the femme fatale Phyllis Dietrichson and the start of his involvement.

This type of strategy works well with the mystery code in particular because, although the audience knows something of the outcome, we do not know the series of events leading up to the ending presented.

Tellers of tales can reorder events. This can involve ***flash forwards*** which create suspense because the audience knows the outcome but does not know the causes of a series of events.

Sometimes these can be used in television as ***inducements to watch***. They are mini-trailers: 'After the break....so and so is faced with a dilemma.'

In television news stories or in documentary, footage of events from different times is often juxtaposed. The famous television documentary ***The World at War*** (UK 1973 Thames Television) opens the first of its 26 episodes with contemporary footage of a ruined French village left as a memorial. The voice-over narration explains that, in 1944, Nazi soldiers massacred the entire population. The film then cuts to the credits and moves back to the beginning of its narrative scope with the Nazi party taking control in Germany in 1933.

Film-makers have developed techniques for showing different things happening at the same time such as ***cross-cutting on parallel action***. In the car chase sequence in ***The French Connection*** (described on p 39), for instance, the editing cuts between shots from inside a car chasing a train to a chase inside the train itself and back again. Cross-cutting increases the melodramatic effect of the action.

Time can be ***condensed*** by showing in a few seconds a montage of events that, in reality, spanned many hours, days or years.

The editing process involving cutting from one action to another and missing out the intervening action also condenses time. When a character in a film or television programme drives from one location to another, we do not see the whole journey. All we need to see are the start, finish and maybe a shot from somewhere along the way.

Activity

Draw a storyboard using cross-cutting between two simultaneous actions, e.g. cutting between shots of a person trying to rescue someone from a burning building and shots of the fire engine on its way to the incident.

STORYBOARD

TITLE ____________ NAME ____________ DATE ________

LOCATION ____________ SEQUENCE ____________ PAGE ____ of __

DIRECTOR ____________ SCRIPT ____________

PARTICIPANTS ____________ CAMERA/VIDEO ____________

PICTURE	ACTION/EFFECT/PROPS	SOUND/SPEECH
Shot No. ____ Time ____ Camera ____		
Shot No. ____ Time ____ Camera ____		
Shot No. ____ Time ____ Camera ____		
Shot No. ____ Time ____ Camera ____		

Example of a blank storyboard

Sometimes time is ***extended*** by the use of ***slow motion***. This is used for emphasis or emotional impact or sometimes, as in television, for clarification – did the ball cross the line or not? ***Freeze frame***, where a single image is isolated, is an extension of this technique.

A useful concept in relation to media narrative is that of '***real time***'. If your watch is accurate it is recording the passing of real time. In particular, soap operas try to tell stories as if they are happening in real time. Though they are recorded several weeks in advance, they will be scheduled so that their Guy Fawkes' episode is transmitted on 5 November and their Christmas programme is shown on 25 December. They create the impression that the audience is peeping in at real events and that the life of the soap opera goes on between episodes. The fiction maintains the illusion that the events which take place pass in the same daily and weekly time scale as the spectator occupies.

Activity

Using the following checklist, identify and describe the narrative codes and conventions of an episode of *Blind Date* or any current quiz programme shown on commercial television.

1 What role does the main presenter play?

2 What expectations are aroused in the opening sequence and in the sections just before a commercial break?

3 How are music and voice-overs (if any) used?

4 What camera movements or editing effects did you notice?

5 Was there any noticeable pattern to the combination and ordering of different types of camera shots, especially with the use of close-ups?

6 How is the set arranged and with what effect?

7 How are the presenter and the contestants dressed and with what effect?

8 Are there any programme-specific codes – frequently repeated words, phrases, sounds, visual effects, etc., that happen only in this programme?

9 What stories are there?

10 Are there any repeated narrative structures such as 'problem, complication, solution'?

11 Do you find any of Propp's 'spheres of action' or character roles?

12 How are the viewers kept in suspense?

SECTION A **Chapter 3**

Genre

INTRODUCTION

This chapter explains what genres are and why they developed. It examines how genres have developed particular characteristics to do with style and content and shows how they have to develop and adapt if they are to survive. It examines the way there has to be an interaction between audiences and producers and how there is a tendency for modern film producers to mix genres.

The chapter focuses on the film industry, with particular reference to the studio system which was largely responsible for the development of film genres and looks at an example of an 'umbrella genre' – the thriller.

What are genres?

Genres are types of media product. They have developed because the media producers and media audiences need them. If films or television programmes did not fall into recognisable categories then the producers would find programming, marketing and scheduling very difficult.

If *audiences* did not know what to expect, then they would be less likely to turn up to cinemas or tune in to a particular television station. Consequently categorisation has developed.

A look at any listings publication or a visit to a video shop will confirm this. Films will be grouped according to their genre – musicals, crime, horror, adventure, romance, comedy and so on. Television programmes will have similar labels, with the addition of documentaries, sports programmes, DIY shows, quiz and game shows, news and perhaps 'reality' programmes. Whole TV channels will be devoted to a single genre such as sport, wildlife, comedy or pop music.

Activity

Organise a genre quiz.

Work in pairs and test each other. Collect old copies of listings magazines, such as the *Radio Times*, and cut out a selection of the publicity pictures from different types of programmes and films and paste them onto a sheet of card as in the figure on the previous page. Your partner tries to identify the genre of each picture, giving reasons. Keep a list of all the reasons as these will be the characteristics of different genres.

The studio system

The studio system refers to the practices of film-making from 1930 to 1960 in Hollywood, which were similar to the production line in a factory.

The major studios in those times, i.e. MGM, Twentieth Century Fox, Warner Brothers, Paramount and RKO, made pictures and leased them through their own distribution companies to cinemas which they themselves owned.

By turning up to watch films in huge numbers during these years, audiences encouraged the mass distribution of films and, to some extent, determined the format of the films themselves. Because people liked particular stories and techniques, this led to ***repetition*** and certain cinematic ***conventions*** became established. The relationship worked both ways.

> 'The filmmaker's inventive impulse is tempered by his or her practical recognition of certain conventions and audience expectations. The audience demands creative variation but only within the extent of a familiar narrative experience.'
>
> (Thomas Shatz, *Hollywood Genre: Formulas, Film Making, and the Studio System* 1981, p 6)

There was a huge demand for films during this period when the majority of the population went to the cinema. The average attendance was twice a week and each programme consisted of an A, or main, film and a B, or support, film. At its peak the Hollywood studio system was producing between 400 and 700 films per year.

This huge demand led to a ***division of labour***, where people concentrated on one small job rather than lots of jobs. This meant that people became specialists rather than 'jacks of all trades'. Actors became proficient at certain types of role. Scriptwriters developed talents for different sorts of stories and directors specialised in certain styles of film.

The costs of making a film could be kept down by ***repeating successful formulas***. For instance, certain sorts of sets, costumes and props were repeatedly used. It is worth remembering that some B films were completed in as little as a fortnight from scripting to editing, so innovation was kept to a minimum.

> 'Thus, many aspects of studio production were refined to accommodate genre film making: the 'stables' of writers and technical crews whose

> work was limited to certain types of films; the studio sets and sound stages designed for specific genres; even the star system which capitalised upon the familiar, easily categorised qualities of individual performers.'
>
> (Shatz, *ibid.* p 10)

One of the consequences of this process was the establishing of certain genres. Genres developed familiar, ***one-dimensional characters*** who acted out a ***predictable story*** within a ***familiar setting***.

The plots developed through conventional conflicts to a predictable resolution. But there had to be some ***degree of variation*** to keep audiences interested. The producers of the films had to balance predictability and novelty. Genres were produced by the interaction of the studios and the mass audience and they survived as long as they satisfied the needs and expectations of the audience.

Genres involve particular ***themes*** as well as narrative elements, such as plot, character and setting, and to this extent they have a ***socialising effect***. That is, they affect the way we see ourselves and our roles in the society we belong to.

This is important when it comes to analysing a film because that analysis must be based on an understanding of the genre and the production system which has led to its existence.

So film genres express the perceptions, feelings and ideas not only of Hollywood film-makers but of the mass audience as well. If this is accepted, then it changes the way critics assess films, as characteristics sometimes seen as shortcomings become significant, e.g. the hero who is not a complex character or the 'predictable' plot.

> 'Film genres are not organised or discovered by analysts but are the result of the material conditions of commercial filmmaking itself, whereby popular stories are varied and repeated as long as they satisfy audience demand and turn a profit for the studios.'
>
> (Shatz, *ibid.* p 16)

The genre film is less about a specific place than about a ***recognisable network of characters, actions, values and attitudes***. This produces familiar characters performing familiar actions which celebrate familiar values. The audience learns to understand certain images and sounds so that, for instance, the white hat and white horse in a traditional Western tell us we are seeing a hero, while a bunch of men dressed in overcoats and trilby hats and carrying what look like musical instruments as they emerge from a 1920s saloon car says 'gangsters'.

Each genre has a ***system of values*** which determines its characters, dramatic conflicts and solutions to problems. In early stages of development genres are, in fact, social problem-solving operations. The static, uncomplicated genre hero and the familiar character types help to focus the audience's attention on ***social issues and conflicts***.

For instance, in the detective genre the hero is the ***man in the middle*** of the forces of anarchy and order, who still remains separate from each. He has his own code and value system which coincides with the forces of law and order, but at the end of the film he returns to his office and refuses to adopt fully the lifestyle of the community he serves. On the other hand, the gangster protagonist aligns himself clearly with the forces of crime and social disorder, so that his eventual destruction is demanded.

Genre progression – the Western

Genres are not static. They develop and change and the changes usually have some connection to the way society is developing. An account of the Western genre can illustrate this process.

Westerns are films about a short period of American history roughly from 1840 to 1900 when settlers from the east moved into territories inhabited by Native American Indians. The films developed certain kinds of stories concentrating on particular themes. The Western's essential conflicts involve the clash between civilisation and savagery and this is expressed in a variety of ***oppositions***:

east v west
garden v desert
America v Europe
social order v anarchy
individual v community
town v wilderness
cowboy v Indian
schoolma'am v dance hall girl

and so on. Perhaps the most significant conflict in the Western is that concerning a community's need for order through cooperation and compromise and the physical environment's demand for rugged individualism and the survival of the fittest.

Clare Trevor as Dallas and John Wayne as Ringo in *Stagecoach*, the first modern Western

The ***locations*** usually show a vast wilderness dotted with oases of civilisation which are tenuously linked by railroad, stagecoach and telegraph. Each oasis is a small community which is plagued by conflicts both internal and external.

There are ***set pieces*** which occur frequently, such as the main street shoot-out, the bar-room brawl, the cavalry riding to the rescue, the attack on the Indian settlement, the ambush and the talk around the camp fire.

Typically in early Westerns, ***a hero acts out the American Dream***. John Ford's ***Stagecoach*** (1939) presents a vision of the West as a place where there is a chance of a fresh start, the promise of a new world. Two characters start off as misfits, Ringo has been accused of murder, while Dallas is a prostitute. They are both social outcasts. However, Ringo first saves the stagecoach from an attack by Indians, then he rids the town (Lordsburg) of the menacing Plummer brothers. He and Dallas fall in love. At the end of the film Dallas and Ringo are allowed to escape by the sheriff to start a new life elsewhere 'saved from the blessings of civilisation'. So the misfit becomes hero and there is a promise of new beginnings when the two reach a new community.

Americans' acceptance of this version of the American Dream waned, however. Society became less idealistic and more sceptical. As this happened the Western hero ***changed***. He became more aloof, more independent, more concerned with his own moral code. A ***vengeful hero*** emerged, a hero who acts because society is too weak to do so but, having acted, moves on. The hero rids society of a menace but cannot share the community's values. Examples of vengeful hero films are ***Shane*** (1953), ***The Searchers*** (1956) and ***One Eyed Jacks*** (1961).

After the vengeful hero came the ***professional hero***. As Westerns became more sophisticated the central question being asked was how can a morally upright, independent, idealistic Westerner defend communities which were repressive, institutionalised, cowardly and thankless. There were two answers: the hero either

Clint Eastwood as a vengeful hero in *Unforgiven*

sells his skills and lets the community evaluate his actions or else he becomes an outlaw. Gone is the isolated heroic cowboy with no visible means of support whose moral vision and spiritual values set him apart from, and above, the community he defends. Instead he is cynical, self-conscious, increasingly unheroic – more like ourselves. Examples of films with such heroes are *The Magnificent Seven* (1960), *The Culpepper Cattle Co*. (1972), *Butch Cassidy and the Sundance Kid* (1969) and *Unforgiven* (1992).

An umbrella genre – the thriller

In his book *Thrillers*, Martin Rubin (Cambridge University Press 1999) tries to define the underlying concepts that make thrillers different from other types of movies, but has to accept that it is an 'umbrella genre' that 'cuts across more clearly defined genres' such as spy, detective, police, adventure and disaster films.

He argues that thrillers have the following characteristics:

- the hero is cut off from former security gained from community, habit, tradition or religious assurance;
- the hero is uniquely competent, not an amateur or average citizen;
- the hero is self-reliant and isolated;
- the hero defeats a conspiracy;
- the conspiracy is the evil design the hero opposes;
- the conspiracy must pose some danger to society;
- the conspiracy must be largely hidden, otherwise it is an obstacle not a conspiracy;
- realism;
- a strong sense of contrast between the ordinary world of the hero and some extraordinary occurrence;
- there is a labyrinth or maze into which the hero is drawn and from which (s)he has to escape by cracking a code or solving a mystery;
- they are modern and urban and the urban environment is depicted as wild and adventurous (this is what makes it different from the adventure film, which needs exotic locations).

Rubin admits that the dividing line between adventure and thriller is hazy and has to accept that there are ***hybrids*** such as *King Kong* (USA 1933), *Jaws* (USA 1975) and *The Poseidon Adventure* (USA 1972).

His chapter on the modern period identifies a variety of ***subgenres***:

- heist (carefully planned robberies)
- Bond and mock Bond
- supercops
- black action
- revisionist
- conspiracy and disaster
- splatter
- stalkers
- neo-noir.

Rubin argues that by the 1960s the thriller had gone through its formative period and now began to ***debunk*** or ***revitalise*** the formula. This was partly due to the decline of the studio system, so that fewer films were produced on an assembly line process.

There was also the challenging of the ***Production Code*** which had influenced so much of film-making from the mid-1930s. The Code, which was written in 1930, particularly affected the way ***sex, violence*** and ***criminality*** were represented in the American cinema.

The effects were diminished partly by Federal court rulings about the differences between sex and obscenity, which weakened the influence of local censorship rulings, so that films became more explicit in their portrayal of sex.

They were also diminished by the effects of ***foreign films*** such as ***The Wages of Fear*** (France/Italy 1953) which, according to Rubin, 'treated American audiences to a number of ingredients not likely to be found in Hollywood films of the era, such as the sordid atmosphere of the opening scenes, the beyond buddiness bonding of the male characters, the dim view taken of American corporate imperialism, and the stark presentation of sudden death and drawn-out violence.'

Early heist films, such as the French film ***Rififi*** (1955), ***The Asphalt Jungle*** (USA 1950) and ***Odds Against Tomorrow*** (USA 1959) exerted pressure on the Production Code by ***presenting criminality in morally neutral terms***. The Code specified that criminals had to be punished for their misdeeds, and that all lawbreakers had to be caught and punished. It also specified that criminal activities should not be shown in detail. The films mentioned above and others such as Sam Peckinpah's ***Getaway*** (USA 1972), in which the hero and heroine robbers escape with a bag full of stolen money, ***ignored the Code completely***.

Latter-day examples of the heist film include ***Thief*** (USA 1981), ***Reservoir Dogs*** (USA 1992) and ***Out of Sight*** (USA 1998).

The ***spy movie*** had enjoyed a period of success from 1935 to 1946 but had become less successful after the Second World War and the anticommunist movement in the US. It was revitalised in 1962/3 by the surprise success of the first Bond movie ***Dr No*** (UK 1962). It had a series of action set pieces and its violence (considered unusually strong for its day) was mixed with humour and Bond's sexual banter with a series of females. It also featured exotic locations.

The Bond films were products of the Cold War, the strained relations between the West and Communist USSR heightened by the U2 spy plane incident (1960), the abortive Bay of Pigs invasion (1961), the erection of the Berlin Wall (1961), the increase in the American military presence in Vietnam (1961) and the Cuban missile crisis (1962). But the Bond movies tended to depoliticise confrontations and the villains are motivated not by ideology but by a lust for power, greed, sexual inadequacy and a simple delight in spreading chaos. The films avoided the Cold War hotspots, such as Cuba, and gravitated instead to tourist venues such as Jamaica, the Bahamas and Venice.

Although Rubin categorises Bond films as thrillers, he does say that their thrilleresque qualities are limited. The suspense sequences are 'moderate' and the hero is not as vulnerable as in, for instance, Hitchcock thrillers. There is much action but the sense of danger is weak. Emotionally Bond is invulnerable, his friendships not developed and women used and discarded.

The ***anti-Bond*** movies of the time widened the field of anxiety. The spy had to contend with enemies from all sides and traitors were everywhere. The spy hero, as in ***The Ipcress File*** (UK 1965), becomes a man in the middle with his top priority simply staying alive. In ***The Quiller Memorandum*** (UK/USA 1966), the British spy chief Pol uses two ashtrays and a peanut to illustrate the situation: two armies obscured by fog, with the agent Quiller alone in the gap. Pol then impassively pops the peanut into his mouth and swallows it.

The settings are not glamorous, as in the Bond movies, and there is more emphasis on the routine and drudgery of the spy's routine.

Genres are problematic

Genres are not watertight, unproblematic categories. Rick Altman in his book ***Film/Genre*** (British Film Institute 1999) argues that strict categorisation suits critics and reviewers, whereas film producers are aware that assigning a film to a particular genre might alienate potential spectators who systematically avoid that genre. Hollywood studios, he says, prefer to imply rather than state a particular genre. The aim is to attract people who recognise and appreciate the signs of a particular genre while avoiding putting people off who avoid the genre. Films which are specifically designed to take advantage of a 'hot' genre are an exception.

Sometimes there is a problem of different names being given to the same genre. In the 1970s and 1980s ***stalker films*** emerged. They typically depicted a group of adolescents or young adults being menaced and systematically slaughtered by a prowling off-screen psychopath. Examples are ***Halloween*** (USA 1978), ***Nightmare on Elm Street*** (USA 1984) and ***Friday the 13th*** (USA 1980). They are a kind of horror movie and are categorised as such in the ***Time Out*** film guide, but they have also been categorised as 'slashers', 'slice-and-dice', 'body count' and 'teenie-kill'.

Altman argues that more ***subtle audience profiling***, which describes audiences not just in terms of age and gender but in terms of ethnicity, class, education, preferred activities, geographical location and income level, puts pressure on producers to think of films as a ***mix of as many genres*** as called for by targetted audiences. Whereas classically Hollywood preferred genre purity it now prefers ***genre mixing***.

So studios come up with marketing jargon such as '***The Player*** – a psychic political thriller with a heart', ***Ghost***, a 'comedy-romance-thriller', or alternatively 'a tingling political paranoia thriller'. It is a compliment, says Altman, for an already composite title like ***Kiss and Kill*** to be called 'a film-noir thriller, a love story, a psychological drama, a whodunit and even a bit of a Western.'

The mixing of genres is easier if the mix is between a genre which is identified by location (science fiction, horror, war films, Western) and those identified by plot type (comedy, melodrama, suspense, thriller).

Activities

1 Design two separate posters for a film you have seen recently. Each poster should emphasise a different genre characteristic.

You could, for instance, describe a Harry Potter film as an action/adventure film or as a supernatural fantasy.

2 Read the following and then answer the questions on it.

Rick Altman in *Film/Genre* argues that modern Hollywood prefers to think in terms of *brand names* rather than genres. Whereas a genre can belong to any studio, a brand film can be linked to a particular studio. The studio has exclusive rights over actors, house directors, proprietary characters and patented processes. Hollywood is in favour therefore of series such as *The Lord of the Rings* trilogy or the series of Harry Potter films. In these cases marketing does not have to start from scratch but can point to the continuity with a previous film.

In recent years proprietary characters, such as *James Bond*, *Rambo*, *Indiana Jones*, *Conan*, *Batman or Superman*, and repeatable titles, like *Godfather*, *Grease*, *Jaws*, *Halloween*, *Star Trek*, *Lethal Weapon* and *Die Hard*, have helped Hollywood reap record profits.

'Though it has been generally assumed that Hollywood makes and publicises genre films, careful inspection of advertising campaigns reveals that generic claims have never constituted a substantial portion of feature film publicity strategy, except when capitalising on some other studio's success. Although even the most rudimentary posters and the shortest trailers provide some information about a film's generic connections, even if only through clothing and setting ...poster texts and trailer voice-overs systematically stress proprietary characteristics (star, director and related successful films by the same studio) over shareable determinants like genre.... Paramount doesn't call Raiders of the Lost Ark an adventure film; instead it touts 'Indiana Jones – the new hero from the creators of Jaws and Star Wars'. The function of publicity is as much to advertise a film's makers as the film itself.'

1 Why are successful brand names rather than genres more useful to individual film studios?

2 What assumption about genre does Altman challenge?

3 Why did Paramount advertise the makers of *Raiders of the Lost Ark*?

4 Analyse the publicity for a new film – its posters and trailers – and compare this with the way reviewers and critics describe it. How far do your findings agree with Altman's assertions about genre and brand names?

Action/adventure films

INTRODUCTION

According to the BFI's *Cinema Book* the term 'action/adventure films' refers to a range of films and genres including thrillers, swashbucklers, science fiction, Westerns and war films.

Their characteristics include:

- spectacular physical action
- narratives involving fights
- the lone hero who often leads a quest
- the hero reacting with a small group to a survival challenge
- plots allowing moments of spectacle
- 'knowing' humour
- wide variety of locations
- heroes often physically aggressive as well as doing good deeds
- chases and explosions
- special effects and stunts.

This chapter shows you how to analyse a chase sequence and a fight sequence from action movies with two specific case studies. It also gives advice about note-taking in exams where you have to analyse extracts from films. There are activities based on analysing the openings of thrillers.

How to analyse a chase sequence

Case study: the car chase in *The French Connection* (USA 1971)

CASE STUDY CASE STUDY CASE STUDY CASE

The chase was described as 'The greatest chase in movie history' by film critic Mark Kermode but dismissed by *Time Out* as 'efficient but unremarkable'. Judge for yourself. The chase sequence starts from about 1 hour 4 minutes into the film.

Chases in films are meant to *entertain and excite*. They may also tell an important part of the story but basically they are used to *thrill* an audience. They have been a stock ingredient of action films over the years. In fact, very early films were often no more than chases.

A chase is often a *story within a story* and has its own *beginning, middle and end*. In *The French Connection* the chase begins with the sudden shock of the attack on the detective Doyle, played by Gene Hackman. A shot from a hidden sniper comes without warning as Doyle is walking

Doyle (Gene Hackman) dodges a sniper's bullet

home through the city streets. The shot misses its target but seems to strike a woman pushing a pram.

The *middle* part of the narrative is the chase itself with all its complications while the ending is when the sniper is shot in the back by Doyle. The poster advertising the film depicted this moment and the audience had been so positioned to identify with the detective that at an early showing in Manhattan about 1000 people stood up and cheered and applauded the killing.

The *character functions* in the mini-story are the hero and the villain who become the hunter and the hunted. The guard and policeman on the train can be regarded as helpers and the only other people we see are innocent observers.

Hitman Pierre Nicoli (Marcel Bozzuffi) on the run

CASE STUDY CASE STUDY CASE STUDY CASE STUDY CASE STUDY CASE STUDY CASE STUDY CASE STUDY CASE STUDY CASE STUDY

The *audience gets its thrills* partly from feeling directly involved in the chase. In this case the effects are particularly *realistic*. The view from the speeding car is authentic. The car was driven by actor Bill Hickman at speeds of up to 90 mph. Hickman was a stunt driver and had driven the car involved in another famous chase sequence in the film *Bullitt*. The realism of the shots from behind the car windscreen as it hurtles through crowded traffic in pursuit of the train was partly achieved by the director, William Friedkin, defying the rules of film-making and not asking permission to film and arranging for the streets to be cleared. Instead he told a stunt driver to drive full speed through the traffic while he himself strapped a camera to his chest and did the filming.

There was no preparation for the filming. No permission had been given, no streets cleared. Hickman was told to go as fast as he could, ignoring traffic signals. As director Bill Friedkin said, 'It was dangerous. It was life threatening. It was illegal.'

Gene Hackman (Doyle) followed in the maroon car seen in the sequence. The lead car was equipped with three cameras: one on the front of the car and two inside, one taking a driver's point of view and one filming Hackman. Crashes and scrapes actually happened. No special effects were involved. It is this degree of realism which makes it such a thrilling experience for the audience.

The realism is enhanced by the sequence being shot on *location* in the streets of New York.

The excitement of the chase is increased because of *cross-cutting*. While Doyle is driving crazily through the streets below the railway, there is another chase on the train itself as the gunman tries to evade capture. The director cuts between the two *parallel actions*. As the chase progresses the cross-cutting becomes quicker, more urgent.

The film gives the audience *different perspectives* of the chase which allow them to experience the excitement of the hunter after a quarry, the fear of the pursued as he tries to escape, and the horror of the bystander observing violence.

Different *camera placements* allow for different points of view during the chase. Several times the audience sees events from Doyle's point of view. At the station, as he is looking for the gunman the camera whips quickly, scanning the travellers standing on the platform. The sudden movements and the panning back as Doyle sees the gunman hiding behind a pillar imitate Doyle's eye movements.

This feeling is reinforced by showing us the *driver's perspective* as the car speeds along under the elevated railway. Sometimes this is further enhanced by positioning the viewer not just behind the windscreen but, as the speed increases, on the front of the car itself. This is echoed by the shots from the moving train where initially we see the train driver's perspective and then, as the train is out of control, we seem to be on the front of the train at the same level as the wheels.

Though the chase is exciting throughout, the excitement is heightened towards its conclusion by the increasing *gravity* of events. There are peaks of tension within the continuing excitement. On the train these involve the shooting first of a policeman and then a guard and the collapse of the train driver followed by the train being brought to an abrupt emergency halt and the passengers and the gunman being thrown about in chaos. The way the camera itself seems to be caught up in the turbulence heightens the realism of this climax.

You could compare the *editing* of the search of the building with that of the chase when Doyle sees the gunman running away. It takes much longer, six shots, for the search than the chase – one shot of Doyle racing through the front doors of the apartment building. Building suspense needs more shots but it would be pointless retracing the editorial steps as it were, so one shot of the return suffices, emphasising the speed of the chase.

The *misè en scene* of the sequence is almost incidental as most of the chase was filmed without planning or preparation. However, there are a couple of shots which have been contrived to emphasise one of Friedkin's aims: 'I had to have a chase where there were innocent people all over the streets'. This is why we see a woman pushing a pram being accidentally shot by the sniper, passers-by rushing to her aid, two children waving cheerily to Doyle as he crouches armed beneath their window and a shot of the speeding train and car taken from a moving truck from behind a children's playground.

Swift editing and a mix of action shots with *close-ups* of emotional expressions increase the emotional impact. A good example of this is where Doyle almost crashes into a woman pushing a pram. At this point the editing is rapid and the shots dramatic as we cut from the driver's perspective of the woman to an extreme close-up of Hackman's eyes, to a screaming mother, a screaming Hackman as he frantically spins the driving wheel and then a shot of the car ploughing through some rubbish. The speed of editing and the *sound effects* of screams and squealing brakes combine to make this a climactic moment in the sequence.

In terms of the film's *narrative*, the sequence showed that the criminals knew about the detectives pursuing them and had decided to use a hitman to get rid of them. It displayed the gunman's cold-blooded attitudes to violence but presented Doyle's violence as heroic.

In terms of *audience pleasure*, chases provide excitement and thrills for their own sake. If they also have a narrative function of enhancing the story or revealing character all well and good, but primarily their function is to thrill.

How to analyse a swashbuckling fight sequence

Case study: *The Mask of Zorro* (USA 1998)

An interesting sequence to analyse begins approximately 3 minutes 45 seconds into the film. It starts with the Spanish governor of California (then Mexican territory) announcing: 'Get the children out of the Plaza immediately' and ends with the escape of Zorro and his silhouette on horseback against the sun.

The sequence shows one of the *conventional features* of action films: the fight of a hero against impossible odds, featuring hand-to-hand fighting and stunts.

The *setting* is in the past (1821). This gives the audience the impression that they are watching something which really happened and gives a realistic foundation for the fantastic feats of the *lone hero*. The *location* is a town square in California which allows lots of space for the elaborate fight scenes involving large numbers of people. There is *conflict* between Spanish colonialists and Mexican outlaws/freedom fighters, one of whom is the lone hero Zorro.

The contrast between the Mexican people and the Spanish governor and troops is mainly achieved by *costume*. The governor, Montero, is extravagantly dressed in colourful military attire and his soldiers in smart uniforms. The Mexicans are simply dressed in earth-coloured clothes. Their clothes seem to blend with the surroundings, suggesting they belong here whereas the governor and the soldiers are too gaudy, suggesting they are alien. They also seem to be arrogant and powerful. This is partly suggested by *facial expressions* which are haughty or cold and partly by *camera angles*. Low-angle shots, especially of Montero standing on the balcony, emphasise power, while high-angle shots showing his point of view of the shouting crowds below emphasise his control. Zorro's black costume and horse make him stand out from the rest, emphasising his outlaw status and his independence.

There are three *narrative segments* to the sequence. First there is the arrival of Zorro and the build-up to the execution, creating suspense and expectation, then there is the release of the prisoners and finally the fight followed by Zorro's triumphant escape.

The build-up of ***suspense*** depends on the audience identifying with Zorro as hero. This is done by showing the hero worship and expectations of the young boys and the portrayal of the Spanish governor as cruel. The governor has no idea who the three men are who are to be executed: 'Three peasants pulled at random from the crowd,' as he says dismissively. So the audience eagerly anticipates and craves a rescue. But suspense demands that the rescue is delayed as long as possible.

Tension is built by the *choice of shots* and the *pace of editing* as the firing squad is prepared. The set-up is displayed from different angles with various *over-the-shoulder shots*. A close-up of the beating drum signals the imminent execution. This is followed by a speedy *tracking shot* as the camera follows the two boys on the roof top as they race forward to peer over the edge to look down on the square and ask 'Where is he?'

The suspense is further protracted as we see a *close-up* of the rifles ready to shoot. Then there is a sudden silhouette of Zorro as we look over his shoulder. He uses his whip to encircle the rifles and redirect them as they are fired so that the bullets strike the officer in charge. Here, and in the subsequent fight, the emphasis is on excitement and athleticism which have to seem realistic, but there is no *realism* in terms of death or bloodshed. In fact, bloodless killings of Spaniards prompt cheering and amusement from the watching young boys. This shows that the film-makers intend the *audience* to be thrilled and excited rather than shocked or disturbed.

A fight scene from *The Mask of Zorro*

The fight sequence is *edited quickly* to prolong the excitement. The impossible speed and strength of Zorro's swordsmanship emphasise that this is an amusement and a fun fight where both the film-makers and the audience accept that this is all fantasy. Zorro's escape through the gallows trapdoor and his trapping of a soldier's head in the guillotine are examples of the *tongue-in-cheek humour* of a swashbuckling fight. There must be times, however, where the hero is seriously threatened. It must not seem too easy for him.

The *stunts* also have to be convincing and not over-edited so that the audience feels cheated. The fall of the soldiers from the rooftop when the boys send the statue tumbling down on them has just one edit; we see them from above and then cut to a low-angle shot as they fall through and demolish the gallows structure. The most effective stunts are during Zorro's escape. These look realistic as he uses his whip as a rope to swing from building to building, though the way he evades a barrage of rifle shots as he runs across the roof tops seems unlikely.

The ***music*** of the soundtrack is expansive orchestral, suggesting excitement and adventure, and rising to a grand, triumphant climax as Zorro on his rearing black horse is silhouetted against the setting sun.

Note-taking in exams

To prepare for externally set exams where you are allowed to make notes before analysing film and television extracts you should practise using notes and abbreviations.

Your first set of notes should be aimed at ***summarising*** the extract so that it is easy to recall specific shots. Devising your own shorthand will save time. Leave space for more details to be added for a second set of notes as in this ***example*** on an extract from ***The French Connection*** car chase:

Trn. gnmn on mv (= Train. Gunman on move)
Arl sh car (= Aerial shot of car)
CU drvr (= Close up of driver)
Ob POV cr swrvng (= Observer's point-of-view of car swerving)
By observer I mean where the camera acts as an unseen bystander observing events, that is showing no particular character's point of view.
CU drvr (= Close up of driver)
Car fr outsde (= Car seen from outside)
Dr POV ovrtkng (= Driver's point-of-view as he is overtaking)
Ob POV tr frm blw (= Observer's point-of-view of train from below)
Tr gnmn to cmr (= On the train with the gunman coming towards the camera)
Tr plcmn chsng (= On the train showing the policeman chasing)
Tr gnmn trappd (= On the train showing gunman trapped)
Tr plcmn closing in (= On the train with policeman closing in)
Tr gnmn draws rev (= On the train showing the gunman drawing a revolver)
Tr plcmn shot (= On the train as the policman is shot)

Then add details after the next viewing:

Trn. Gnmn on mv
Gunman seen running through train with policeman in pursuit. Doors are barriers.
Arl sh car
High-angle shot shows speeding car. Camera pans with it.
CU drvr
Shot from outside of car showing Doyle leaning forward over steering wheel. Reflection of rail track on windscreen.
Ob POV cr swrvng
Shot of car from observer's point of view. Avoids collision. Blaring of car horns. Swift pan.
CU drvr
From inside car we see a close-up of Doyle in profile.
Car fr outsd
Observer's point of view from car in front. Car swerving at high speed. Engine noise.
Dr POV ovrtkng
Driver's point of view. Narrowly miss pedestrian. Facing oncoming traffic.
Ob POV tr frm blw
Observer's view of train from below. Camera pans.
Tr gnmn to cmr
On the train we see gunman coming towards camera which seems to move out of way.
Tr plcmn chsng
The chasing policeman is closer and draws gun.
Tr gnmn trappd
The hand-held camera moves with the gunman along the carriage. We see him close up. He is trapped.
Tr plcmn closing in
The policeman closes in and shouts 'Hold it!'

Tr gnmn draws rev

The gunman draws a powerful looking revolver and fires without warning.

Tr plcmn shot

The policeman is hit and staggers back. We see blood and flesh briefly.

The passengers scream.

Activities

1 Analyse the opening sequence of a thriller, for example *The Usual Suspects* (USA 1995), *Manhunter* (USA 1986), *Charley Varrick* (USA 1973), *Scream* (USA 1996) or *Se7en* (USA 1995).

- What *genre* of film is this and how can you tell? Examine some of the genre codes and conventions which you notice. Things you might consider are:

  types of camera shots used and their purpose,
  pace of editing,
  use of music and sound effects,
  lighting and use of colour,
  settings and locations.

- What *narrative techniques* are being used and what are the intended effects on the audience? You might consider:

  creation of suspense or mystery,
  techniques of revealing and concealing information,
  use of dialogue,
  characters and their functions (e.g. heroes, villains, victims),
  inciting incidents which disturb an equilibrium.

2 View a short fight sequence from an action or adventure film (e.g. the opening of *Gladiator* or any James Bond or Indiana Jones film) and then answer the following questions.

- What *genre* of film is the sequence from and how can you tell? You might consider:

  types of camera shots used and their purpose,
  pace of editing,
  use of music and sound effects,
  lighting and use of colour,
  settings and locations.

- What *narrative techniques* are used and what are their intended effects? You might consider:

  characters such as heroes and villains,
  portrayal of nationalities,
  the nature of the conflict,
  how the sequence begins and ends,
  whether there are peaks of excitement as the fight progresses,
  use of suspense.

Documentaries

INTRODUCTION

A documentary is different from fiction in that it aims to portray the 'real' world. It is usually based on real events, places and people and is intended primarily to record and inform. It can also be used to investigate, educate, spread propaganda or campaign for a cause as well as entertain. In this chapter you will find information about documentary techniques and a guide to different types of documentary.

There are model analyses of a classic drama documentary, *Cathy Come Home*, and a spoof documentary, *People Like Us – The Headteacher*.

Documentary definition and techniques

Interviews

Documentaries have to be carefully researched and part of the research involves identifying people with expert or ***specialist knowledge***. These people can be interviewed and edited versions of the interviews are used in the final programme. The interviews are sometimes with authoritative figures who may be filmed in academic locations, such as libraries, or they can be with members of the public who have experienced or witnessed events.

Cameras

The camera is used to record people being ***natural***, sometimes not being aware they are being filmed. This may involve the use of concealed miniature cameras.

This Is Spinal Tap – a spoof documentary

This can lead to poor quality shots with bad lighting, camera shake, poor sound, subjects being out of focus and so on. Such quality is sometimes seen as an indication of ***realism***. Fictional films that want to give the illusion of realism sometimes use hand-held, unsteady cameras to produce a documentary style.

The documentary-look camera movement, apparently unplanned or unpremeditated, is shot as if the camera has been surprised, with an objective but recognised (by the person being filmed) camera as opposed to the unrecognised camera in drama. There are some good examples of recognised and unrecognised cameras in the sitcom *The Office* which is shot in a documentary style.

The documentary conventions are designed to give the impression that the camera has happened upon a piece of unpremeditated reality which it shows to us objectively and truthfully. These techniques tend to shift the emphasis onto the environment of the protagonists, onto social factors and away from individuals. This does not apply to character-based documentaries though.

The talking head

Someone ***talks directly*** to the camera. In early documentaries this is usually a presenter or expert who has more authority because he or she is talking direct to the audience. Interviewees are usually shown talking to someone to one side of the camera and they carry less authority: but remember that conventions like these are sometimes broken.

Voice-over

Usually this is an actor who has a controlling role, ***telling the story***, rather than participating in it. This person often has the role of detective, solving the mystery, or is the equivalent of a newsreader. There can, however, be several narrators in a documentary, who may be experts or people with specialist knowledge or members of the public directly involved in events.

Archive film

Film shot for other purposes, such as news broadcasts, can be used in the documentary. There are many film libraries and archives which store films and video.

Documents

Written evidence is sometimes presented such as newspaper headlines, legal documents, letters and quotations from books and magazines.

Graphics and still photographs

These are used if there is a shortage of suitable moving pictures. These may include maps, cartoons, graphs, tables and charts.

Music

This can be used to influence the mood and emotional response of the viewer. Sometimes, as with the use of popular music, it can be used to indicate a certain historical period.

Vox pops

These are interviews with ordinary members of the public in ordinary surroundings, such as shopping centres.

Simulation

In early documentary films, because of the bulky filming equipment people reconstructed their everyday activities in studios.

Reconstruction using actors

These are usually made clear and cover things such as court cases where filming of actual events can't be done.

It is arguable that, though documentaries are expected to stay as close to the truth as possible, they may also contain some entertainment, which means having interesting characters, stories, dramatic climaxes and complications. They are therefore always likely to be made up of both ***fact*** and ***fiction***, thus blurring the distinction between these.

Technology

When TV documentaries could only be filmed using cumbersome 35mm cameras, huge cables and heavy lighting equipment, it would be difficult to imagine them giving insights into the 'real world'. The practice was generally to film people at work and then invite them into the studio to talk, or else workplaces were reconstructed in the studio. The early examples of these in the 1940s were dramatised 'how to' guides to the professions with titles such as *I Want to Be an Actor* and *I Want to Be a Doctor*.

The advent of videotape in the late 1950s and the introduction of ***lightweight film equipment*** in the 1960s led to different filming techniques. The Drama Documentary Group (at the BBC) was formed in 1961 and produced programmes which were hailed at the time as 'the birth of dramatised documentary' by *The Times*.

A four-part series on crime called *Jacks and Knaves* acted as a kind of pilot for a crime series called *Z Cars*. The documentary style could be seen in *Z Cars*, which had lots of filmed location shots making it seem more 'real' than, say, *Dixon of Dock Green* which was studio based. ITV produced programmes which they called drama documentaries but which today we would call soap operas – *Emergency Ward Ten* and *Coronation Street*.

In 1964 a film called *Culloden* was another development. It was about the Jacobite rebellion in Scotland in 1745. Conventionally it could have been a documentary with historians talking and lots of maps and relics. Instead the director, Peter Watkins, reconstructed the battle itself with an amateur cast and then filmed it in newsreel style, using lightweight 16mm ***hand-held cameras***. The events were narrated by an off-screen news reporter.

In 1964 the BBC launched a new single drama slot called *The Wednesday Play*. This featured the naturalistic portrayal of social problems and mixed techniques of drama, newsreel, interviews and reporting. The new lightweight technology allowed TV crews into places which they hadn't previously filmed, such as working class streets and factory floors. The slot led to significant works such as *Up The Junction*, about abortion, *Cathy Come Home*, homelessness, and *In Two Minds*, schizophrenia, which all had an impact on British social life and attitudes.

Types of documentary

- *Fly-on-the-wall* where people become so used to the cameras that they behave, in theory, as if they are not there.
- *Historical* with the use of stills, archive films and eyewitness accounts to examine past events on subjects such as the First World War or the Holocaust.
- *Current affairs* which examine in detail the background of controversial topics in the news such as crime rates or outbreaks of disease.
- *The investigation into controversial subjects*, especially those that organisations or governments want to cover up, such as miscarriages of justice or misuse of public funds. For example, Michael Moore's *Bowling for Columbine* (USA 2002) is a searching and disturbing analysis of America's gun culture. Another example is Moore's *Roger and Me* (USA 1989) a hilarious and scathing film which traces the effects of the closure of a car factory in Flint, Michigan. Moore himself described this as a 'docucomedy'.
- *Drama documentary*, where real events are re-created by actors such as in *Hillsborough*.
- *The docusoap*, which spans a number of weeks and focuses on characters who develop through time. Often they focus on a particular working community such as hotel staff or the crew of a cruise liner.
- *Personality based*, where the presenter takes the viewer through the topic and links sections of film together. The treatment can be serious or entertaining. Louis Theroux's programmes on the Hamiltons and Jimmy Saville are examples.
- *Spoof documentaries*, which are meant to entertain and amuse and maybe to satirise. Serious documentary techniques are used but the content is absurd or comical, as in *Best In Show* (USA 2000) or *Cane Toads* (Australia 1987).

Docusoaps

Docusoaps were one of the success stories of British television at the turn of the century. At £65,000 production costs per episode, they were about half the price of a drama that would fill the same spot and they sometimes pulled in ratings that exceeded even popular soap operas.

The ingredients for a successful docusoap seem to be a contained location with a manageable cast of characters who interact with the public, a couple of characters who are interesting enough to become stars, and a bit of conflict including a row.

The programmes should be about places where most viewers would like to see what goes on behind the scenes. The setting could be glamorous, such as the Royal Opera House in ***The House***, or it could be the kind of place which viewers are familiar with, such as an amusement park (***Pleasure Beach***) or a shopping centre (***Lakesiders***). There are a whole series of docusoaps about young people behaving badly on holiday (***Holiday Reps***, ***On the Piste*** and ***Ibiza Uncovered***). The most successful series seemed to feature nasty bosses: people who put others under pressure and seem to enjoy it.

At the time of writing the docusoap looked as if it was in need of revitalising. Programme makers were looking for something a little more than the usual suspects and the usual argy bargy. There seemed to be an opportunity for the genre to tackle more serious subjects and to inform as well as just entertain. The BBC seemed to be getting into more serious areas with productions planned on RSPCA inspectors, maternity nurses and women's prison officers

Examples of docusoaps with their viewing figures:

Animal Hospital	BBC	10.3 million
The Driving School	BBC	12.45 million
The Cruise	BBC	12.86 million
Vets' School	BBC	10.04 million
Airline	ITV	11.77 million

Case study

ANALYSING A DOCUMENTARY

CASE STUDY CASE STUDY CASE STUDY CASE STUDY

Cathy Come Home (1966)

Cathy Come Home is a good example of a pre-1990 documentary because it was an early drama documentary which had a huge *public impact* when it was broadcast within BBC's regular *Wednesday Play* slot. The documentary was written by Jeremy Sandford, produced by Tony Garnett and directed by Ken Loach.

The aim of the programme was to highlight a particular *social problem* – homelessness. After its screening the issue became an urgent topic of public debate and led to local authorities taking action to deal with the problem and to the formation of the charity Shelter.

The *story* is about Cathy (Carol White) who marries and has children. Her husband Reg (Ray Brooks) has an accident at work and loses his job. The family become poor and eventually homeless, at which point the authorities take Cathy's children into care. The programme shows stages of Cathy's decline over a number of years with Cathy herself giving a

Reg (Ray Brooks) and Cathy (Carol White) in the influential TV drama documentary *Cathy Come Home*

Cathy and Reg barricading the house

voice-over commentary in the past tense. The story is a personalisation of a general problem.

ANALYSIS OF THE OPENING

The opening sequence of *Cathy Come Home* combines both conventional documentary and fictional drama techniques.

We see a close-up of a character who is unaware of the camera. She looks anxiously left and right as she stands by the side of the road. Intermittently she is obscured by passing traffic. The early introduction of a character, especially in close-up, suggests a drama while the voyeuristic camera, which gives the feeling that we have come across this person by chance, is a documentary technique.

The song of parting and lonely travelling on the soundtrack tells the audience how to feel. Though music is sometimes used to produce emotional effects in documentaries it is a more common device in fiction.

We are initially given a person's story. The *voice-over* is not an authoritative male one, the voice of an anonymous but trustworthy narrator. Instead it is a woman talking informally and confidentially about her past. She is introducing her story which will be told as a flashback, another convention belonging mainly to fictional drama.

Cathy's monologue is scripted but sounds as if she is thinking aloud:

> 'Well I was a bit fed up you know, there didn't seem much there for me. You know how these little towns are, one coffee bar and it was closed on a Sunday. Didn't even tell 'em I was going.'

CASE STUDY CASE STUDY CASE STUDY CASE STUDY CASE STUDY CASE STUDY CASE STUDY CASE STUDY

We also are put in Cathy's position as the camera shows her *point of view* from the van window as she describes the town she is leaving: 'That house over there, that one with the broken step...'

Next there is a montage of *actuality* shots which are meant to show the kind of place she is leaving. We see a close-up of a middle-aged woman crossing a street, an old man walking slowly along a pavement, a group of women standing on a street corner, gossiping. The people are grim faced and poorly dressed.

The impression of down-at-heel urban living given by these images is in contrast to the next sequence which shows Cathy and Reg talking happily as they walk along. This leads us into a scene which is shot very much in the style of a romantic *drama*. We see in a park lake a reflection of Cathy and Reg as they embrace. They are next to a tree and we can just glimpse them through the sunlit, shimmering leaves. The camera dwells on this moment of beauty and love for a while as a popular love song fills the sound track – 'Stand By Me'.

This tender and beautiful scene is important for the progression of the story as it sets a high point in the relationship against which the couple's subsequent decline becomes more poignant. It also encourages the audience to *identify* emotionally with the couple and therefore react emotionally later against the officials and property owners who seem to treat them harshly. That at least seems to be the preferred or intended meaning of this opening of the drama documentary.

The scene is a good starting point for equilibrium theory analysis (see Narrative, chapter 2, p 9). The scene suggests harmony and happiness and hope for the future. This *equilibrium* is disturbed by a series of misfortunes and by unhelpful officialdom until the final *disruption* with Cathy having her children taken from her. This emotive scene leads to a final equilibrium – a restoration of Cathy to her former single and lonely status. Seeing the story in these terms makes us focus on the values of the programme and ask questions about its attitudes to housing policy, the harshness of social services, self-reliance, irresponsibility and so on.

Activity

Continue the analysis of *Cathy Come Home* using the following guidelines:

1 Compare the scene with Cathy and her children climbing the stairs of the hostel (about 26 minutes into the programme) which lasts for approximately 2 minutes with the scene immediately afterwards with Reg and Cathy together. There is a good contrast here between the conventional documentary filming technique of the first scene and the drama style of the second.

Which seems more realistic and why?

Describe the types of camera shots you are shown, the camera movement, the editing and the sound.

2 How does the final scene in the railway station combine documentary fly-on-the-wall camera techniques with drama-style close-ups and sound effects?

3 How are the officials portrayed in the film?

In the 1960s the programme was criticised for giving a biased account of the problem and depicting officials as uncaring and hostile in a way which would have been unacceptable in a conventional documentary.

4 How are the audience invited to feel sympathy for Cathy and Reg? Think about the love story aspect and the casting of likeable, attractive actors for the parts.

5 How far do the portrayals of officials as 'heartless' and main characters as 'likeable victims' make this documentary biased and propagandist?

6 Describe two or three examples of commentary and viewpoint.

7 Give two examples of shots of ordinary people (not actors) being natural, and two of montage shots of places which establish an atmosphere.

8 What is the purpose of including the anonymous voices of women recounting their experiences and the anonymous voice giving statistics about housing?

Activity

When *Cathy Come Home* was broadcast on BBC Choice at the end of 2001 the organisation Shelter, worried that the circumstances which had led to the problem in the first place were recurring, issued the press release printed below. Use the release and your own viewing of the documentary and write a 200 word article for a 'What's on the Box' feature in a popular newspaper for Sunday 23 December 2001.

13/12/2001

EMBARGO: Immediate Release 13/12/01

CATHY COMES HOME TO THE BBC AND HIGHLIGHTS THE PLIGHT OF HOMELESS FAMILIES ONCE AGAIN

Cathy Come Home, the film that first brought the plight of homeless families to the public's attention 35 years ago, is being shown again on BBC Choice at 8.00pm on Sunday, 23rd December. Thirty-five years after *Cathy Come Home* was first broadcast, homeless families are again facing the threat of separation.

Recent case law has seriously weakened the homelessness safety net. Previously, when housing departments have refused to house homeless families, social services would provide housing help to the family as a whole under the Children Act. Yet recently Shelter has worked directly with increasing numbers of families who have been told by social services that the Act means they have a duty to house the children but not the parents. This means children would be taken into care. Some families have opted to sleep rough or simply disappear, rather than be split up.

Cathy Come Home tells the story of a young family who find themselves trapped in a downward spiral of homelessness after Cathy's partner suffers an accident at work. It follows the family's move from one form of accommodation to another: from a relative's house to a squat, to a hostel and finally onto the street as Cathy tries to prevent social services taking her children into care. The powerful film shocked viewers when it was first screened with its emotive subject matter and realistic style of filming. As homeless families once again face the prospect of being separated from their children, it is hoped that broadcasting Cathy will again shock the public into action.

Chris Holmes, Director of Shelter, said: 'The events depicted in *Cathy Come Home* are happening once again, 35 years on. An increasing number of homeless families are being threatened by social services with having their children taken into care, rather than being offered housing help. Shelter is campaigning for an urgent change to the law to stop this happening.'

When *Cathy Come Home*, written by Jeremy Sandford and directed by Ken Loach, was first broadcast in December 1965, it won support for Shelter, which was founded only one week later. Ever since, the film and the charity for homeless and badly housed people have been closely linked in the public's mind. The programme came second in the British Film Institute's TV 100 and was voted the most popular one-off TV drama ever in the same poll.

Jeremy Sandford, writer of *Cathy Come Home*, said: '*Cathy Come Home* was written to bring an end to the dreadful practice of separating children from their mothers and fathers because they had become homeless, and taking them into care. For many years I thought that with the help of Shelter this procedure, so traumatic for both parents and children, had been brought to an end. It is very sad news that some local authorities are now proposing to do this again. It is shocking that young children should again be taken into care for no other reason than that their parents have become homeless.'

(Shelter 2001, reproduced with permission)

Case study

THE SPOOF DOCUMENTARY

CASE STUDY CASE STUDY CASE STUDY CASE STUDY CASE STUDY CASE STUDY CASE STUDY

People Like Us – The Headteacher

Spoof documentaries are worth studying because they draw attention to the techniques of documentary making by using them for comic purposes:

- The interviewees may sound important or real but often talk nonsense.
- The interviewer sounds at first to be authoritative but is both incompetent and often distracted.
- The camera techniques may suggest realistic fly-on-the-wall shots but show actors doing absurd things.
- The editing does not omit gaffes.
- The voice-over may sound trustworthy but is meaningless and so on.

ANALYSIS OF THE OPENING SEQUENCE

The Headteacher is part of a series of spoof documentaries based on people's occupations. The opening is of interest because of the way it combines *conventional* documentary techniques with nonsensical and *comical* content.

It starts with an *establishing shot* of the school and *actuality shots* of pupils going into school at the start of the day. A *voice-over* provides what seems to be a factual account. It is a male voice which sounds authoritative and trustworthy. It tells us that this is King Edward VII Comprehensive at Ashford in Kent. The information that follows sounds superficially like the kind of statistics documentaries usually provide us with:

'Every morning anywhere between 1200 mostly mixed sexed children between the ages of 11 and 18 pass between these gates together with between 130 teaching and administrative staff between the ages of 24 and

CASE STUDY CASE STUDY CASE STUDY CASE STUDY CASE STUDY CASE STUDY CASE STUDY CASE STUDY

70.' The tone of the delivery makes it all sounds very *plausible* until you notice it is nonsense.

The shots of pupils going into school look like *actuality* shots and the mix of different camera angles and placements and the *smooth editing* between them suggest that this is a real-life documentary. So when we have an internal shot of the headmaster's morning management meeting this seems to be 'real' as well. There is now dialogue which seems to be natural conversation but which turns out to be a *comic script*. It seems that the deputy head is talking about how to deal with a pupil who has been drinking in a local pub through the lunchtime and then has come into school and been sick over a desk before passing out. The punchline comes as a casual remark, 'Apart from anything else it sets a bad example for the kids,' and we realise he has been talking about a member of staff.

A voice-over cuts into the conversation and it seems to give *background information*: 'Stuart Simmons has been headmaster of Edward VII for 3 years. He was deputy head for 9 years and was promoted to acting head on the strength of the previous head's stroke before becoming permanent gradually.'

The conversation then becomes more bizarre as a pupil's conduct is discussed. The deputy head asks about his parents:

> Deputy: Do they seem like reasonable people?
> Head: Well his father's a QC.
> Deputy: I see.
> Head: Oh an IC is it? Quite possibly.

Though this scene is clearly scripted the camera movement around the room gives us the impression that we are observing a 'real' meeting.

The actual and the acted are blended in the next two shots, one of a school staircase with a voice-over saying: 'Meanwhile the preliminary rounds of the school day are already being fired.' This is followed by an actor calling the register in what looks like an authentic classroom. It must be a scripted scene, however, because all the pupils are called Emma.

Activity

Continue analysing this spoof documentary using the following guidelines.

1 Trace the references to the interviewer's parked car through the programme and show how it is used to humorous effect. Why do such references to the production crew's personal lives and circumstances not appear in conventional documentaries?

2 Another topic running through the film is 'child centred learning' and its variations. Make a list of these. How does this show that the film is not 'natural' but has been scripted? Does it still make an important point in the way a conventional documentary would?

3 How does the interviewer become a *character* in the documentary and why is this unconventional?

4 Look at the scene when the head takes an assembly. Analyse this to show different documentary *techniques* such as a 'behind the scenes', 'intimate' interview, scriptwriting, actuality film and acting. How real is the assembly?

5 Look at the interview in the playground with the schoolboys and say whether it is real or acted and why.

6 Documentaries often cite statistics in order to prove a point. What examples of spurious *statistics* are there in *The Headteacher*?

7 Which bits of the lessons are real and which acted?

8 Though the spoof is primarily meant to be entertaining, does it also make some important points about schools? Give examples of sequences which are 'true-to-life'.

Extension activity

Analyse *Bowling for Columbine* (USA 2002) concentrating on these techniques and their effectiveness:

- the different sorts of interviews (e.g. celebrity, eyewitness, with experts, with members of the public, sympathetic, challenging, interrupted);
- the use of archive material (e.g. film of shootings);
- voice-over interpretations of events (e.g. Moore's view of 'working for welfare');
- confrontation and deception (e.g. the interview with Charlton Heston);
- the use of cartoons (e.g. American History);
- the polemic (aggressive and controversial) style;
- your own responses to the film.

Advertising and marketing

Introduction

This chapter shows you how to analyse an advertising campaign using key questions about:

- purpose
- branding
- information and persuasion
- selling points
- celebrities
- action lines
- continuity in TV ads
- editing techniques
- media planning
- audience reaction.

It goes on to look at the effects of changing technology on marketing and at 'stealth' advertising techniques, such as product placement. It also suggests how you might go about investigating the marketing of a local newspaper.

Analysing advertising campaigns: key questions

Advertising campaigns are often about selling goods and services, but they may also be about heightening people's awareness of problems, giving information or changing attitudes. There is an example of an advertising campaign in chapter 16 Other examples can be found on the Newspaper Society web site: www.newspapersoc.org.uk.

Here are some important questions to ask when you analyse a campaign.

- What is the *purpose* of the campaign?

These are some of the kinds of campaign you may come across:

spreading important information to large numbers of people, e.g. about health issues such as outbreaks of diseases like meningitis;
changing people's behaviour, e.g. appealing for blood donors;
encouraging recruitment, e.g. armed forces or teaching;
introducing a new product or brand, e.g. Daewoo cars;
maintaining awareness of an existing brand, e.g. Nescafé Gold Blend;
increasing a product's share of the market, e.g. Walker's crisps;

changing attitudes, e.g. men's attitudes about women's 'overuse' of phones.

It is of course possible that an advertising campaign could have several of these purposes.

- How does the campaign create, reinforce or manoeuvre a ***brand identity***?

Where there are lots of similar products, branding is used to try to set individual items apart. Manufacturers do this by emphasising repeatedly the name of the product/service and its logo or slogan. They can also emphasise a particular quality the product/service has.

Successful brands are those which have connotations of good quality so that consumers choose one product over another because they believe it is superior, although in fact there may be little or no difference between the products. For instance, shoppers tend to believe that superstores' own brands are inferior to 'well known' brands whereas the products are often supplied by the same manufacturer.

Brand names can be significant in people's choice of clothing, with some brands being considered fashionable and socially desirable, while products without brand names are scorned. You can consider your own attitude to branding and how far it determines what you buy and compare it with the attitudes of your peers.

- Does the campaign need to ***convey information***? If it does, how clearly and effectively does it do this?

Advertising agencies will check this out by using market research findings, but your investigation will have to be restricted to your own observations and some small-scale survey of friends and family.

For example, record a TV advert or cut out a print advert from a newspaper or magazine and show it to the sort of people it is aimed at. Find out how much information they can recall five minutes later and how accurate it is.

A full page advert for Ford Fiestas taken from the ***Daily Mail*** of 28 January 2002 listed the following information:

interest-free finance for three years
minimum 35% deposit
Ford Fiesta Freestyle for £8,760
1.25i 16v 3dr
14" 5-spoke alloy wheels
central locking
electric front windows
front fog lights
cd player
air conditioning at no extra cost
3 year warranty

You should think about which sorts of products are advertised in this way and which are not and why there are differences.

- What ***persuasive techniques*** does the campaign use?

Adverts frequently appeal to people's emotions by associating products with ***desirable images*** of happy families, successful careers, romance, escape to glamorous locations, good humour and fun, nature, luxury, etc.

Sometimes '***before and after***' techniques are used depicting an undesirable condition or situation which is improved by someone using a particular product. These techniques are often linked with exploiting people's ***feelings of guilt or fear***, e.g. of loneliness or illness or old age.

Another common persuasive technique is to use ***scientific fact*** or 'scientists' who apparently endorse a product.

Many persuasive techniques work at a ***subconscious level***. In ***The Hidden Persuaders*** (Penguin 1960) Vance Packard identified the following in the chapter on 'Marketing Eight Hidden Needs':

i) Selling ***emotional security***, e.g. selling fridge freezers as an assurance that there is always food in the house as insecure people apparently need more food around than they can eat.
ii) Selling ***reassurance of worth***, e.g. selling soap products to houseworkers by fostering their feeling of 'worth and esteem' and getting away from the feeling that housework is unappreciated drudgery.
iii) Selling ***ego-gratification***, e.g. the vanity press which prints people's books if they pay the publishing costs themselves. Though no one ever reads the books, the authors are made to feel important.
iv) Selling ***creative outlets***, e.g. selling gardening products to older women as a way of their going on growing things after they have passed the child-bearing stage.
v) Selling ***love objects***, e.g. the promoters of American TV pianist Liberace, who appealed to older women (who apparently wanted to stroke his greasy, roguish curls), made sure that his TV shows always included a picture of his real-life mom beaming in her rocking chair.
vi) Selling ***sense of power***, e.g. new cars sold to males as a way of renewing their sense of power and reinforcing their masculinity which their old car fails to deliver.
vii) Selling a ***sense of roots***, e.g. associating a product such as bread with 'the good old days' which by implication were warm, homely and friendly.
viii) Selling ***immortality***, e.g. selling life insurance to men by promising the prospect of immortality through the perpetuation of their influence. Apparently, though men can stand the thought of physical death, what they cannot accept is their obliteration.

Often adverts will combine information and persuasive techniques as in this advert for a Sony digital camcorder:

'The world's first Network Handycam IP. Not just the world's lightest, most compact recorder. For the ultimate freedom to shoot and share, on the fly. Capture the action on superb quality digital video. Then flip the LCD screen and you've got an internet device ready to surf the web and e-mail still images or MPEG e-movies via Bluetooth.'

- What ***selling points*** are there? These are the things that are special about the product/service. For example this is from an advert trying to sell holidays to single travellers:

  'Your own room – no sharing.
  Inclusive prices – no single supplements.
  Many excursions and meals included.
  Experienced tour manager.
  Optional pre-tour get-togethers.'

- Is there a *unique selling point* (USP)?

A USP is one which points out a feature or characteristic of the product/service which no rivals have. For example, in an AOL advert 'The only FREE trial with FREE help'.

- Are ***celebrities*** used and, if so, how appropriate are they?

The celebrity commercial is where a famous person recommends a product either directly or just by being associated with it.

- Is there a contact or ***action line***?

This urges you to act quickly, e.g. 'Buy now' or 'Sale ends tomorrow'.

- Do TV adverts have any ***continuity***?

For example, there are ***mini soap operas*** as in the Nescafé Gold Blend adverts. How do these small dramas encourage audiences to become involved? What qualities of the product are linked to the drama? For instance, invitations to coffee are associated with romance or intimacy.

- In moving image adverts, are the ***editing techniques*** used to associate two different objects or objects and people?

For instance, a picture of a beautiful woman can be dissolved into a picture of a car, or a handsome Arab can become a bar of Turkish Delight, thereby creating an association between the two for the viewer.

- Are there characters to ***identify with*** or ***envy***?

The kinds of images which we are invited to imitate or envy are of people who are healthy, often young and attractive, or rich, happy and successful.

- In moving image adverts how effectively is ***sound*** used?

Bright music and an enthusiastic voice may give the impression of excitement or friendliness. A more intimate, seductive voice or sultry music can suggest sex appeal.

Regional accents can suggest down-to-earth ordinariness or familiarity, while standard accents can be authoritative.

- How are ***different media*** used to disseminate the messages?

The main ones are: television, newspapers (national, regional, local, free-sheets), magazines, radio, cinema, outdoors (e.g. posters, bus sides).

While television offers a mass audience, other media outlets which could be less costly might offer a more specialised audience.

- How significant is the ***timing*** of the campaign?

For instance, adverts and publicity events (such as celebrity interviews) for a new film have to be scheduled precisely to coincide with the film's launch. ***Press kits*** are sent to newspapers some two weeks before the film is to be shown. The kits include film stills, credits, production notes, biographies and filmographies of the cast, director and producer. Broadcast journalists also receive video or audio clips from the film.

There is no guarantee that this information will be used, so the film distributors may also book ***advertising space*** for the film in newspapers, magazines and on TV and radio in the fortnight before the launch.

A ***poster campaign*** may be scheduled to begin a couple of weeks before the press packs are released in order to arouse curiosity in the public. The poster will have a striking image which will try to emphasise the main selling point of the film, which could be its dramatic content or its stars or even its director.

Trailers are usually scheduled to be shown in cinemas around six weeks before the release date. They continue to play until the film itself is shown.

Star interviews are carefully planned. Touring a star is expensive but it is effective publicity. The tour has to be organised to allow the maximum number of interviews and there has to be a spread of media covered so that publications or programmes with similar audiences do not clash. You can see an amusing example of such an interview in ***Notting Hill*** (USA/UK 1999).

Previews with invited audiences are sometimes arranged just before the release date. The purpose is to invite people who are from the target audience to see the film in the expectation that they will tell their friends and the people they work with about it. These sometimes double up as ***press screenings***, where journalists are invited to see the film so that they can write or broadcast previews and opinion pieces. (More information about marketing films can be obtained from ***Film Education***: www.filmeducation.org)

- How does the ***audience*** react to an advert?

Even the best laid plans of advertisers can go wrong. Audience reaction is unpredictable. There can be regional differences, for instance. Northerners were distinctly less impressed with Jamie Oliver in his Sainsbury's adverts than were southerners, apparently.

Though advertising can be effective, it would be too glib to assume that people are gullible and easily influenced. When consumers consider buying something they have seen advertised they may also take into account:

Their own experience of the product: 'Well this fragrance did make me irresistible to the opposite sex, but I was allergic to it.'
The experience of people they trust: 'Janine said that Harry Potter was a bore and I trust her judgement.'
The approval of friends: 'I always buy 17 Eye Dazzle because it sends my boyfriend crazy.'
What they read in the press: 'This film's been advertised a lot but the reviews were dreadful.'
The price: '£25 for a hi-fi? It must be rubbish!'

Activity

Analyse a current advertising campaign using the key questions suggested above.

- Choose a campaign that has at least two sorts of media, e.g. television and print.
- Contact the organisation responsible for commissioning the campaign and ask for materials that might be of help, such as sample posters and flyers. If you can obtain a copy of a 'media schedule' that would be very useful in helping you analyse the reasons for certain media being used at particular times.

The effects of changing technology on marketing

As schedules become less important in the way people watch television and people can compile their own schedules and take out the adverts from the programmes they record, techniques such as ***sponsoring*** and ***product placement*** will become more common. Increasingly advertisers will make their own programmes.

In the film ***The Truman Show*** (USA 1998) Truman Burbank, the main character, notices that people appear to listen to him but never really connect, that his marriage is not real and that every time he tries to leave the community he is thwarted.

It is as if he were programmed and indeed he has been, because he is part of television's most audacious experiment, a real-life soap opera following a person from birth to death. Everything around him is part of a gigantic set and all the people are actors, a secret that must be kept from him at all costs.

The show is broadcast twenty-four hours a day to a world-wide audience and there are no commercial breaks. It is all paid for by product placement.

Everything in the 'town' has been placed there and paid for by companies wanting to get their products or services noticed.

In 1994 the ***internet*** was virtually an advertisement-free zone. By 1996 Yahoo had over 50,000 companies advertising on their sites.

Advertising on the net ranges from simple information about a company and its products to lavish promotions like Pepsi or Levi's, rich in trickery and more like lifestyle magazines than simple advertising.

Advertisers attract viewers by having interactive banners on web sites. These are advertising strips along the side of a site which, when clicked, lead you into the advertiser's own web site.

The reason for this is that advertising on the web is different from other advertising. You have to make a decision to visit the site. It's not just dropped on you because you are watching something else.

Location-based advertising is possible on the internet. This allows advertisers to direct their message to a specific locality, based on postcodes. For instance, Pizza Hut can send online pizza ads from local restaurants to nearby office workers when they are thinking about getting their lunch. Chrysler car dealers in Holland have started sending web ads only to people in their vicinity.

Guinness came up with the idea of using one of their television ads as a ***screensaver*** which could be downloaded. The result was that in offices all over the country Guinness advertising is being shown on computer screens and it costs the company nothing.

Interactive advertising works by a viewer who has a digital television with a set top box responding to an on-screen message. The message is in a normal advert and says that it is interactive. When the viewer presses a remote control button the advert shrinks to a quarter. For a food ad the rest of the screen has recipes, orders for money-off vouchers, competitions, quizzes, anything to make the viewer think about the product the advertiser wants to sell. The advertiser is getting the viewer's attention for several minutes rather than 30 seconds.

The first interactive television advert was in March 2000 and was for Chicken Tonight. It was 70% more successful than an ordinary TV commercial.

Renault advertised the Clio with an interactive TV commercial as part of its 'VaVaVoom' campaign in 2002/3. When the ad was shown viewers saw a graphic asking 'Lost it? Press red'. When the red button was pressed, the ad reduced to quarter screen size and the viewer was offered a number of ways to recapture their VaVaVoom – such as order a brochure, or a test drive, or take part in a competition to win a drive in a Formula One car.

Tom Cruise in *Top Gun*

Stealth advertising

PlayStation 2 was advertised with adverts that did not seem to be advertising anything. One showed a weird image of a hyper-wrinkled old woman above the line 'I am horse, sinew, muscle and hoof. I am thunder across your land.'

The thinking behind the campaign was that the audience were getting jaded with conventional adverts. The manufacturers of PlayStation wanted to have an image of being a cutting edge, alternative games provider. The campaign was aimed at intriguing people and making them wonder what was going on. Once the word got round the people who were in the know felt special.

Another example was in the film ***Top Gun***, where financial backing for the film was partly provided by the American Air Force and the makers of sunglasses. The recruits in the film wore sunglasses much of the time and the result was a glut of eager Air Force recruits and an unprecedented rise in the sale of sunglasses.

Activity

Can newspaper articles be a form of stealth advertising? Read this article and then answer the questions on it.

Scruton in media plot to push the sale of cigarettes

By Kevin Maguire and Julian Borger

Professor Roger Scruton, darling of the right, asked one of the world's biggest tobacco companies for £5,500 a month to help place pro-smoking articles in some of Britain's most influential newspapers, and magazines.

The controversial conservative academic offered to use his Fleet Street contacts to get pieces published in his own name and those of others on 'major topics of current concern' to the tobacco industry. In a leaked e-mail to Japan Tobacco International seeking a £1,000 rise in his existing £4,500 monthly fee, Prof Scruton...[said] 'We would aim to place an article every two months in one or other of the *WSJ* [Wall Street Journal], the Times, the Telegraph, the Spectator, the Financial Times, the Economist, the Independent or the New Statesman.'

[The] note, [was] sent last October under the name of Sophie, his wife and business partner.

'Whilst one or more of these articles might be written by RS, we would do our best to get other journalists to join in.'

He advised Japan Tobacco to shift the onus on to health risks posed by other products.

'For example, fast food of the McDonald's variety, which seems to be addictive, is aimed at the young, is a serious risk to health, with a worse effect on life expectancy than cigarettes, and, unlike cigarettes, has a seriously corrosive effect on social relations and family life,' he wrote.

The proposal was one of a series made by Prof Scruton, editor of the *Salisbury Review* and once a regular on Radio 4's Moral Maze, in a long e-mail. He suggested he could help the multinational – the world's third largest cigarette combine and manufacturer of brands including Camel and Winston – with everything from education and licensing to dealing with the World Health Organisation....

Denounced by the left as a reactionary and apologist for the political right, the visiting professor at the philosophy department of London's Birkbeck College was distinctly unphilosophical yesterday when asked about the leaked e-mail.

'The whole thing is quite immoral – the stealing of private correspondence and making it public,' he said....

'We have never concealed the fact that we work for Japan Tobacco,' he said, complaining that the company never adopted his October proposals....

Professor Scruton has denounced single mothers, homosexuals, socialists, feminists and popular culture, while defending Enoch Powell and fox hunting.

Clive Bates, director of the ASH anti-smoking campaign, said last night: 'Scruton likes to pass himself off as a leading intellectual of the right, but it seems he is just a grimy hack for the tobacco industry.'...

(*Guardian* 24/1/02, reproduced with permission)

1 What work has Professor Scruton done for the tobacco industry?

2 How far can placing articles in the press be regarded as a form of advertising?

3 What is Professor Scruton's proposed main tactic for promoting cigarettes?

4 What is the source of this article?

5 How fair is it to publish details of someone's e-mail?

6 How does the article position its readers to discredit Professor Scruton?

7 How far can this article be seen as an 'advert' for ASH?

Activity

Advertising: good or bad?

Discuss in a class or small group the role of advertising. These are some of the points which you might want to raise.

Good:

- it encourages the sale of mass-produced goods and is therefore a stimulus to production and a creator of employment;
- it provides information about products so that consumers can make an informed choice about what they want to buy;
- it is not brainwashing because people can ignore the messages if they want to;
- it is strictly regulated and tries to be 'legal, decent, honest and truthful';
- without money from advertising much of the huge variety of modern media would not exist;
- most radio and television stations, newspapers and magazines and cinemas derive part or all of their revenues from advertising;

- all independent radio and television companies would fold and newspapers would become so expensive they would only be bought by the few who could afford them.

The media have large audiences which the advertising industry needs. The audience becomes the market. The media can provide large *mass audiences*, so that the *Sun* newspaper and, say, Coronation Street can provide an audience/market of about 10 million readers/viewers. Other specialised publications/programmes can provide *niche markets*, smaller numbers of people but sharing a common interest. The magazine *Webuser* carries lots of adverts for computer software, for instance.

Bad:

- it encourages people to neglect urgent human needs and buy things which are not really needed;
- it encourages people to be greedy and selfish and makes us wasteful because we are always wanting new products and discarding old ones which could still be useful;
- while advertising is telling us about products it is also encouraging certain lifestyles;
- it creates desires that did not previously exist and this in turn can make us dissatisfied with our lives if we cannot afford the products which advertising is suggesting we need to be happy and successful;
- in a consumer society we seem to have a huge choice of goods, but the choices are made by the producers of goods rather than the consumers. When we are offered a choice between different washing-up liquids the actual differences between brands are small and trivial and the important decisions about the products have already been made. Our choice is a bit of an illusion.

Collect examples from your own experience and that of friends and relatives of advertisements which have:

- led directly to you buying something,
- changed opinions or behaviour,
- been simply entertaining,
- been controversial and talked-about,
- offended or caused disapproval.

Activity

Gender representation in adverts

Track the advertisements on prime time commercial television over a number of days and check to see if the following observations are accurate. Suggest reasons for your findings.

- there are strong links made between attractiveness and women,
- authoritative voice-overs are generally male,

- women are very often shown in the home,
- women are shown as dependent on men,
- in adverts aimed predominantly at females, men are depicted as sex objects or buffoons,
- in adverts aimed predominantly at males, men are portrayed as gregarious but self-reliant, daring and adventurous and athletic,
- giving orders and advice is more associated with males than females,
- men are more likely to be shown as having expertise or authority,
- women are three times more likely than men to be shown in the home,
- nine out of ten on-camera product representatives are males,
- people portrayed at work are mostly male,
- women are more likely than men to be shown as product users,
- elegant and sophisticated women tend to advertise beauty and personal hygiene products, cars, clothes and alcoholic drinks,
- more reserved women with less make up who are not so fashion conscious advertise baby products, children's products, pharmacy items and food.

Activity

Investigate the marketing of a local newspaper

You can find information about local newspapers on the Newspaper Society web site at www.newspapersoc.org.uk. Some newspaper companies have Newspapers in Education departments which should be able to organise visits and meetings with promotions and marketing experts. In March 2003 the following companies were listed as being part of the Newspapers in Education Forum:

Belfast Telegraph, Lincolnshire Echo, Berks & Bucks Examiner, Liverpool Daily Post & Echo, Biggleswade Chronicle, Lynn News, Bolton Evening News, Maidenhead Advertiser, Cambridge Evening News, Manchester Evening News, Chester Chronicle, Middlesex County Press, Chronicle Newspapers, Milton Keynes Citizen Group, Coventry Evening Telegraph, Newcastle Chronicle & Journal, Creative Media Concepts, Newsquest North London, Cumbrian Newspapers, The (Portsmouth) News, Daily Echo (Bournemouth), Rochdale Observer, Derby Telegraph, Slough Observer, South Essex Recorder Group, Eastern Counties Newspapers, Staffordshire Newsletter, Evening Gazette (Middlesbrough), Sunderland Echo, Gazette Media Company, Surrey Herald Newspapers, The Guardian, Uxbridge Gazette Newspapers, Hampshire Chronicle, Welwyn & Hatfield Times, Herts & Essex Newspapers, West Ferry Printers, Hull Daily Mail, Western Mail & Echo, Informer Publications, Western Morning News, K M Group, Whitehaven News, Lancashire Publications Ltd, Wigan Observer, Yorkshire Post.

You should find information about the following.

1. What proportion of revenue comes from cover price, and what proportion from selling advertising space? How is revenue linked to circulation figures and how might this influence the newspaper's content?
2. Why are links with newsagents vital?
3. How is distribution organised and why is timing crucial?
4. Why is branding important?
5. How does the organisation find information about its target market (readers) and how is this information used?
6. What competition (for readers and advertisers) does the organisation have and how does it track its competitors?
7. How does the newspaper promote itself? (Most newspapers have a department called 'Promotions'.)
8. How does the newspaper try to find new markets? (It could, for example, try to attract new readers or extend its circulation area.)

SECTION A **Chapter 7**

British newspapers

INTRODUCTION

This chapter has a case study showing you how to compare tabloid and broadsheet reporting of the same story.

It shows you how to investigate the current political stance of newspapers and the values they assert or defend, values concerning questions such as sex, patriotism, class, hierarchy, leisure, money and family life. In particular there is a detailed example of how to track a newspaper over a period of time as a means of investigation.

This chapter shows you how to find information about newspaper audiences and what this information has to do with circulation trends and advertising rates.

There is a section on how newspapers construct an audience. That is, how stories and features are written with a *target audience* in mind which has certain *responses* or *values*. A successful newspaper has to deliver a product that is appreciated by its target audience.

The chapter shows you how stories can be angled in different ways and there is a final section on the question of privacy and intrusion.

Tabloid and broadsheet reporting of the same story

Sometimes two very different style newspapers attach the same importance to a particular story. It then becomes interesting to see how they report and present the story in contrasting ways. In particular, contrasts between broadsheet and 'downmarket' tabloid styles can be illuminating. This is an example of what to look for when you contrast them.

Case study

THE TYSON/LEWIS BRAWL

CASE STUDY CA

Before looking at the different styles of reporting of this story it is useful to clarify the differences between tabloid and broadsheet newspapers.

Tabloid is a technical term for the size of a newspaper. It is a newspaper whose pages are half the size of broadsheet pages. When some titles wanted to produce smaller newspapers that were easy to handle and easy to read, it was convenient to use the standard size rolls of newsprint and adapt the printing machinery to fold and cut it in a different way.

Broadsheet refers to large format newspapers with pages twice the size of tabloid newspapers. In the UK the broadsheet format is used by the 'upmarket' newspapers such as the *Daily Telegraph*, *The Times*, the *Independent* and the *Guardian*. These papers sometimes also produce tabloid sized supplements.

The popular newspapers in the UK are all tabloids, though some broadsheets outsell some tabloids. The word 'tabloid' is often used as a term of disdain, if not abuse, and especially to indicate low journalistic standards. However, this often simply serves to indicate the snobbery and sometimes the ignorance of the critic, as people who criticise tabloid journalism tend to pride themselves on not being readers of such trivial stuff.

There is a wide range of journalistic styles and content in England and Wales's national tabloid press. At the lower end of the market are the *Sun*, the *Mirror* and the *Star*. In the middle market are the *Daily Mail* and the *Daily Express*. You should know something about each of these titles and be able to describe their differences as well as their similarities and know something about the different audiences they aim to attract.

THE STORY

The story concerns boxers Mike Tyson and Lennox Lewis who had a brawl during a press conference. Both *The Times* and the *Sun* featured the story on their front pages. The *Sun* continued the story in a double page spread on pages 4 and 5 and in its sports section on pages 54, 55 and 56. The *Times* had an article on Tyson in its Sports Daily supplement.

PICTURES AND TYPOGRAPHY

The *Sun* illustrates the story liberally with pictures. It uses two on the front page, eight on pages 4 and 5 and ten in its sports section. The *Times* has three on its front page and one in its sports section.

The papers have used the same picture on their front pages but in the *Sun* it is much more dramatic. It is printed at more than twice the size of the version in *The Times* and it has been cropped to highlight the most dramatic part with Tyson, we are told, biting Lewis's leg. The image is then used as the background for the dramatic headline and tagline:

> CANNIBAL
> First Tyson chomps ear, now he eats Lennox leg

Four emphasising techniques are used in the headlines – white on black (reverse print), capitals, large font and underlining.

Barristers should beware, the Prime Minister may not always be one of them – Simon Jenkins, page 16

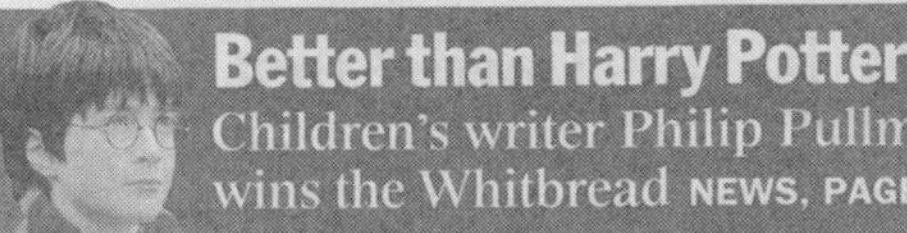

Better than Harry Potter?
Children's writer Philip Pullman wins the Whitbread NEWS, PAGE 3

Paris – London
Rachel Campbell-Johnston at the Royal Academy TIMES 2

THE  TIMES 40P

No. 67355 WEDNESDAY JANUARY 23 2002 SL SL www.thetimes.co.uk

Our industry needs euro, says Hewitt

By Tom Baldwin, Peter Riddell and Lea Paterson

MANUFACTURING industry is struggling to export into the eurozone and would benefit from British membership of the single currency, Patricia Hewitt, the Trade and Industry Secretary, says today.

Her comments, in an interview with *The Times*, will be seen as the latest evidence of an offensive by supporters in the Cabinet of an early referendum on the euro.

Ms Hewitt, who returned from a trade mission in the Far East last week, says that the views of Japanese and Asian investors in Britain about the euro were "very clear".

"The issue of concern for inward investors in Japan is, of course, the euro and the exchange rate. There does have to be something wrong when some of the most productive plants in the world are struggling to export profitably into the eurozone. It suggests that *there is something fundamentally wrong in the current euro/pound exchange rate."*

She says that further inward investment is "extremely important" to the future of manufacturing industry and points out that it is one of Gordon Brown's five economic tests that will decide whether the Government calls a referendum on euro entry.

In recent weeks, the Treasury has sought to dampen speculation about an early referendum by highlighting that its economic assessment must first conclude that there is a "clear and unambiguous" case for entry.

However, Charles Clarke, the Labour chairman and a long-term ally of Ms Hewitt, has said that there is a "political imperative" for joining the single currency and that "if it was a 50-50 call, I would still go for it".

Pro-euro campaigners are poised to step up their pressure on the Government following the disclosure yesterday that a network of Labour MPs had been set up to extol the benefits of the single currency. The network, being organised by the Labour Movement for Europe, includes Gareth Thomas and Caroline *Flint, the parliamentary aides* to Mr Clarke and Peter Hain, the Minister for Europe.

In a further sign that a cross-party "yes" campaign is being mobilised, Lord Heseltine, the former Deputy Prime Minister, yesterday made an impassioned call for the Government to come off the fence on the issue.

He said: "The Prime Minister has said that he recognises the dangers of Britain drifting apart from the decision-making processes of Europe. Yet, when public opinion reveals the hunger for a clear lead over the single currency, all we get is brief and counter-brief. It is time to end this cavilling."

In her interview today, Ms Hewitt says that while Britain is "holding its own" on inward investment, much of the new capital coming in was the result of decisions taken three or four years ago.

In a clear hint that she fears that delaying a euro referendum beyond the next election could discourage new investment, she adds: "What I'm concerned about is the decisions which are being taken at the moment and in the next year or two.

"We will assess the five tests together but the views of the inward investors, certainly from Japan and Asia, are very clear.

"Indeed, I've made it very clear that there are real potential benefits of membership of the euro particularly for manufacturing industry in terms of things like currency stability and transparency of costs."

The Department of Trade and Industry is already engaged in the process of "gathering information" from inward investors which will be fed into the Treasury once work begins on the assessment.

Manufacturing is currently mired in its deepest recession since 1992 and has been declining steadily as a share of national income over the past 30 years. Since 1995 the sector has barely registered any growth and in November recorded the largest year-on-year fall in output for more than a decade.

Economists say the strength of sterling against the euro – *which remains well above the* level that many consider compatible with sustainable growth – has been the key cause of difficulties.

A recent survey by Ernst & Young, the accountancy firm, suggested that indecision on euro membership may have already begun to damage the outlook for inward investment. The survey showed that Britain's share of European inward investment projects fell sharply to 21 per cent in the first half of 2001.

However, in a speech to City investors today, Ms Hewitt will emphasise that the euro is not the only issue facing manufacturing and launch a "sustained campaign" to eradicate the myths which hold back investment in industry. She will call on their help to strengthen the link between science and manufacturing, ensuring that "invented in Britain" becomes "made in Britain".

Mrs Hewitt says that the long-term prospects remain bright and that people should stop "talking it down".

Full interview, page 9
Leading article, page 17

Tyson cut, Lewis bitten – and the fight hasn't started yet

Lewis throws a punch at Tyson (top), who then ducks under the people crowded round, upends Lewis and apparently bites into his thigh

Cut but defiant: Tyson leaves the media circus

From Oliver Holt
in New York

A £100 million boxing match that took 18 months to finalise may have evaporated in 60 seconds of madness here last night when Mike Tyson went berserk and bit a lump out of Lennox Lewis's leg.

The two boxers had been brought to New York's Hudson Theatre to announce that arrangements had been agreed for their long-awaited fight to take place at the MGM Grand in Las Vegas on April 6. Shadow boxing and taunts at such events have become almost a ritual. But this time it was clearly no stunt.

When Lewis, the British world heavyweight champion, took his place on the stage opposite Tyson, the American strode towards him and then lost control when a minder tried to get between them. He threw a punch and Lewis responded with a righthander.

In the ensuing mêlée, Tyson's forehead was gashed and Lewis's thigh was bitten in a savage reminder of the moment Tyson chewed Evander Holyfield's ear during their fight in 1997. As the pair were pulled apart Jose Sulaiman, the President of the World Boxing Council, was knocked out and organisers had to abandon the press conference.

Last night there were unconfirmed reports that Lewis had been taken to hospital for a tetanus injection. The Briton later released a statement that hinted he may no longer wish to have any part in the fight. "I will evaluate my options after the relevant boxing commission has ruled," he said.

The Nevada State Athletic Commission is due to meet on Tuesday to decide whether to grant Tyson a boxing licence. If he is turned down the match may not go ahead.

Some suggested that Tyson may have behaved like a wild animal because he secretly feared a fight with Lewis.

Tyson chaos, S5

INSIDE

"You have one hour to see how many mistakes you can spot in your exam paper"

Board examined

A senior government adviser has been sent in to help to run the troubled Edexcel examination board after the Prime Minister's spokesman condemned its performance as sloppy 6

Gun rampage

A gunman opened fire in Jerusalem yesterday, wounding eight people. The attack came after the terror group Hamas said it was returning to "all-out war" against Israel........14

Liverpool joy

After eight consecutive victories in the Premiership, Manchester United's title charge was stopped in its tracks when they were beaten 1-0 by Liverpool........**Sports Daily**

Golden Jubilee mastermind quit in protest at 'shambles'

By Andrew Pierce and Richard Ford

THE shambolic state of Britain's official preparations for the Queen's Golden Jubilee year led to the resignation of the man chosen by Buckingham Palace to organise the celebrations in the capital.

Lord Levene of Portsoken, a former Lord Mayor of London and former efficiency adviser to Tony Blair, was appalled by the chaos he discovered.

The job of making a success of the public celebrations has now fallen to Philippa Drew, the civil servant who lost responsibility for jail security after two prison escapes in the 1990s.

Lord Levene, who enjoys the confidence of the Queen, was put in charge in 2000 of the Government's formal preparations for the anniversary. *The Times* has learnt he was so dismayed by the work of the "Golden Jubilee Office" set up by ministers to co-ordinate the events that he insisted on setting up his own independent operation.

Ministers keen to retain his expertise and avoid another Millennium Dome-style fiasco agreed to provide public funds for him and his team to move to a separate Whitehall office.

It was in vain. He resigned last summer, to the disappointment of the Queen, because of the lack of strategy and co-ordination and failure of the Golden Jubilee Office – which is staffed by 20 civil servants – to make any public impact.

A senior Whitehall figure, referring to yesterday's report in *The Times* that Buckingham Palace feared a jubilee flop would damage the monarchy, confirmed that Lord Levene had gone in protest. The official explanation to date had been that Lord Levene had too many business commitments. Lord Levene was not available for comment yesterday.

"That story was only the tip of the iceberg. The whole thing was shambolic which is why Levene went," the Whitehall source said.

"The Golden Jubilee Office has been going for more than a year and yet most people have never heard of it or know what it does. The whole thing is drowning in bureaucracy. Levene was sympathetic to the Palace. They are in the hands of the civil servants and politicians. Levene complained about the bureaucracy which is stopping things being done.

"The civil servants would spend hours debating whether bunting for official jubilee events should be fireproof or red, white and blue rather than devising a big picture strategy. There is no co-ordination around the country. It drove Levene to distraction."

The Times reported yesterday that even in the Royal Boroughs of Kensington and Chelsea, Windsor and Maidenhead, and Kingston upon Thames there were only a handful of applications for street parties and community events. The cost of public liability insurance and road closures for street parties was cited in a *Times* survey as a major deterrent to people staging community events.

A Buckingham Palace source said that they were content if expectation was downplayed. "We are not trying to ramp this up into the most fantastic few days of people's lives. I am not going to complain if people say it is going to be a bit bleak."

The planning of the jubilee was also disrupted when the Home Office surrendered the task to the Department for Culture, Media and Sport after the general election. A Home Office official said that they were relieved to see the back of the jubilee. "It was not a task any of us looked forward to."

In the past the Home Office has always been the Whitehall department dealing with royal matters, including state occasions.

Planning for the Golden Jubilee has been beset by difficulties from the start. The Home Office source said they had been astonished when Buckingham Palace said that it had no plans to increase the press operation to handle an event expected to generate worldwide media interest. The Palace also opposed plans to allow 24-hour drinking, because it feared that drunkenness would spoil the celebrations.

Red tape, page 10

Omagh terrorist faces life

By David Lister
Ireland Correspondent

A DISSIDENT republican who spent 30 years working for terrorist groups in Northern Ireland yesterday became the first person to be convicted in connection with the 1998 Omagh bombing, the worst atrocity of the Troubles.

Colm Murphy, 49, a contractor and publican from Dundalk, Co Louth, sat motionless with his hands clasped in front of him as Mr Justice Robert Barr found him guilty of conspiring to cause the blast which killed 29 in August 1998. He will be sentenced on Friday and faces the prospect of life imprisonment.

His conviction, at the end of a five-week trial without a jury, marks the first real success after a multimillion-pound cross-border investigation.

The judge at Dublin's Special Criminal Court described him as a "longstanding republican terrorist" who had served time in jail in the Irish

Continued on page 4, col 4

The Times Today: page 2. Crossword: 26. Property: Times 2, 19-21. TV & radio: Times 2, 23-28

Front page of the *Times* 23/1/02

Wednesday, January 23, 2002 30p www.thesun.co.uk

CANNIBAL

First Tyson chomps ear, now he eats Lennox leg

From PAT SHEEHAN in New York

THIS is the amazing moment yesterday when snarling Mike Tyson BIT Britain's Lennox Lewis in the thigh.

Tyson, 35, sank his teeth into world champ Lewis as a New York press conference for their heavyweight showdown erupted in a brawl.

It was the second time disgraced ex-world champ Tyson had bitten an opponent. In 1997 he chomped on Evander Holyfield's ear during a title fight.

Harold Knight, assistant trainer to Lewis, 36, said: "Tyson bit a gash in Lennox's leg. I can only think

Continued on Page Four

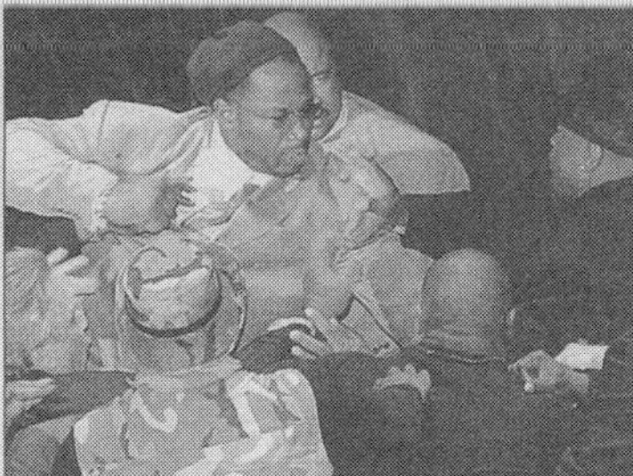

Punches fly . . Lewis (light suit) and Tyson (dark top)

FOOTBALL EXTRA

MAN UTD.......0
LIVERPOOL....1

SunSport PAGES 52 & 53

50 years . . . the Queen

SAVE THE JUBILEE

By PAUL THOMPSON

THE race was on last night to save the Queen's Golden Jubilee from being a flop.

Only 300 communities have so far applied to hold street parties — compared to more than 12,000 for the 1977 Silver Jubilee.

Experts say council red tape is putting off many organisers — and stress England's opening World Cup match on June 2 clashes with the four-day celebration. Palace officials fear the jubilee has failed to capture the nation's imagination. But they hope a wave of enthusiasm for England's soccer heroes

Continued on Page Six

Front page of the *Sun* 23/1/02

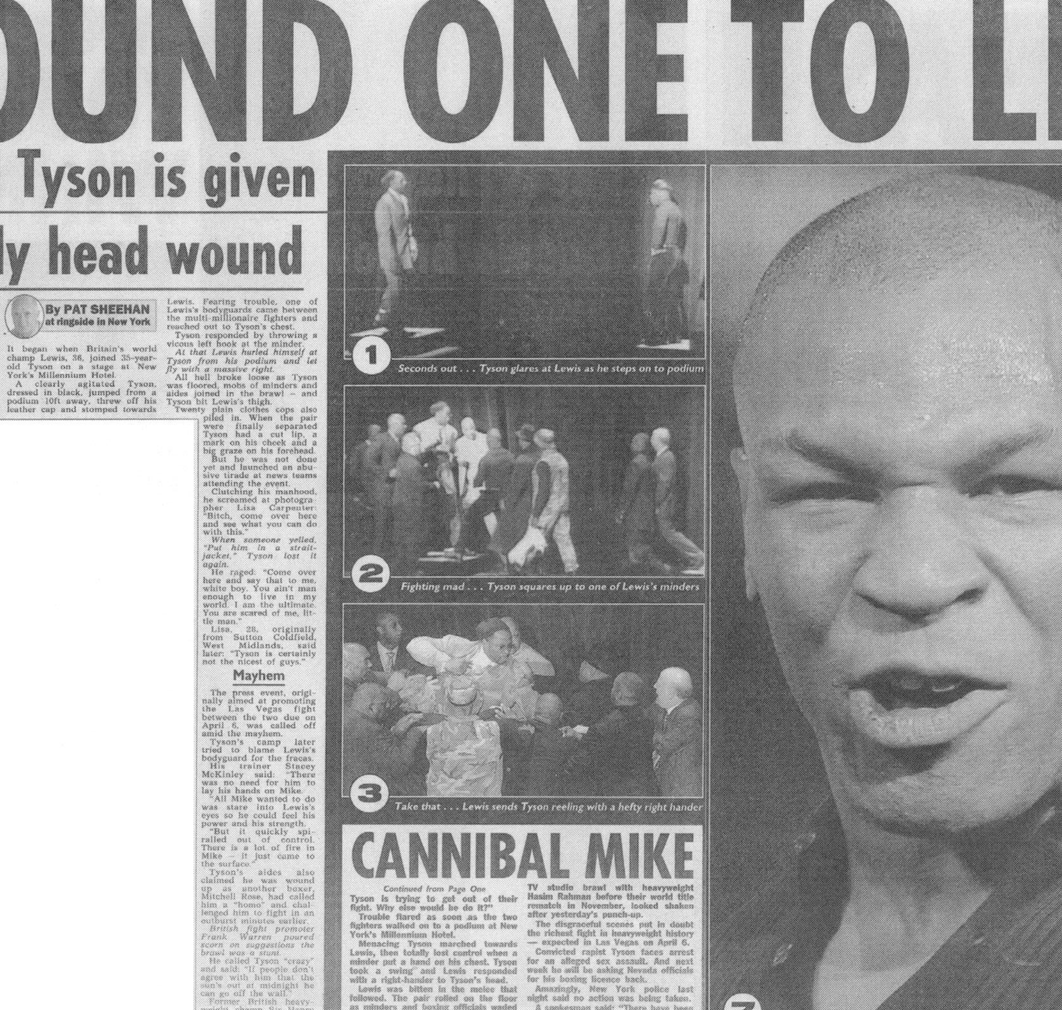

4 THE SUN, Wednesday, January 23, 2002 3G

3GSL THE SUN, Wednesday, January 23, 2002 5

ROUND ONE TO LENNOX

Floored Tyson is given a bloody head wound

By PAT SHEEHAN at ringside in New York

LENNOX Lewis won Round 1 of his clash with Mike Tyson yesterday by giving his crazed rival a bloody head wound.

The two heavyweights dragged boxing through the gutter yet again as they triggered a disgraceful brawl during a promotional face-to-face.

It began when Britain's world champ Lewis, 36, joined 35-year-old Tyson on a stage at New York's Millennium Hotel.

A clearly agitated Tyson, dressed in black, jumped from a podium 10ft away, threw off his leather cap and stomped towards Lewis. Fearing trouble, one of Lewis's bodyguards came between the multi-millionaire fighters and reached out to Tyson's chest.

Tyson responded by throwing a vicous left hook at the minder.

At that Lewis hurled himself at Tyson from his podium and let fly with a massive right.

All hell broke loose as Tyson was floored, mobs of minders and aides joined in the brawl – and Tyson bit Lewis's thigh.

Twenty plain clothes cops also piled in. When the pair were finally separated Tyson had a cut lip, a mark on his cheek and a big graze on his forehead.

But he was not done yet and launched an abusive tirade at news teams attending the event.

Clutching his manhood, he screamed at photographer Lisa Carpenter: "Bitch, come over here and see what you can do with this."

When someone yelled, "Put him in a strait-jacket," Tyson lost it again.

He raged: "Come over here and say that to me, white boy. You ain't man enough to live in my world. I am the ultimate. You are scared of me, little man."

Lisa, 28, originally from Sutton Coldfield, West Midlands, said later: "Tyson is certainly not the nicest of guys."

Mayhem

The press event, originally aimed at promoting the Las Vegas fight between the two due on April 6, was called off amid the mayhem.

Tyson's camp later tried to blame Lewis's bodyguard for the fracas.

His trainer Stacey McKinley said: "There was no need for him to lay his hands on Mike.

"All Mike wanted to do was stare into Lewis's eyes so he could feel his power and his strength.

"But it quickly spiralled out of control. There is a lot of fire in Mike – it just came to the surface."

Tyson's aides also claimed he was wound up as another boxer, Mitchell Rose, had called him a "homo" and challenged him to fight in an outburst minutes earlier.

British fight promoter Frank Warren poured scorn on suggestions the brawl was a stunt.

He called Tyson "crazy" and said: "If people don't agree with him that the sun's out at midnight he can go off the wall."

Former British heavyweight champ Sir Henry Cooper said Tyson was "out of control" and had to be stopped before he kills boxing.

1 Seconds out . . . Tyson glares at Lewis as he steps on to podium

2 Fighting mad . . . Tyson squares up to one of Lewis's minders

3 Take that . . . Lewis sends Tyson reeling with a hefty right hander

CANNIBAL MIKE

Continued from Page One

Tyson is trying to get out of their fight. Why else would he do it?"

Trouble flared as soon as the two fighters walked on to a podium at New York's Millennium Hotel.

Menacing Tyson marched towards Lewis, then totally lost control when a minder put a hand on his chest. Tyson took a swing and Lewis responded with a right-hander to Tyson's head.

Lewis was bitten in the melee that followed. The pair rolled on the floor as minders and boxing officials waded in. Lewis, who was also involved in a TV studio brawl with heavyweight Hasim Rahman before their world title rematch in November, looked shaken after yesterday's punch-up.

The disgraceful scenes put in doubt the richest fight in heavyweight history — expected in Las Vegas on April 6.

Convicted rapist Tyson faces arrest for an alleged sex assault. And next week he will be asking Nevada officials for his boxing licence back.

Amazingly, New York police last night said no action was being taken.

A spokesman said: "There have been no complaints against any parties."

7 Loser on many points . . . growling Tyson sports bloodied face after yesterday's shameful clash

4 Brawl or nothing . . . minders from both camps wade in

5 Do you want some? . . . now Tyson clashes with a minder

6 Below the belt . . . he grabs crotch as he insults girl in crowd

£70M KO — SEE BACK PAGE

Pages 4 and 5 of the *Sun* 23/1/02

CASE STUDY CASE STUDY CASE STUDY CASE STUDY CASE STUDY CASE STUDY CASE STUDY CASE STUDY CASE STUDY CASE STUDY CASE STUDY

The start of the story, together with a smaller picture of the start of the fight, are printed in a box which covers part of the photograph.

In *The Times,* two pictures of the same shape and size are printed one above the other. There is a small headline above: 'Tyson cut, Lewis bitten – and the fight hasn't started yet', and a caption below: 'Lewis throws a punch at Tyson, top, then finds himself upended, with feet in the air after the American went berserk at the pre-fight news conference'. Though the pictures draw attention to this story, the lead on this page in terms of headline size is 'Hewitt joins new push for the euro'.

The difference in style of presentation is between a restrained and a dramatic use of pictures and typography.

The word 'Cannibal' is emotive and it is printed so large that it is striking and forceful. The reverse print (white on black) of the headline and tagline make them grab the reader's attention. The close cropping of the photograph emphasises the violence and drama of the incident. In *The Times*' version the surrounding figures detract from the dramatic part of the picture.

Inside the *Sun* there is a montage of photographs of the whole incident and a huge close-up of a scowling Tyson looking directly and threateningly at the camera. The smaller pictures are numbered and seem like a series of stills from a filmed version of the conflict. The story and the pictures cover a two-page spread.

STYLE OF REPORTING

The *Times* report
From Oliver Holt

A boxing match that took 18 months to finalise and was thought to be worth up to £100 million to its two combatants may have evaporated in 60 seconds of madness here yesterday when Mike Tyson went berserk and bit a lump out of Lennox Lewis's leg.

The world's two most famous boxers had been brought to New York's Hudson Theatre for the announcement that the labyrinthine arrangements for their long-awaited fight had been agreed and that it would take place at the MGM Grand in Las Vegas on April 6.

When Lewis, the British world heavyweight champion, took his place on the stage opposite Tyson, the American strode towards him and threw a punch. In the ensuing melee, Tyson's forehead was gashed and Lewis's thigh was bitten in a savage reminder of the moment when Tyson chewed Evander Holyfield's ear during a fight.

Jose Sulaiman, the President of the World Boxing Council, was knocked out. The scheduled press conference was abandoned. There were also unconfirmed reports that Lewis was taken to hospital for a tetanus injection.

The Briton later released a statement that hinted he may no longer wish to have any part in the fight. 'As a result of today's events,' Lewis said, 'I will evaluate my options after the relevant boxing commission has ruled.'

The Nevada State Athletic Commission is due to meet on Tuesday to decide whether to grant Tyson a boxing licence in the state. If he is refused a licence, the fight will not be allowed to take place in Las Vegas. Some have suggested that Tyson may have behaved like a wild animal because he secretly feared a fight with Lewis.

The *Sun* report
From Pat Sheehan

This is the amazing moment yesterday when snarling Mike Tyson BIT Britain's Lennox Lewis in the thigh.

Tyson, 35, sank his teeth into world champ Lewis as a New York press conference for their heavyweight showdown erupted in a brawl.

It was the second time disgraced ex-world champ Tyson had bitten an opponent. In 1997 he chomped on Evander Holyfield's ear during a title fight.

Harold Knight, assistant trainer to Lewis, 36, said: 'Tyson bit a gash in Lennox's leg. I can only think Tyson is trying to get out of their fight. Why else would he do it?'

Trouble flared as soon as the two fighters walked on to a podium at New York's Millenium Hotel.

Menacing Tyson marched towards Lewis, then totally lost control when a minder put a hand on his chest. Tyson took a swing and then Lewis responded with a right-hander to Tyson's head.

Lewis was bitten in the melee that followed. The pair rolled on the floor as minders and boxing officials waded in. Lewis, who was also involved in a TV studio brawl with heavyweight Hasim Rahman before their world title rematch in November, looked shaken after yesterday's punch-up.

The disgraceful scenes put in doubt the richest fight in heavyweight history – expected in Las Vegas on April 6.

Convicted rapist Tyson faces arrest for an alleged sex assault. And next week he will be asking Nevada officials for his boxing licence back.

Amazingly, New York police last night said no action was being taken.

A spokesman said: 'There have been no complaints against any parties.'

THE FACTS

Are there any differences in the facts reported?

The *Sun* mentions the action of a minder in trying to restrain Tyson. This is not mentioned in the *Times*. The *Sun* also reports that other people joined in.

The Times makes no mention of the brawl between Lewis and Hasim Rahman, nor does it refer to Tyson's rape conviction and the allegations of sexual assault.

The Times does say that Jose Sulaiman, the President of the World Boxing Council, was 'knocked out'. It also refers to the rumour that Lewis was taken to hospital for a tetanus injection. The *Sun* mentions the New York police response which is not in the *Times* report.

VOCABULARY

Are there any differences in the language?

The words used to describe the violence are similar:

Times – '60 seconds of madness', 'went berserk', 'bit a lump', 'threw a punch', 'melee', 'forehead gashed', 'thigh bitten', 'savage reminder', 'chewed an ear'.

Sun – 'BIT', 'sank his teeth', 'trouble flared', 'brawl', 'took a swing', 'right hander', 'bitten in the melee that followed', 'chomped an ear'.

There seems to be little difference here between the choice of vocabulary. What is noticeable, however, is the way the first three paragraphs of the *Sun* report have dramatic verbs about the fight: 'BIT', 'sank his teeth', 'erupted', 'bitten' and 'chomped'.

The Times is less dramatic, with its first paragraph mentioning money and location before the violence and its second paragraph explaining the reason for the press conference, with no mention of violence.

The *Sun* uses more adjectives than *The Times* and they tend to be used to guide the reader's judgement, to tell the reader how to respond: 'snarling Mike Tyson' makes us see him as an animal, 'disgraced' tells us how to judge him, 'menacing' makes him sound evil and dangerous, 'disgraceful' tells us how to pass judgement on the event and 'amazingly' tells us to be astonished at the fact that the two men have not been punished.

Activity

The tabloid papers are often condemned for their sensationalism. Use the above stories and/or two from contemporary papers as evidence and discuss this definition of sensationalism:

'Sensationalism does not mean distorting the truth. It means vivid and dramatic presentation of events so as to give them a forceful impact on the mind of the reader. It means big headlines, vigorous writing, simplification into familiar, everyday language and the wide use of illustration...' (Silvester Bolam, former editor of the *Daily Mirror*)

Press politics and values

You should investigate the current political stance of newspapers and the values they assert or defend. The values can be seen in the newspaper's attitudes to questions such as sex, patriotism, class, hierarchy, leisure, money and family life.

Most British newspapers seem to support a series of propositions such as:

- we have freedom of speech
- we have a free press
- everyone would like to own their own house
- everyone wants strict law enforcement
- democracy is the best form of government
- class differences are a thing of the past
- moderation is better than extremism
- cooperation is better than confrontation
- peace is better than violence
- industriousness is better than idleness
- equality is better than inequality
- openness is better than secrecy
- firmness is better than weakness
- constructiveness is better than destructiveness
- freedom of choice is better than uniformity
- order is better than chaos.

People who do not support these ***core values*** are treated in one of two ways. If the deviation is not too extreme, newspapers take the position either that 'everyone is entitled to their own opinion' or 'it takes all sorts to make a world'. If the deviation is extreme then the people are 'subversives', 'deviants', 'troublemakers', 'perverts' and so on.

The core values are then expressed as the things that 'we' as a population value which are being threatened by 'them' who can be variously criminals, trade union activists, foreigners, homosexuals, paedophiles, asylum seekers, etc.

These values and political attitudes can be studied by looking at:

- the editorials,
- opinion pieces written by regular columnists,
- the way stories are reported,
- the language used to describe the people and organisations or groups involved in conflicts.

Activity

Tracking the *Daily Mail*

To get a clear picture of a newspaper's values you need to track it over several days, keeping records as you do. Track the *Daily Mail* for at least a week and compare your findings with the following. One is by the author from one week in January 2002. The other is by Roy Greenslade from August 2002. Then describe, with examples, the core values of the paper and the activities, people and values it disapproves of.

The *Daily Mail* January 2002

MONDAY

A dispute over wages for railway workers is presented as:

> *dangerous, left wing militants* versus responsible employers and a long-suffering public.

In a story about a rail strike by the Rail Maritime and Transport Union over a pay claim made to the rail company South West Trains the strikers are described as:

> 'far left activists',
>
> 'militant',
>
> 'a clique of union militants' who have a 'stranglehold' on other workers,
>
> behind the strike is 'hard-left union militant Greg Tucker'.

The employers, however, are depicted as *generous victims*:

> they have already given 'an inflation-busting 7.5% pay rise',
>
> the company's boss is 'being held to ransom',
>
> he is 'on the side of the millions of commuters who are forced to endure another 48 hours of rail chaos',
>
> he is quoted as saying: 'We are not prepared to watch our customers suffer.'

These same values and political attitudes are reflected in the paper's editorial entitled, 'Time to face down rail militants'. The *Mail* polarises the conflict, depicting it as being between the *militant unions, with possible Labour party support, and the company and customers*.

'At last someone is prepared to face down the union militants cynically exploiting the current shambles on the railways for their own political ends. And for a change the rail company taking this stand is likely to win the applause of its hapless customers....

South West Trains strike-breaking strategy is a further sign that it does not intend knuckling under to politically motivated union obduracy.'

The editorial also detects a 'resurgent union militancy' in the public sector which could 'drag Britain back into crippling strike chaos', before going on to say that government ministers 'seem only too ready to put themselves on the side of the unions rather than the customers'.

The paper's *antagonism towards the Labour government* can also be seen in its reporting of *problems in the National Health Service*, as in the opening paragraph of a story headlined 'Bed-blocking crisis hits 500,000 patients', which begins: 'Up to half a million NHS patients have missed out on operations since Labour came to power because of lack of places in care homes it emerged yesterday.'

The attack is sustained with a cartoon by Mahood showing a nurse talking to a patient and saying: 'We're hoping to get you fit and well enough to vote Tony Blair out at the next election!' Another cartoon by Mac has a picture of hospital patients lying in a room labelled 'Storeroom'. The place is filthy with an old woman strapped into a bed, and a man with his limbs in plaster casts sitting in a chair next to a coffin. A patient opposite has been fitted with a wooden leg which resembles a furniture leg with a castor on it, while a fourth patient looks as if he has died. A nurse and a doctor stand at the door and the nurse says: 'Good news everybody! We're planning a hanging around unwashed in a corridor party to celebrate the Queen's Golden Jubilee'.

Next to an article headlined, 'Our nurses go round in tears, say surgeons' the *Mail appeals for bad news stories*:

'The *Daily Mail* supports the work of dedicated NHS staff, many of whom are struggling to cope in difficult conditions. We also support the right of patients to speak freely about their experiences. If you or your relative has suffered due to lack of NHS resources contact the *Daily Mail*.'

'We're hoping to get you fit and well enough to vote Tony Blair out at the next election!'

Mahood cartoon

Columnist Melanie Phillips writes an article *criticising the NHS* and supporting an alternative private system: 'If Tony Blair really wants to champion doctors and nurses, he should make all hospitals properly independent, revolutionise health funding so that clinical staff become accountable to patients...and remove himself and all politicians from health care altogether.'

Another target for *Mail* attacks is *Moslem extremism*. A story about *'Moslem fanatics'* refers to 'The son of a controversial Moslem cleric' and 'Mohammed Mustafa Kamel, 20, the son of claw-handed fundamentalist Abu Hamaz' and refers to 'His father, who has caused controversy with his radical views'.

Other *government figures attacked* are Foreign Secretary Jack Straw, described as a 'former student rabble rouser' and Deputy Prime Minister John Prescott, the 'minister of silly talks'.

TUESDAY

The rail strike is reported again and the blame for 'stoppages causing misery for thousands of commuters' is placed on *'militant trade unions'*.

An article about South West Trains boss Brian Souter portrays him as a successful, *'no-nonsense'*, *entrepreneur* who 'is one of the toughest business brains in Britain'.

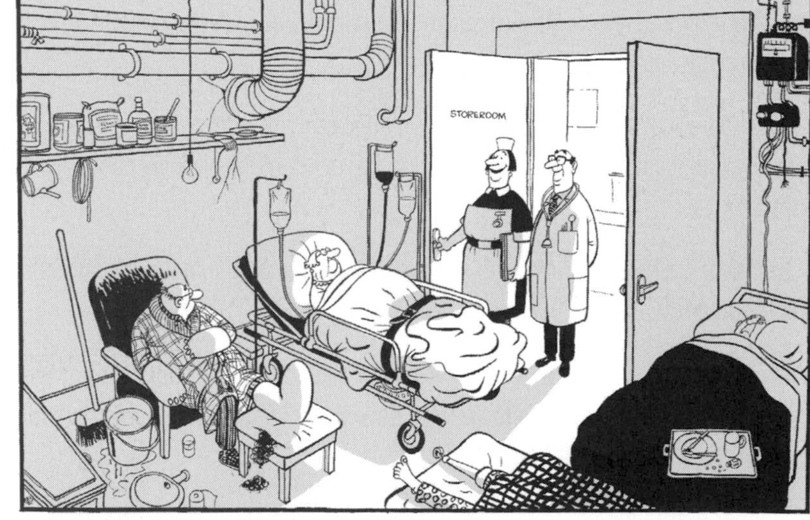

Good news, everybody! We're planning a hanging around unwashed in a corridor party to celebrate the Queen's Golden Jubilee.'

Mac cartoon

The *continuing attack on Labour* hits the front page with the headline ENRON SLEAZE ENGULFS LABOUR over a story about the government 'facing accusations of a cash-for-access scandal to dwarf those which plagued the Major administration'. A double page feature is headlined, 'ENRON: The questions that Labour must answer and *Blair's fatal attraction to the rich*'.

As far as sex and marriage are concerned the *Mail* seems to favour *traditional attitudes*. A story about an unexpected rise in marriages emphasises that live-in relationships are short-lived and often fail, 'plunging women into single motherhood'. It refers to 'damage caused by cohabitation' while emphasising that marriage makes you better off and living longer in better health.

WEDNESDAY

There are more attacks on *militants* in the coverage of the rail strike. The editorial tries to raise fears of a return to the 'mad, militant Seventies, when bullying union barons called the shots'. The editorial also pursues the possible scandal over ENRON: 'New Labour and a suspicious smell.'

Columnist Lynda Lee-Potter joins in the *jibes at the National Health Service* in a nostalgia piece remembering when Britain was great:

> 'We had an absolute belief that we were part of the finest nation in the world.
>
> 'If we were ill the local GP came to visit the same day. If we had to go to hospital the sheets were dazzlingly white and crisp and the matron patrolled the wards like a ferocious general.'

She insists that everything is much worse now and that poor conditions in hospital are due to *'lack of discipline, lack of organisation and an uneasy air of sloppiness'*. Later in the article she complains that everywhere in British society we have 'abandoned cleanliness, discipline, politeness and formality'.

This belief that the past was better and that the future will be even worse unless old-fashioned toughness returns is a common theme in the *Mail*.

Asylum seekers do not get a good press in the story 'Refugees force cuts in Chunnel freight link', being accused of 'forcing hundreds more lorries a day on to Britain's overcrowded roads' because they cause cancellations of freight trains through the Channel Tunnel.

THURSDAY

The *Mail* seems *to oppose genetically modified food*. In a story headlined 'Bread with "hidden" GM ingredient' it gives prominence to the director of the Food Commission's view that 'The Government knows that the majority of people don't want to eat genetically modified food. Now we find it is creeping in to staple foods like bread and cake, without any law to stop it or any label to warn customers.'

The campaign to highlight the *deficiencies of the NHS* continues with a story about a hospital where 'slapdash procedures in its mortuary led to a baby's body being sent to a laundry'.

FRIDAY

Things aren't what they used to be. A photograph of the Royal Family taken in 1957 has the headline, 'From a gentler age, an image of the perfect family'. The story that goes with it maintains that the family were 'adored and revered by their loyal subjects' but have now become 'end-of-the-pier-show grotesques.'

Happy Family: the royals circa 1957

The writer paints a picture of a time of civilised behaviour when:

> 'marriage was made to last'
>
> 'divorce was .... alien'
>
> people believed that the Queen 'had been anointed to reign by God'
>
> 'everyone stood up for the national anthem',
>
> 'in the street, gentlemen raised their hats and always gave up their seats on buses, trains and trams for ladies'.

The editorial paints a picture of a *nation in decline*: 'In shabby, cash-strapped, down-at-heel Britain, our Third World health service stumbles from failure to failure. A shambolic rail system is mired in industrial militancy. Motorists are murdered for the price of their cars. Nothing works as it should.' It *blames Tony Blair* for not putting things right.

Television is bad for you, and everything is in decline according to an obituary for *Z Cars* actor Stratford Johns. There is reverence, however, for the *good old days* and scorn for the nasty present.

Writer Max Davidson says, 'For boys of my generation growing up in the Sixties, two things above all others kept us on the straight and narrow. The first was schoolmasters who beat us black and blue if we forgot our French irregular verbs. The second was nightmares about Stratford Johns.'

He admires the way Johns interviewed suspects in the crime series and says it was fear of a similar grilling that kept people from crime in those days. 'If that was what happened when you got arrested by the police, then you did not want to get arrested. It was as simple as that.' Instead 'young people watching today' are 'more likely to pick up ideas on new ways to snort cocaine'.

He regrets that TV crime series no longer reinforce the police but *undermine* them. He complains that wrongdoing is 'glamorised through scenes of cartoon-like violence, or treated as a form of psychological disorder which needs to be remedied by counselling'.

There is another *health scare story*, 'Granny with a broken neck sent home by doctors'.

There are two *anti Tony Blair stories*, one in which he is blamed for the rail strike and the other where he is criticised for spending too much time abroad.

SATURDAY

There is a '*good old days*' story about a marble statue of Margaret Thatcher, 'Gathering dust under a railway arch, this statue of our greatest post-war Premier shames the MPs too timid to put it on show.'

A crime story is used to continue the theme of *contemporary national decline*, the recalling of a better past and the fear of an even worse future unless tough action is taken. In the Saturday essay, James Jackson lists a catalogue of street crimes – someone stabbed to death trying to stop thieves stealing his car, an 80-year-old who had his face slashed, a woman who had her fingers broken as her mobile phone was snatched from her grasp. 'My city [London] is sinking into a *cesspit of crime*,' he laments.

He lists 'excuses' such as alienation, marginalisation, understandable resentment but dismisses them all. He describes the atmosphere of his neighbourhood: 'I'm talking about knives held to throats, of faces scarred for life, of pervasive threat, of mindless, predatory aggression, of wanton evil...'.

He goes on to complain that *political correctness* prevents people from speaking openly and then claims that 'most street crime is perpetrated by young black men'.

The solution he offers is 'accept responsibility, reintroduce zero tolerance, insist on stop-and-search, demand proper policing, force a change in the law to introduce mandatory prison sentences for those found carrying knives'. Otherwise he predicts in a decade's time we will have 'fled our capital, armed ourselves, or donned stab-proof vests to live in gated, guarded enclaves...'

Columnist Simon Heffer continues the theme on the next page . He mentions recent crimes and then says, 'At the root of our violent crime problem are two things: the widespread *'recreational' use of drugs* and the politically correct obsession with so-called institutional racism that has prevented the police from dealing with the threat posed by organised gangs of black youths'.

There is a *soft-on-criminals* story about shopping vouchers being given to criminals who agree to help with research into their criminality.

There is an *anti-Labour story* about under-investment in public services and a pro-Conservative story about Iain Duncan Smith 'bravely visiting' a staunchly Labour housing estate in Glasgow.

Greenslade's findings

Journalist Roy Greenslade, writing in the *Guardian* on Monday 2 September 2002, describes his own tracking of the *Mail* during August of that year in an article entitled 'So just why is the Daily Meldrew so grumpy?'

> A study of the past month's issues of the Daily Mail proves that its real title should be the Daily Meldrew. Playing to the fears and narrow mindedness of its audience, it magnifies their xenophobia and hypochondria, panders to their envy and, despite its vaunted image as a paper sympathetic to women, disparages feminism.

What follows is a random sample of headlines, stories and features that illustrate those points....

Let's begin with the *knocking of our country*. An article headlined 'Dickensian Britain' suggested life hasn't improved much in the past 150 years....

'How Britain is destroying itself' was followed by a piece which decries 'the insidious and inexorable march of political correctness'.

Now to the specific peril we face, *immigration*, which...accounted for more spreads and page leads than any other topic. The month began with a page about non-white Britons having a higher birth rate, and here is a handful of headlines in subsequent days and weeks:

> 250,000 migrants a year entering Britain
>
> Farce of asylum crackdown
>
> Luxury centre for failed immigrants' last days in UK
>
> Asylum seekers will be bribed to go home
>
> Asylum seekers will get £50,000 for their driving lessons

One story that ran and ran began with a revelation that a group helping people to fight deportation had been given a lottery grant of £340,000: 'Is this the barmiest lottery handout of them all?'

Race relations workers were excoriated...for being the 'fanatical forces of politically correct anti-racism now sweeping Britain'. 'Sorry', said another headline, 'your bedroom is going to a foreign nurse.' A picture of a bridge over a Bradford river was headlined: 'Ganges UK: Hindus may be allowed to scatter the ashes of relatives from this riverbank.'....

Then we come to the *Mail's* coverage – or should that be obsession? – with *matters of health*, much of which was guaranteed to breed Meldrewism:

> Three cigarettes a day can double a woman's risk of a heart attack
>
> Why stretching won't save you from aches and injuries
>
> Vitamin pill danger
>
> How one in five people catch cold from their holiday flight
>
> Poisoned! How a cocktail of 300 chemicals in everyday items pollutes our bodies
>
> British blood too risky for our children....

It was noticeable how the paper ... maintains a traditional view of the *female role*. 'Why women should learn to love doing housework' trilled one headline. Another suggested 'how to practise the lost art of flirting.'....

The *Mail* understands that people love reading about *celebrities* but doesn't appear to like them, consistently presenting them in a poor light, doubtless believing that its readers are jealous of their fame and riches.

...We should note the devious use of the query at the end of these headlines.... It...allows the wildest speculation to be presented as fact.

'He is a miner's son who married an aristocrat...but did Bryan Ferry's marriage ultimately fail because he is too in love with himself?'...'Less Hurley. As her curves shrink alarmingly, is Liz overdoing the diet regime?' ... 'What do women see in this man [Andre Previn]? ... 'Who Dunaway with her [Faye's] money?'....

Knock, knock, knock. The *Mail* presents every facet of life in as gloomy and threatening a light as possible. There were pieces attacking the BBC, the NHS, the education system, GM foods and...the judicial sentencing policy.

If there are so many Meldrews about in Britain, could it be entirely due to the *Daily Mail*?'

(*Guardian* 24/1/02, with permission)

When you do your own comparison you could use the following checklist of topics as a starting point. How many of the core values listed earlier in this chapter does the *Mail* share? You can relate these values to the question of ownership explored in chapter 14. (See the section on 'How and why the papers took sides over Cherie' in particular.) You should also consider how the Mail is both reflecting and reinforcing the opinions and attitudes of its readers.

Topic	*Mail's* attitudes
politics	left, right, neutral?
unions	troublemakers, defenders of workers' rights?
immigration	threat or a help?
law and order/penal system	too soft, too tough?
NHS	badly run or efficient?
television, films, video games	beneficial or damaging?
gender	anti-feminist or pro-female?
transport	in a mess or working well?

Other topics: education, sport, drugs, homosexuality, family life, single parents, the benefits system, the countryside, the environment, demonstrations, poverty, wealth, health, food, national decline, world affairs.

Press audiences

Audience segmentation

All paid-for newspapers depend partly on cover price and partly on advertising revenue for their income. Broadsheet newspapers rely more on advertising revenue than do tabloid papers because their circulations are generally much smaller but they have a readership which has high spending power and is therefore valuable to advertisers. Consequently the broadsheets have developed specialist features sections which often change from day to day. The purpose of these sections is to attract audiences with special interests. These audiences are then 'sold' to advertisers.

Activity

Build up a picture of this aspect of newspapers by compiling a chart to show the range and timing of these sections. Show the link between the specialist feature/supplement and the advertising it attracts. Do this for two of these papers: *The Times*, the *Daily Telegraph*, the *Guardian* or the *Independent*. Say what you can learn about the readership (audience) of these newspapers from your findings. Compare your findings with those below which were recorded in January 2002 for *The Times*.

You should ask why there are more specialist features on Saturdays and what are the links between the topics of the features and the kinds of advertising they attract.

Are there any links between the time of year and the products being advertised?

Specialist sections of *The Times* with accompanying advertising

Day	*Supplement*	*Advertising*
MONDAY	Sport:	sports betting, Subaru cars, Fisherman's Friend lozenges, air travel.
	Times 2: parents, film, fashion, arts	cheap flights, online shopping, opera tickets, National Theatre.
TUESDAY	Sport:	men's fashion shop in London, Dell computers.
	Law:	jobs in legal profession.
	Times 2: lifetime, health, arts	cheap air flights, chair lifts, vasectomy operations
WEDNESDAY	Sport:	Natwest mortgages, Powergen.
	Times 2: books, arts, jazz, property,	Firstplus loans, property for sale, all-season duvets, secretarial appointments, theatres, computers, foreign language courses, low-cost flights.
THURSDAY	Sport:	Easyjet, AMD PC processors.
	Appointments:	18 pages of jobs.
	Times 2: medicine, films, education	jobs in education, films, low cost flights, Acorn stairlifts, Wellman Clinic.
FRIDAY	Sport:	Natwest mortgages, Sky Television football, Dell computers.
	Times 2: arts, media, pop	Scope mountain trek, London Furniture Village sale, Alan Jackson album, Harry Potter film, Lord of the Rings film,Kelly Joe Phelps tour, inexpensive flights.
SATURDAY	Magazine:	VW Passat, Boots cosmetics, Renault Laguna, Swan Hellenic Cruise, Bosch washer, Alfa Romeo 156, holidays in Florida, Skoda Octavia, Portland conservatories, Corsica holidays, Brittany Ferries holidays, Dulux paints, Dolphin bathrooms, English Country Cottages, Sharps home office, MFI, British Gas communications (mobile phones), Page and Moy holidays, Safeway, Saga holidays, Gallery kitchens, Noble Caledonia holidays, Voyages Jules Verne, New England and California skiing, Spanish Paradores (holidays), Toyota Corolla.
	Sport:	Heineken, jamjar.com (car purchase), Subaru Forester Sport, Lloyds TSB, Natwest mortgages, Sportingodds.com (betting).

Money: 20 adverts for financial investment products such as unit trusts, bonds and ISAs, e.g. Fidelity investments, Marks and Spencer finance, Aberdeen Bonds, Financial Discounts direct, Legal and General, Royal Bank of Scotland, Merrill Lynch Investments.

Travel: 31 display adverts for holidays such as Great Rail Journeys, Qantas, Travelsphere holidays in Vietnam, Cox and Kings holidays in India. This is followed by over six pages of classified ads for holidays.

Weekend: RSPB garden birdwatch, Royal (a book about the Queen), Edwardian Hotels, plus four pages of small ads for garden and home products.

Newspapers and their readers

You can discover what newspapers think of their readers by looking closely at the media packs which they produce and which you should be able to get by contacting their advertising departments. The following information was in such packs in 2002.

	Number of Readers in 000's	%of the total population of adults in GB	% of Daily Telegraph readers	Number of Readers in 000's	%of the total population ofadults in GB	%of Telegraph Magazine Readers
All			100.00	2,231	4.8	100.0
Men	1,257	5.5	55.1	1,121	4.9	50.3
Women	1,023	4.3	44.9	1,110	4.6	49.7
Main Shoppers	1,515	5.0	66.5	1,520	5.0	68.1
Age 15-24	182	2.6	8.0	143	2.1	6.4
Age 25-34	208	2.4	9.1	223	2.6	10.0
Age 35-44	306	3.6	13.4	299	3.5	13.4
Age 45-54	456	6.0	20.0	463	6.1	20.7
Age 55-64	406	6.9	17.8	397	6.8	17.8
Age 65+	722	8.0	31.7	707	7.8	31.7
AB Adults	1,299	11.9	57.0	1,255	11.5	56.2
ABC Adults	1,960	8.3	86.0	1,891	8.0	84.7
ABC1C2 Adults	2,147	6.4	94.2	2,089	6.2	93.6
C1 Adults	660	5.2	29.0	636	5.0	28.5
C2 Adults	187	1.8	8.2	199	2.0	8.9
DE Adults	133	1.0	5.8	142	1.1	6.4
London/SE/ East Anglia	1128	6.8	49.5	1,077	6.4	48.3
Greater London	297	5.2	13.0	269	4.7	12.1
South East	743	8.0	32.6	710	7.7	31.8
East Anglia	89	5.0	3.9	97	5.5	4.4
South West/Wales	362	5.6	15.9	379	5.9	17.0
Midlands	323	4.2	14.2	336	4.4	15.1
North West	220	4.3	9.6	212	4.1	9.5
North East/North	187	2.8	8.2	168	2.5	7.5
Scotland	60	1.4	2.6	60	1.5	2.7

Daily Telegraph circulation 2001, reproduced with permission

Daily Telegraph

These figures show that the *Telegraph* is read by 2,231,000 people, which is about 5% of the population. It seems to be more popular with men than women and its biggest readership from an age point of view is in the over-65s. Over half its readers are in the top social classes (ABs). Geographically it is strongest in London and the south-east of England.

This is the image it presents in its publicity brochures:

> 'A newspaper that doesn't just report the news but introduces you to the people who make it. The *Telegraph* can engage, intrigue, amuse and even provoke. It will certainly never be a dull experience.'

It prides itself on being 'enquiring', covering current affairs, politics and world events.

It boasts of its sports coverage and being the first paper to introduce a 'stand-alone' daily sports section. It lists famous sports people who have written for the paper: Gary Lineker, Sebastian Coe, Roy Keane, Nasser Hussain, Graham Taylor and Steve McManaman.

It thinks its coverage of gardening and homes is expert and inspirational with its 'entire section on gardening' on Saturdays and its 14 page 'Guide to modern living' in the *Saturday Magazine*. It tries to appeal to people who see property as an investment: 'The Property section on Saturday is the best location to be for the latest news on the market and the most interesting property investments around the country'. This seems to suggest that it expects many of its readers will be wealthy enough to think of property as a way of investing money rather than simply as somewhere to live.

The *Telegraph* is seen by some as a dull and stuffy newspaper and it tries to counteract that image by emphasising how 'witty' it is. Evidence given for this quality is that Michael Parkinson and Ian Hislop write for it, that it serialised Bridget Jones's diaries and that it has an award-winning cartoonist, Matt.

The other qualities it emphasises are:

- it likes 'mixing with people' because it has searching interviews with celebrities like Kate Winslet and Clive Anderson, and it has a food and drink section. ('Jan Moir takes you on a weekly tour of the tastiest and most interesting places to eat around the country whilst Giles Kime has a nose for a fine wine at a reasonable price.')
- It is adventurous. (It has a travel section.)
- It has good business coverage.

Its trademark qualities are: 'It speaks with a voice that is unmistakably its own: intelligent, witty, questioning and most of all, dependable.'

Sun

The *Sun* is proud of being 'The UK's best selling daily newspaper'.

It thinks of itself as being easy-to-read, fresh, lively and campaigning. It says it speaks to readers in 'a down-to-earth manner which is both easy to understand and empathise with'. It also prides itself on its 'fearless' reporting. It says it 'pulls no punches' in its editorials.

Rupert Murdoch, its owner, says, 'I do think we speak for middle-England common sense and we understand working class values. It's a mixture of morality and hedonism: it sounds contradictory but we want them to have a good time yet have very strong values.'

Former editor Larry Lamb maintained, 'We acknowledged what many journalists at the time were anxious to forget – that the basic interests of the human race are not in politics, philosophy or economics, but in things like food and money, sex and crime, football and television.'

It can boast a young readership with around a quarter of its readers in the 25–35 age range while over three million of its readers are 'female main shoppers', a fact of interest to potential advertisers.

Criticisms of the *Sun*:

- 'That tawdry little journal, the Sun, written for morons by morons.' (*Sunday Express*)
- 'The Sun, a coarse and demented newspaper.' (*Daily Mirror*)
- 'The Sun is a lackey of its financial boss.' (Sir Edward Heath)

- Around a quarter of Sun readers are aged 25-34. Sun readers are 28% more likely than the average person to fall into this age bracket.
- The Sun delivers over three and a half million female shoppers, representing well over a third of readers.
- An equally high percentage of readers live in households with children under 15 and are considerably more likely than the average to do so.
- Seven out of ten readers do not read any other daily tabloid, and 81% read at least three out of four issues of the Sun.
- And it gets even better on a Saturday, when the Sun can boast around 9.9 million readers-
- 86% of whom read the TV Mag, over 8.5 million people, making the Sun's free magazine the UK's best-read TV title

Sun's circulation and readership figures

The Times

The Times emphasises its tradition, 'one of the world's oldest national newspapers' (founded in 1785) and its seriousness – a 'paper of record' or, in other words, it is a reliable recorder of today's major events.

It maintains it is 'the authoritative medium for political, court, legal, business and social news. The Times is synonymous with responsible news gathering and informed comment.'

It boasts that its audience has large numbers of AB business executives, young establishment adults (ABC1s under 45), sophisticated professionals and students, who will 'go on to become successful business executives'.

		(000's)	% of marketplace	% of Times readers	Index (100 = national propensity)
	All	1575	3.4	100	100
	Men	932	4.1	59	121
	Women	644	2.7	41	80
Age	Under 25	213	3.1	13.5	91
	25-34	290	3.4	18.4	99
	35-44	271	3.2	17.2	94
	45-54	354	4.7	22.5	138
	55-64	197	3.4	12.5	99
	65+	250	2.8	15.9	82
Social Grade	AB	954	8.6	60.6	256
	ABC1	1389	5.9	88.1	173
	ABC1C2	1499	4.4	95.2	131
	C1	435	3.4	27.6	102
	C2	110	1.1	7	32
	ABC1's under 45	678	5.3	43.1	158
	AB's under 45	422	7.3	26.8	218

The Times circulation figures 2001

Guardian

According to editor Alan Rusbridger the *Guardian* is a paper of innovation with a tradition 'for investigation, for elegant writing, for irreverence, for wit'.

The paper is owned by the Scott Trust which monitors its progress but does not intervene. It is not owned by its shareholders or a press baron, nor is it influenced by a political party, though generally it supports left-of-centre policies.

The newspaper describes its branding in this way:

> At the core of everything we do at the *Guardian* is a single controlling idea – Free Thinking. The concept originates from our unique ownership by the Scott Trust and enables us to position ourselves as 'open-minded', 'challenging', 'intelligent', 'modern', 'lively', 'questioning', 'innovative' and 'confident'.
> With no proprietor dictating what can and cannot appear in our pages, the *Guardian* is the medium for genuine free thinkers – journalists, readers and advertisers alike...the *Guardian* readers are people who can weigh up complex arguments and make up their own minds. They are people who don't subscribe to bland opinions and who are interested in setting the agenda rather than following the crowd....

The same readers who are attracted to the paper because of its brand values are also an extremely desirable target audience for most advertisers – they are people who are open-minded, value debate and who are individualistic.

- 'I think the *Guardian* is a terrific paper. I just don't like it.' (Rupert Murdoch)

Daily Express

The *Express* lists these as its 'readership strengths':

- a higher proportion of younger and more upmarket readers than any other mid-market or popular newspaper,
- a large proportion of its readers are people who own their homes and have children under fifteen,
- they tend to be in full employment or are self-employed (1 in 10),
- two out of every three readers are main shoppers,
- they tend to be car buyers and have access to the internet,
- they are 50% more likely than the average to hold stocks and shares.

Star

The *Star* is a sister paper of the *Express*. It lists its readership strengths as:

- readers are younger (average 37) than those of any other national newspaper,
- they are mainly in full-time work,
- more likely than other tabloid readers to have a mortgage and be planning a move in the next six months,
- they tend to have higher than average household incomes, use the internet and have satellite television.

Independent

Its brand values are 'a newspaper with a mind of its own and a voice that's clear'. It is free of proprietorial and political party influence. It sees its readers as having 'an independent perspective on life'.

Though it says its readers are 'hard to pigeonhole' because they have eclectic tastes and diverse interests, it boasts of having a high proportion of them who 'have flown on business more than 3 times in the last 12 months'. A high proportion of them also have a net income of over £28,000 and 71% of them access the internet more than once a month.

Circulation trends

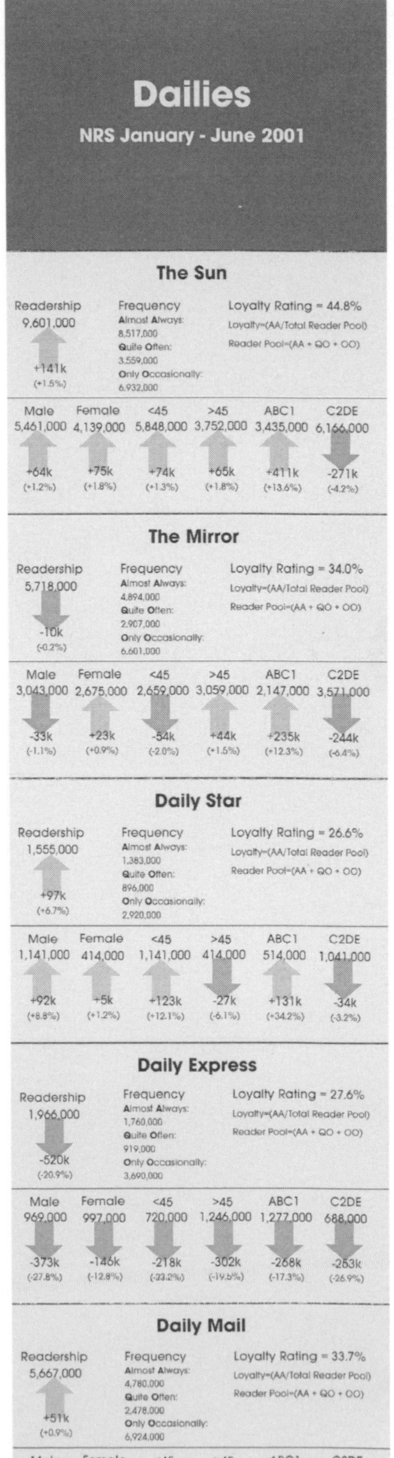

Constructing an audience

Stories and features are written with a ***target audience*** in mind and the way they are written assumes certain ***responses*** or ***values***. A successful newspaper has to deliver a product that is appreciated by its target audience. But newspapers also help to shape the tastes and values, the concerns and worries of the readers. For instance, the public did not spontaneously decide to worry about genetically modified food. Activists and scientists interacting with journalists orchestrated the concern.

Journalists in fact have limited access to the public and they have to invent or imagine their audience. Newspapers decide what matters to their readers when they select what to print and how to report it. The tabloids in particular claim to speak for their readers, often using the terms 'we', 'us' and 'our' as in 'The war against al-Qa'ida is about preserving our way of life', 'Blair is using our taxes to campaign for it', 'Jack Straw, a man we have a lot of time for....'. 'Tell us the truth, Tony.'

The opposite of 'us', 'them', varies from day to day. 'Them' can be Europeans, especially the French and Germans, soft judges, gypsies, the loony left, the BBC, and anything 'liberal'.

According to John Street in ***Mass Media, Politics and Democracy*** (Palgrave 2001) an audience is constructed 'through a series of contrasts and oppositions, through the ...orchestration of 'us' and 'them'. National borders are drawn and redrawn in this way, as are norms of sexuality and of political behaviour. At a trivial level this can be discerned in sports commentary for international competitions where it is assumed that the audience is on one side or another; at a more serious level, it is involved in the construction of an enemy in the prelude to, and the conduct of, war....

The point of this argument is not to suggest that there is, in fact, a single 'people', or that one account of who 'we' are is necessarily more accurate than any other, but that *different forms of address create different versions of the people*. In creating one version, the media marginalise another.' p 55 (my italics).

Activity

Circulation trends

The readership of newspapers has been in gradual decline for many years. The problem almost all newspapers face is how to manage declining circulations. Look at the figures from 2001 (see p90), comparing the circulation of the major national tabloid papers and answer these questions on them.

1 Which newspaper seems to be having the greatest problems in maintaining its sales? What has happened to that paper since 2001?

2 Which paper has the highest ABC1 readership? Why is that attractive to advertisers?

3 Which paper has the highest percentage increase in ABC1 readers?

4 Which paper has the largest female readership?

5 Which paper is read more by women than by men?

6 Which paper has the biggest difference (proportionately) between numbers of male and female readers?

7 Which two papers have a stronger under-45 than over-45 readership? Why is this important?

Advertising rates

The higher the readership the more a newspaper can charge for its advertising space. In 2002 these were some of the rates per page charged by national newspapers:

Telegraph	mono £47,500	colour £62,000
The Times	mono £24,000	colour £34,000
Sun	mono £36,000	colour £45,000
Independent	mono £15,000	colour £24,000
Express	mono £29,000	colour £31,000
Guardian	mono £20,000	

Circulation figures for December 2001 were:

*Mirror**	2,657,482
Star	594,310
Sun	3,307,051
Express	937,006
Mail	2,389,031
Telegraph	1,005,338
Financial Times	501,209
Guardian	397,138
Independent	224,008
The Times	710,309

* includes the ***Daily Record*** in Scotland

A declining market

In 2001 the four red-top dailies – ***Sun***, ***Mirror***, ***Record***, and ***Star*** – together had a 1.4% drop in circulation over the year. The ***Mirror*** was just 46,000 from dropping below 2 million sales. The ***Sun*** had seen its biggest fall in sales since Rupert Murdoch took over in 1969.

The problem for all the popular tabloids is that, as its older readers die, young ones are not taking their place. As ***Mirror*** editor Piers Morgan pointed out in the Media Guardian in February 1997, 'It is a sobering fact that 30,000 of our older readers die every year.'

Roy Greenslade writing in the ***Media Guardian*** in January 2002 said, '...the downmarket quartet are doomed (even if they plan to spend a long time fighting each other in the cemetery).' He wondered if the readers deserting them were moving into middle-market papers, the ***Mail*** and the ***Express***, but thought it more likely that the ***Mail***'s rise of 70,000 sales was largely due to people switching from the ***Express***, down 80,000.

Do falling circulation figures simply reflect a recession in the economy or are people losing the reading habit? Will newspapers go out of fashion?

Roy Greenslade argued in December 2001 that 'mass circulation papers hardly merit the title any more'. The ***Mirror*** at that time was at its lowest sales point since 1946, the ***Sun*** at its lowest since 1974, while the ***Star*** was selling only half of what it did at its height. Greenslade believes that 'some people have certainly given up on reading, preferring to take their news from television, the radio and the internet'.

Other factors are the effects of wide circulation in some cities of the ***Metro*** freesheets, the increase in people driving to work, the reluctance of newsagents in inner cities to deliver newspapers and the decline of interest in politics. 'The rejection of newspapers goes hand in hand with the rejection of politics.'

Activity

Investigate the reasons for young people not reading newspapers on a regular basis.

Construct a focus group of about six people. They should be either non-readers of papers or occasional readers.

Compile questions that will allow you to find out about their reasons for not reading or seldom reading papers.

Are they:

- practical (e.g. not easily available, make your hands dirty, too much bother to carry around, not enough time to read them);
- to do with people choosing other news sources such as television;
- to do with apathy about the news – 'not bothered', 'not interested';
- to do with principles – 'they're all capitalist propaganda sheets'?

Find out what changes, if any, in content, pricing or design would make people more likely to read papers.

Find out how the members of the group think their reading habits will change as they grow older.

Write a report on your findings.

Competition

A declining market leads to fiercer competition between titles. In the broadsheet market the *Telegraph* competes with the *Guardian*, the *Independent*, the *Financial Times* and, mainly, *The Times*.

In 1993 a price war started. *The Times* cut its cover price to win customers from other broadsheets and from the middle-market papers, the *Daily Mail* and *Daily Express*. It was able to do this because it was part of a larger organisation, News International, which in turn is part of News Corporation, a multinational company owned by Rupert Murdoch. Profits from the larger organisations were used to subsidise the price cuts. Winning over readers means that advertising revenue can increase while competitors lose out. Ultimately, if a competing newspaper can be put out of business it means a huge potential new market for the survivors.

In the middle market in 2002 there were only two competitors, the *Mail* and the *Express*. The Express's circulation declined rapidly after the title was bought by Richard Desmond who had gained his wealth from publishing pornographic magazines. The rival *Mail* exploited Desmond's background by offering *Express* readers 'a cleaner, brighter daily read' and emphasising Desmond's seedy publications. Newsagents were offered inducements to persuade buyers of the *Express* to take the *Mail* on a six-week trial period. The *Express* responded by running a feature about the Rothermere family which had owned the *Mail* from its start in 1896. The feature mentioned the first Lord Rothermere's fascism in the 1930s and the third Lord Rothermere's colourful private life.

In the battle for circulation the *Mail* has greater long-term strength. It is much better resourced than the *Express*, which sacked its reps, the people on the ground who maintain contact with the newsagents, and cut back on its editorial staff.

Privacy and intrusion

The essential problem with this topic is how to draw a line between an individual's right to ***privacy*** and the public's ***right to know***. The Press Complaints Commission, which is run by newspaper professionals though it has non-specialist people on it as well, passes judgement on individual cases and advises the press how it should behave.

In January 2002 Vanessa Feltz complained to the Press Complaints Commission about an article in the *Sunday Mirror* which claimed she had a new boyfriend and then went into intimate detail about their alleged sex life. The Commission ruled against Feltz because she had already talked publicly about the breakdown of her marriage, saying that celebrities who talk publicly about their private life undermine their right to privacy. Some people argued, however, that the revelation of personal details without consent can never be justified.

Some members of the public, in particular celebrities facing unflattering publicity, have found this arrangement unsatisfactory and have taken to using the Human Rights Act to stop newspapers printing stories and pictures. In November 2001 a court ruled that the *Sunday People* could not print a story about a married Premiership footballer's affairs with two women because it was an invasion of his privacy as defined by the Human Rights Act. The editor of the paper argued that this was a dangerous precedent. 'What this ruling says is that any sexual liaison, no matter how immoral...is by definition confidential and cannot be disclosed.... The breadth of this ruling needs to be understood. According to this, we wouldn't be able to report if Tony Blair was visiting a prostitute'. Lord Wakeham, then head of the PCC, said, 'It is a very serious attack on the freedom of the press.... It is not in the interest of the public or anyone that this sort of gagging order should be there.'

In December 2001 actress Amanda Holden and her husband comedian Les Dennis struck a blow against tabloid press intrusion by suing the *Star* under the Human Rights legislation. They won £40,000 in damages for infringement of privacy. The *Star* had published sneak photographs of them on holiday in a private villa in Tuscany.

NEWS OF THE WORLD

FREE MAGAZINE 28 days to a NEW BODY INSIDE TODAY

WORLD EXCLUSIVE

HARRY'S DRUGS SHAME

- Prince admits: I smoked pot at Highgrove
- Charles orders him to heroin rehab clinic
- Agony started with illegal pub sessions

THE ONLY PAPER WITH THE FULL SHOCKING STORY

Activity

Prince Harry and the *News of the World*

Imagine you are sitting in judgement over this case and give your verdict with reasons on whether the newspaper should have been allowed to print the story.

- Prince Harry was sixteen. He is second son to the heir to the throne. He had drunk alcohol to excess on several occasions at private parties and at the Rattlebone Inn in Sherston. He had smoked cannabis on several occasions, mainly in outdoor locations. He had been involved in fights over after-hours drinking sessions at the pub and had been banned for a short time. His father, Prince Charles, took him to a drug rehabilitation clinic to listen to former addicts to shock him into realising what could be the consequences of his behaviour.

- The *News of the World* argued that, because of Prince Harry's exalted position, it would be wrong to cover up his misbehaviour. Because of his privileged position, the public should know what he gets up to.
- The editors' code says that 'where material about the private life of a child is published, there must be justification for the publication other than the fame, notoriety or position of his or her parents or guardian'.

(See p 163 for more information about privacy laws.)

Choosing an angle for a story

In January 2002 a story appeared in the *Evening Standard* about Rose Addis, aged 94, who was apparently left in the casualty department of Whittington Hospital in north London for three days because no hospital bed was available, a claim denied by the hospital. Having been admitted with a head injury, Mrs Addis was allegedly left unwashed in the same clothes for 48 hours.

This basic story was presented in different ways, with papers choosing different angles as it became more complicated.

- Story 1 is about an old woman suffering from allegedly incompetent staff.
- Story 2 is about a failing National Health Service.
- Story 3 developed when the Conservative leader, Iain Duncan Smith, raised the matter in Parliament. Now it was about blaming the Labour Party.
- Story 4 was when the hospital spokesperson blamed years of underfunding by the Conservative Party for the state of the NHS.
- Story 5 It turned out that the spokesperson was a Labour Party activist, so the story is about Labour trying to hide the truth.
- Story 6 It transpired that the old woman's family had not visited her for two days, suggesting some kind of neglect on their part, so it is a 'heartless relatives' story.
- Story 7 There are suggestions that Mrs Addis was not changed from her clothes because she refused to be attended by an ethnic minority nurse. It's a racist story.
- Story 8 Mrs Addis is no Hitler! She is a Jew so it couldn't be a racist story!
- Story 9 A photograph taken by the old woman's grandson appears in all the papers. He is a freelance photographer and it was he who took (or perhaps sold) the story to the Evening Standard in the first place. So now it's a story about a 'mercenary' opportunist.

Activity

Think of as many angles as you can for each of these stories. Invent contrasting headlines for different aspects of the same story.

- A gynaecologist has refused to help a cancer patient try for a baby because she is dying. He says that treating the woman is 'pointless'.
- A Sikh priest who tried to smuggle two grammes of cannabis into a prison by hiding it in his turban has been jailed for 12 months. He made weekly visits to the jail to pray with Sikh inmates.
- The garage group So Solid Crew, banned from touring after a shooting at a concert at the Brixton Astoria last month, are to perform for schoolchildren. There will be extra security at the gigs. This is part of the West Sussex County Council youth project.
- Fiona Mont, dubbed by *Crimewatch* as 'Britain's most wanted woman' has been arrested at a campsite in Spain. The former public schoolgirl has been on the run for two years. She is accused of a £300,000 computer fraud. She was with her boyfriend and her two young children when found.

SECTION B **Chapter 8**

Representation

INTRODUCTION

In media studies the term '*representation*' refers to the ways the media portray people, groups, values and issues and how those portrayals are inevitably linked with power. It is also linked with the notions of reality and truth.

Representation is about what producers choose to depict and what not to depict. Because it is selective, it is about how the producers of media texts determine what the audience sees, reads, hears and how they disguise this process.

Representation of nations and ethnic groups

Representation is linked with ***dominant beliefs***. For instance, the notion that black Africans were uncivilised and savage was a dominant belief in nineteenth-century Britain and this made their slavery appear justified. The dominant Victorian belief that it is God's will for there to be people born rich and that poor people will be rewarded in the next life gave justification to those who wanted to perpetuate the class system.

The ***key questions*** you need to ask are:

- Who is being represented?
- How are they represented?
- By whom are they represented, and why are they represented in this way?
- Is the representation fair and accurate and are there opportunities for self-representation?

Activity

Here are two examples of writers objecting to the way their own ethnic groups have been portrayed. Read the two examples carefully and then discuss the questions posed.

Example A

The first example concerns the way the British and others are portrayed in the American film *The Patriot* (USA/Germany 2000). This in essence is the critical analysis of the film by the critic Jonathan Foreman (*Guardian* G2 10 July 2000).

Mel Gibson in *The Patriot*

The film is an epic about the war of American Independence and showed British redcoats as 'bloodthirsty and unprincipled stormtroopers' and 'bloodthirsty child-killers'.

Foreman quotes from the *Daily Express*, which pointed out that this film was the latest in a series of essentially racist films such as *Titanic*, *Michael Collins* and *The Jungle Book* remake, all of which depict the British as 'treacherous, cowardly, evil and sadistic'.

Braveheart (USA 1995), which like *The Patriot* stars Mel Gibson, attributes these characteristics specifically to the English. Foreman agrees with the historian Andrew Roberts' opinion that, 'With their own record of killing 12 million American Indians and supporting slavery for four decades after the British abolished it, Americans wish to project their historical guilt onto someone else'.

Foreman maintains that the film *distorts history* 'in a way that goes well beyond Hollywood's traditional poetic licence'. But he also argues that it is fascist in the deepest sense of that word.

He maintains that it presents a deeply sentimental image of the family, that it casts particularly *Aryan-looking actors* as heroes and avoids any kind of democratic or political context in its portrayal of the revolution. Its imagery is of blonde pre-teen soldiers, reminiscent of the Third Reich's boy soldiers, Mel Gibson looking like the kind of axe-wielding Superman admired in Nazi imagery, and of the black population of South Carolina depicted as *happy*, *loyal slaves*.

Foreman goes on to point out that the German director of *The Patriot*, Roland Emmerich, also directed the 'jingoistic' Independence Day (USA 1996) and that the screenwriter, Robert Rodat, was criticised for excluding British and Allied troops from Saving Private Ryan (USA 1998).

In *The Patriot* the two portray British troops committing the same kind of atrocities as those committed by German forces, particularly the SS, in the Second World War. Foreman recalls in particular the massacre of women and children in the French town of Oradour, when the Nazis herded them into a church and set fire to it. In *The Patriot* British troops are depicted locking scores of women and children in a church and setting it alight. No such incident took place in the actual revolution.

Foreman argues that this portrayal of the British has *sinister implications*. 'By transposing Oradour to South Carolina and making 18th century Britons the first moderns to commit this particular war crime, Emmerich and Rodat have done something unpleasantly akin to Holocaust revisionism. They have made a film that will have the effect of *inoculating audiences* against the unique historical horror of Oradour – and implicitly rehabilitating the Nazis.'

Example B

The second example is from the *Guardian*'s Middle East editor Brian Whitaker in his article 'Why the rules of racism are different for Arabs' (*Guardian*, 18/8/00).

Whitaker argues that many people seem to talk about Arabs in terms which they would never use about black people, yet they do not regard this as racist. He goes on to refer to an American film, *Rules of Engagement* (USA/Germany 2000), which he maintains is the *most racist film ever made* against the Arabs. He says that he is not alone in thinking that Arabs are the 'only really *vicious racial stereotypes* still considered acceptable by Hollywood'.

The film portrays the Arabs, in this case Yemenis, as *deceitful*, *bloodthirsty fanatics*. Eighty-three of them are massacred by the hero, an American Marine colonel, with the film suggesting that this is justified for the greater good of America.

Whitaker goes on to note that on the day *Rules of Engagement* was released in the UK, the American media reported on the investigation of the crash of EgyptAir flight 990. The media had learned that the co-pilot repeated an Arabic phrase "tawakilt 'ala Allah" (I rely on God) and suggested that the man was an Islamic fundamentalist who had deliberately crashed the plane. The Egyptians pointed out that the phrase is used by Muslims when facing difficult situations and accused American investigators of being reluctant to explore the possibility of a mechanical failure in an American-built Boeing 707.

The suicide theory began to look improbable and the media then turned to another stereotype – *the Arab as the over-sexed villain*. They discovered that the co-pilot was noted for sexually harassing hotel chambermaids and had once exposed himself at a hotel window. The implication was that he was an unstable character who should not have been allowed to fly.

Whitaker is unsure about why such anti-Arab racism is considered acceptable but speculates that it might have something to do with the political role of the West in the Middle East which *needs to arouse suspicion about Arabs* in order to reinforce its policies, particularly those which support Israel.

He also wonders how far it is based on *ignorance*, the belief that all Arabs are Muslims for instance, and fear of Islamic extremism.

1 How are the British and the Arabs portrayed in the examples above?

2 How far does your own media experience support the views expressed? Describe specific examples.

3 What examples are cited of the distortion of truth as part of the portrayal? Describe any similar examples which you know about.

4 What reasons are suggested for these negative representations and how convincing are they?

5 What other examples of ignorance contributing to negative stereotypes have you encountered?

Activity

Read the following account of how the *Sesame Street* programme helped inter-racial understanding. Write a treatment about how a particular contemporary television programme – or one of your own devising – could be used to influence people's attitudes to particular racial groups. Show how you mean to challenge racial stereotypes.

Writing a treatment

A treatment is the outline of how a subject or story line of a film or TV programme is to be presented so that others can visualise what is intended. You might like to break it down into headings like these:

1 The title and the type of programme.
2 The target audience.
3 The purposes of the programme (e.g. to inform, entertain, question).
4 The content of the programme.
5 The values and messages of the programme.
6 The characters/presenters.
7 The settings and/or locations.

You can illustrate the outline with sketches.

A bilingual production of *Sesame Street* has helped Arab and Jewish children to be more positive about each other's racial group.

Before watching the programmes, four-year-old Jewish children were likely to make statements such as 'An Arab is the one who wants to hurt Jews in the strongest way'. Arab children were likely to make statements such as 'The Jew is the one shooting the children throwing rocks'.

But after four months of them watching the *Sesame Street* programme, researcher Nathan Fox from Maryland University found that the number of children who chose positive adjectives to describe the other side rose from 21% to 42%.

Fox was astounded at the degree of negative stereotyping among Jewish and Arab children but maintained that watching the *Sesame Street* programmes was 'like an early inoculation' against that. After watching the programmes, a significant number of children said they would invite a friend named Moshe or Mahmoud over to their homes to play. Before watching, most of the children chose only a playmate from their own culture.

On the show, Hebrew and Arabic speaking puppets live on different streets but cross over to each other's neighbourhoods. This gives them the chance to learn each other's language and become familiar with cultural, religious and national symbols.

Some people worried that the programme would present too rosy a picture of co-existence and be out of touch with reality, but researchers found that the children's ingrained unfavourable views of the other side were modified by alternative images of what life could be like in the future.

(Adapted from: 'Big Bird teaches peace to old and young' by Ilene Prusher, *Guardian* 4/11/99.)

How to question representations

Analysis of representations in media texts must recognise that the media do not offer universal truths, which cannot be contested, but particular ***constructions of the world*** and 'reality'.

Every media text carries ***meanings and implications*** to do with how society functions, what people believe and the values they have.

This does not mean that every media producer is consciously trying to influence people with a particular philosophy, though some might, or that there is some vast conspiracy. Rather, these ***meanings are embodied in the systems and techniques*** employed by media organisations.

These ideas and values influence how we see ourselves and the groups we belong to. They influence us in the way we behave in terms of gender, social class, age group, race and so on.

Producers' guidelines

Some media organisations have guidelines on how groups of people are portrayed. The BBC in its Producers' Guidelines makes it clear that it acknowledges that its programmes should 'reflect and represent the composition of the nation accurately'. 'Programme makers must always be aware of the sensitivities of groups in society who feel unjustly treated or discriminated against.'

It goes on to insist that producers should not perpetuate myths or reinforce stereotypes: 'Those who feel they are misrepresented or neglected by society in general should feel they are dealt with and portrayed fairly and accurately by the BBC.'

The areas of concern include the following regular portrayals:

- black people as criminals
- women as housewives
- disabled people as victims
- gay people as ineffectual
- old people as incapable.

The document does recognise that there has to be care taken not to depict a society which does not exist and that it should report and reflect prejudice and disadvantage, but 'should do nothing to perpetuate them'.

There are specific guidelines about these groups: women, ethnic minorities, the disabled, lesbians, gays and old people. They are mainly about the language used to describe them and the roles they play or do not play.

Key questions

- How have the contents of the media text been selected? Almost anything could be said about any event, so who decides, why and to what effect?

In ***Language in the News*** Roger Fowler explains it like this: 'How the medium is used implies options for the producer or editor...these choices are made with systematic regularity according to circumstances and they become associated with conventional meanings. For example, the television newsreader is generally shown full-face, head and shoulders almost filling the screen, from a camera position at just below eye level: this arrangement signifies authority. The meaning changes when the newsreader turns to the side towards an interviewee, and is seen at a greater distance, signifying a diminution of status.'

(Fowler, ***Language in the News*** Routledge 1991 p 25)

The media producers choose and their choices are part of the meaning of whatever is produced. They may not always be aware of this but it is nevertheless true. Choices are inevitably bound up with values but in the case of factual media products they give the impression of ideological innocence, which needs to be questioned. So, as far as possible, you should be concerned with ***alternatives***, asking how else could this story be told and with what effect.

In terms of newspaper stories the selection process could involve a journalist picking a story from a range of press releases which have been produced by public relations people who have themselves chosen from a range of events. The choice may be conditioned by:

the journalist's perception of her editor's preferences or biases
her awareness of the style and tone of the publication
her own interests
her awareness or otherwise of the audience's expectations and preferences
the space and time available
the context in which the story will appear.

Activity

Record twenty minutes of a breakfast news programme and buy two morning papers for the same day. After viewing and reading these, discuss in small groups which news stories you would choose from them to feature in the evening's *Newsround* on children's television. Record *Newsround* and compare your choices with those the programme producers made.

- Is visual evidence being interpreted for the audience?

Any visual image can have many different meanings and media practitioners usually give a ***preferred meaning***, as when the caption on a photograph tells the reader how to interpret the image or the commentary on a film directs the viewer towards a meaning.

This imposition of meaning is called ***anchorage***, which can also include the context in which an image is placed. So, whether we see an activist, a protester, a troublemaker, a hard-working salt-of-the-earth British taxpayer or a destructive yob depends on the caption writer or the reporter's script as well as our own observation.

Each visual image is the product of a photographer's or camera person's own choices, which include:

deciding what to picture
how to frame it
what angle to use
what lighting effects to aim for and so on.
The image is then edited, which can mean altering the composition of the picture and, with digital technology, the content of the picture. Details can be exaggerated or suppressed.

Activity

Rewrite the captions and headlines of each of the pictures on the next page so as to change the 'meaning'. Which picture and caption would be best suited to:

a) being critical of the behaviour of the protesters;

b) being in support of the protesters;

c) being critical of the police?

Picture and caption from *Daily Mail* 17/12/02 page 7, 'Confrontation: a bloodied protestor remonstrates with police in Parliament Square yesterday. Eight people were arrested in a series of scuffles.'

Picture from the *Guardian* 17/12/02 page 9, 'Police hold back pro-hunt supporters outside the Palace of Westmnster yesterday.'

Picture from the Sun 17/12/02 page 2, 'Burning effigy ... pro-hunt demonstrators roar support as dummy of Tony Blair is torched in Parliament Square.'

- Does the presence of media producers affect what happens?

The presence of a television camera and crew can affect the situation which is being filmed. People can become more extrovert when conscious of being filmed or can freeze when being interviewed. Some interviews are shot several times until the required performance is achieved. The media work hard to convince us of the authenticity of their representations, but try their best to conceal the ways they have produced meaning and the effect that they have on the events portrayed.

- Has anything been set up?

The events that television producers want to film or photographers want to illustrate do not usually happen conveniently. Frequently, events have to be staged. The author recalls observing a minute's silence at a football match in respect for a famous former player who had just died. The silence then had to be repeated for Sky Television which had missed the event because of a commercial break.

If you see pictures on the television news of people in white protective clothing destroying GM crops in some remote field it is very likely that the camera crew has been invited to witness the event and not just stumbled on it by accident.

Such happenings are not, generally, intended to deceive, but to clarify. The potential for deception, however, is present and cheating does occur.

Occasionally deception is revealed. When a BBC reporter told the viewers in a live report from a rowing boat that the floods in North Yorkshire were so bad that this was the only way of getting around, her contention was undermined by the sudden appearance in the background of a cyclist merrily riding through what turned out to be a couple of inches of water.

Activity

Imagine you are a photographer for a local newspaper. You have been sent to get some pictures to illustrate this story.

Residents near a shopping centre have been complaining that students from a local school have been causing a nuisance by using a bus shelter as a gathering place during the lunch hour. Members of the public have not been able to use the shelter because of the unruly and antisocial behaviour of the students.

When you arrive at the scene, however, everything appears calm. Some old people are in the shelter waiting for a bus. Some students are wandering about, eating their lunch. There is no sign of any intimidating or unruly behaviour.

Describe how you would set up a photo to illustrate the story you were sent to cover. If the original complaints were valid, have you clarified or distorted the truth?

- How has the text been edited?

This is a process used in all media which imposes order on chaotic material. In newspapers stories are given labels (e.g. headlines), stories are made to fit the available space and the flow of text is planned so that it is easy for the reader to follow.

In broadcasting, material is ***compressed*** in order to fit the available time. Then bits of recorded material are ***joined together*** to provide a continuous flow. Thus new meanings are created from original material, and what seems to be real is in fact an illusion.

Activity

Develop the story from the previous activity. In groups of three, appoint a student, a complaining resident and a reporter. The student and the resident ad-lib, using the following ideas. The reporter takes notes and then writes up the story with a headline, deciding what angle to take. The student and the resident can write letters to the paper explaining their views.

Student

You spend your lunch hour in the shopping centre because it is a change from school. Along with your friends you usually buy some food and soft drinks and consume them while walking about. Sometimes there is a bit of horseplay, but it is all good-natured and friendly. You get lots of moans from some older people because they don't have much sense of fun and they are easily upset by little things. Occasionally some people do get carried away but not often. (Add details to this from your imagination.)

Resident

You live in a flat above a shop in the centre. You are fed up with the noise, the litter and the antics of students at lunchtime. They swear, shout and lark about, making shopping a nightmare for respectable, civilised people. You can make up some examples of bad behaviour from your imagination. You would like to see the students banned from the centre.

- What influence has the anchor person?

Newsreaders or presenters often have a powerful influence on their audiences and they can indicate how their audience should react. This can be done quite subtly by using phrases which at first hearing do not seem to be particularly significant, such as 'they claim', 'he says', 'so you say'.

- What visual codings influence us?

People have greater impact and carry more authority if they are pictured full face. This privilege is accorded to newsreaders, ministers making ministerial broadcasts and weather forecasters. This authority is reinforced by appearance and dress and by being named on a caption.

Sets are also designed with the purpose of suggesting qualities such as professionalism – the inside of a studio or office – or cheerful informality – the sofa on GMTV.

- Who is telling the story and what is their motive?

Such questions can be asked even of factual programmes such as the news and sporting events. Football commentators, for instance, focus on famous individuals rather than on team performance and determine what are the 'key moments' in games in order to make games seem more dramatic and so retain the audience.

- How real is it?

There are many ways in which the media can distort reality. Some of them are easy to spot, others are more obscure.

Activity

In small groups discuss the following findings about news and fiction. Describe examples of each finding. Then choose either news or fiction and write an essay on how the media distort reality.

News in the media

a) News presenters go to people in *positions of power* to find their stories and they over-represent official voices.

b) Attention tends to focus on *elite members* of society and political parties.

c) News tends to support *traditional values* and not challenge the status quo.

d) Foreign news tends to be about the *richer and more powerful* nations rather than poor, weak ones.

e) News tends to be *nationalistic* (patriotic) in its opinions and they way it portrays the world.

f) News tends to reflect *male values*.

g) *Minorities* are neglected or criticised.

h) News *exaggerates* violent and personal *crime*.

i) Political news tends to be *neutral* or to support parties to the right of the spectrum.

Fiction in the media

a) Characters tend to come from *higher status occupations*, especially the police, medicine and the military.

b) *Ethnic minorities* are often shown in lower status or socially dubious roles.

c) *Women* have tended to appear in domestic and passive roles.

d) Fictional violence is portrayed in a wildly *unrealistic* light.

e) Fiction which is about *social problems* tends to avoid the issues and support the status quo.

f) *Homosexuality* tends to be ignored or treated negatively.

Representation and ideology

All media products express and/or imply certain values, beliefs and ideas. The people who buy, use or experience these products are conditioned to accept these values, beliefs and ideas as natural, obvious, or just plain common sense. This process perpetuates the status quo in society and maintains dominant class interests.

This involves the process of ***hegemony*** (pronounced 'hegg em on ee') which Fiske in ***Introduction to Communication Studies*** (Routledge 1982) defines as 'the constant winning and rewinning of the consent of the majority to the system that subordinates them'. One of the key strategies in hegemony is the notion of 'common sense'. If an idea can be accepted as not belonging to a particular class but as common to everyone, then resistance evaporates.

Fiske gives as an example the 'common sense' notion that criminals are wicked or deficient people who need punishment or correction. 'Such common sense disguises the fact that lawbreakers are disproportionately men from disadvantaged or disempowered social groups.... Common sense rules out the possible sense that the causes of criminality are social rather than individual, that our society teaches men that their masculinity depends upon successful performance...and then denies many of them the means of achieving this success'.

This, he says, is a comforting process for the law abiding because they don't have to suffer the consequences of changing a social system and losing their advantages. 'The common sense that criminality is a function of the wicked individual rather than the unfair society is thus part of bourgeois ideology and, in so far as it is accepted by the subordinate (and even by the criminals themselves, who may well believe that they deserve their punishment and that the criminal justice system is therefore fair to all), it is hegemony at work.'

(John Fiske, ***Introduction to Communication Studies*** Routledge 1982, ch 9)

Questioning 'common sense'

It is part of the function of media studies to ***challenge the naturalness*** of what is offered and to ***question apparent common sense***. This can be done in a number of ways.

- First, by encouraging the practice of ***negotiated or oppositional*** readings of texts. These terms were coined by David Morley in his book *The Nationwide Audience* (BFI 1980).

A negotiated reading is where the 'reader' broadly accepts the dominant message but modifies parts of it in the light of his/her own knowledge or experience.

An oppositional reading means realising what you are supposed to think or accept and then interpreting the text in a completely different way as in Matthew Engel's deviant reading of Cinderella.

An 'oppositional' reading of Cinderella

'The treatment of the Ugly Sisters in this pantomime is one of the worst examples of prejudice in the whole of drama. They are ridiculed because they are not slim and beautiful. They are mocked for having big feet. It is assumed that because they are not good looking they must be unpleasant characters. This is an out-of-date attitude. Instead of laughing at them we should celebrate them.

Then there is the heroine's disgraceful treatment of Buttons. Cinderella first ignores him and then mocks his psycho-sexual longing for her. She proclaims undying friendship for him while ignoring his basic needs. Then she is ridiculously besotted by an upper class twit she hardly even knows. Cinderella is mean and a snob.

And what about the glass slipper? Surely this a dangerous thing to show when there are so many children in the audience? Even if glass slippers don't smash into lethal fragments, they create bunions in later life.

There is the prince who only comes round the houses when he is driven by lustful longings. Where has he been the rest of the time? Anyway let's get this straight: any girl who thinks she can be happy ever after by marrying a prince just hasn't been listening these last few years.'

(Adapted from 'Panto Shock for All Right Minded Folk' by Matthew Engel, *Guardian* 14/12/99, with permission)

Activity

Produce a storyboard with dialogue and/or voice-over which gives an oppositional reading of a familiar children's story. For instance, Goldilocks as a criminal who breaks into a house, steals food, vandalises furniture and sets up a squat.

- Second, by understanding that ***ideas permeate every aspect of media production*** – finance, conventions and working practices of media producers, distribution and consumption.

For instance, the highly successful quiz show ***Who Wants To Be A Millionaire?*** owes much of its popularity to the way it purports to offer ordinary people a chance of winning enough money to change their lives significantly.

This offering of transforming riches is vital to the popular appeal of the programme because it encourages ***identification***. Viewers can feel that they are actually participating, but it is also crucial for the financing of the programme. The host appeals to the viewers by saying this could be you winning a fortune just by ringing this number. The more calls, the more revenue for the programme makers.

Contestants on the show are encouraged to speculate on how their lives will change if they win the next huge chunk of money. The audience sees shots of their relatives in the audience sweating on the answer to a question. Extra drama is added to the proceedings because of the possibility of losing large sums of money by giving a wrong answer.

That the programme had some effect on the nation as a whole was illustrated when the then Education Minister, David Blunkett, blamed the killing of a ten-year-old boy on what he called the ***Who Wants To Be A Millionaire?*** society and the outrage when the first million pound winner in the UK turned out to be a woman who was relatively wealthy already. The 'ordinary people' who saw the programme as a way of allowing their own kind some escape from a life of wishing they were richer saw this as a betrayal.

There are of course all manner of ways of reading this programme but it can be seen that notions of 'money brings happiness', 'being lucky rather than earning wealth is OK', and taking pleasure in other people's success are present. To tease some of these issues out it can be worth trying some subversive techniques.

- Third, by using ***connotation*** and ***denotation*** as two different sorts of textual analysis as shown on p6 and after.

Activity

Write a treatment (see p 99) for a subversive version of *Who Wants To Be a Millionaire?* which challenges the notion of 'money brings happiness'.

Activity

Watch a current documentary and then discuss as a class or in small groups which of the following most accurately describes its effects.

1 It gave you a *window* on the world, allowing you to see for yourselves what is going on without other people interfering.

2 It acted as a *mirror*, giving you a reflection of the world as it is, though with some distortion, with the angle and direction of the mirror being decided by others.

3 It acted as a *gatekeeper*, choosing certain experiences and views and ignoring others.

4 It was a *signpost*, pointing the way and making sense of what is otherwise confusing.

5 It was like a *forum*, providing information and ideas and offering possibilities for response and feedback.

6 It was a *screen* or *barrier*, providing a false view of the world either through escapist fantasy or propaganda.

Gender

INTRODUCTION

This chapter encourages you to examine the way males and females are portrayed in the media and to think about the effects that these portrayals have.

The kind of questions that you need to think about are whether the mass media are instruments of male-dominated social control and whether they transmit sexist values and beliefs about women and femininity from one generation to the next. This involves looking at the role models which children see on television and in print, the sorts of behaviour depicted as culturally acceptable and desirable and what effect they have on the audience.

Representation of women

Research findings reported in Barry Gunter's ***Television and Gender Representation*** (John Libby 1995) showed that there was a gross ***under-representation*** of women in action-drama shows and that when women do appear they are portrayed in a very ***narrow range of roles***. Other research showed that women tend to be portrayed as being in the home rather than at work and that they are incompetent in any other than marital or familial roles. This chapter tries to help you find out whether these observations are still relevant to television today.

The blonde ***stereotype*** seems to have dogged fair-haired women for decades. Blonde means ***sexy, vulnerable, not too clever***; it means Marilyn Monroe and Jean Harlow.

Research findings from Coventry University seem to show that the stereotype is still powerful. In the study, 120 students were given photographs of a model and asked to rate her intelligence, shyness, aggression and popularity. They were given one of four photos of the same woman, identical except for the colour of her wig – platinum blonde, natural blonde, brown haired or red haired.

The platinum blonde was rated significantly less intelligent than the others and this was more apparent when the viewers were men. The researcher concluded that we do make judgements based on stereotypes, even when we are unaware that we are doing it.

Publicity shot of Jean Harlow

A concerned critic, Dr Linda Seger, in 'How to evaluate media images of women' (Center for Media Literacy: www.medialit.org/Reading Room) says that media images of women still show women as wife, mother or girlfriend, and that these images are not just restricted but negative.

> These images misrepresent who we are, demean us, and make it harder to see women as people. When women are only shown as beautiful and passive or rich and bitchy, it becomes more difficult for both men and women to accept them as the diverse, multifaceted people they really are.... We applaud images of women who require a whole range of adjectives to describe them, women who...are strong, sometimes brassy, sometimes sensual, often compassionate, usually making good decisions but not always, emotionally responsive, at times angry and always interesting.

Activity

Discuss in class Linda Seger's views on media representation of women.

How accurate are her comments about 'misrepresentation' with reference to contemporary media?

What current examples are there in the media of the multifaceted women she applauds?

Images of women in magazines

Feminist writer Rosalind Coward studied the ***portrayal of women in magazines*** and found that the prevailing images present female readers with ideals which are virtually unattainable and likely to leave women feeling ***inadequate*** failures (see ***Female Desire***, Harper Collins 1984, chapter on Pouts And Scowls).

She quotes from ***Ideal Home*** the contention that the perfect female body would be between 5'5" and 5'8", long-legged, tanned and vigorous looking, but above all without a spare inch of flesh. 'Brown, slim, lively and lovely...that's how we would all like to see ourselves on holiday. Here are a few tips on achieving this and maintaining it.'

The consequences of a barrage of such advice were that women, to a large extent, became preoccupied with dieting, feeling guilty about food and exercising.

Magazines made women self-conscious and ***dissatisfied*** with particular parts of their body, such as bottoms, which were defined as 'problem areas', as in this example from ***Women's Own*** 24 July 1982:

> Female behinds – whether sexy and shapely or absolutely enormous – have long been the subject of saucy seaside postcards. But this important structure can make or mar summer clothes...to say nothing of beachwear. If what goes on below your back is no joke to you, join Norma Knox as she looks at ways to smooth down, gently reshape and generally improve the area between your waist and your knees.

Other problem parts are identified in a variety of magazines as flabby thighs, loose stomach muscles and breasts which aren't firm. Coward argues that this preoccupation of the media with an ideal shape for women has cultural consequences. She maintains that the ideal female shape is, in fact, a version of an immature body and that most praise is heaped upon the older woman who 'keeps an adolescent figure'.

This valuation of immaturity is emphasised by such practices as shaving off 'unsightly' hair under the arms and on the legs – the 'very evidence that a girl has reached puberty'.

She argues that the image makes women unhappy because it upholds ***impossible ideals***. She speculates on why women continue to believe in this ideal when they are sceptical of advertising stereotypes and the dieting and exercise regimes that are supposed to produce the ideal. She suggests that it is partly a question of the ***kinds of language*** in which the issue of slimness and beauty is conducted. Women are made to feel that ***fat and flesh are disgusting***.

'Language pertaining to the female body has constructed a whole ***regime of representations*** which can only result in women having a punishing and self-hating relationship with their bodies. Fat is described as if it were a disease: 'if you suffer from cellulite'. Cures for the 'disease' are punishing: you have to pinch the fat away, pummel the flesh, wring, twist, and knead it.'

Coward quotes, from ***Cosmopolitan*** magazine, an actress's beauty philosophy: 'I'm determined to do all I can to help myself. If I cheat on my regime, I write myself abusive notes. Anyway all this masochistic stuff gives me a purpose in life.'

It is the ***mass of advertising images and glamour photographs*** that make women feel they need to achieve an ideal slimness, but that somewhere along the line they know that the image is impossible to achieve. Yet they remain trapped 'because our culture generates such a violent dislike of fat'.

Coward noticed a change in the ***representation of the female face*** in women's magazines in the early 1980s. They stopped smiling. Instead the look portrayed was glum, not exactly aggressive but resistant. Though this could have been a response to feminist objections to the portrayal of women as submissive and anxious to please (signified by the smile), Coward argues that it was simply a change in the notion amongst photographers and the models themselves of what is attractive. She also argues that the new look 'is remarkably similar to representations of female sexual expressions which have long dominated pornography, which is aimed at men'.

Activity

Collect examples of different smiles from media images and produce a short 'smiles dictionary', explaining the different 'meanings' that smiles can have.

In pornography, she argues, the ***woman's look*** is invariably unsmiling – 'sex is signified as a serious business'. The eyes are usually narrowed to suggest sexual interest, the mouth just slightly apart to hint at sexual arousal and the body arranged to suggest that the viewer is making love to the model.

This borrowing of photographic conventions from the world of pornography is not surprising, according to Coward, because of the 'intimate connections between the world of models, photographers and pornographers'. This look is linked with prevailing ideals of sexual attraction. 'The look of defiance, the pouting and scowling faces, are part of the current tendency to represent women as attractive whether or not they work at it. Indeed the look ultimately says, "It's not because of my invitation that you will want me. You will want me anyway." We are meant to read off from the narrowing of the eyes, the perfection of the skin, the posture of the body, that this is a person confident of sexual response whether or not it is sought.' (Coward, *ibid*. 1984)

Just as the images of smiling, simpering models reinforced the idea of ***women's passivity***, so the pouting, scowling look determines for women readers what is attractive and what is attractive is ***sexual readiness***. What is being suggested is that however resistant women may appear, underneath they are sensual, soft and loveable. Coward suggests that this ***underlying ideology*** is similar to that sometimes used to excuse rape – women want it. 'The face says all too clearly that precious moves towards real autonomy for women have been contained. In the look of resistance lies a whole convention of submission.'

This view is echoed by Gillian Dyer in *Advertising as Communication* (Routledge 1982 p 186) where she says that some advertisers, aware of the concerns of feminist critics, tried to use images of cool, professional, liberated women, but that they equated 'liberation' with aggressive sexuality and that the message was still: 'underneath they are all loveable' (from a frilly underwear advertisement). Alternatively the cool professional women are depicted as having weak spots for a man's after-shave or a present of a box of chocolates or sexy underwear.

Activity

Representation of femininity

Analyse the nine images of women – consider expressions, posture, hairstyle, clothing, make-up, composition of image, lighting, and so on. How far do they convey messages about women's power or passivity, and independence /dependence?

Collect images of women from contemporary magazines and describe any patterns or trends you notice, especially concerning female independence and empowerment.

18

castorama

Representations of males

Definitions of masculinity

Ideas of manliness vary and depend on time and culture. For instance, this is what manliness means in the following countries:

- Spain – class loyalty amongst workers;
- Japan – being diligent and disciplined;
- Cyprus –– belonging to male social groups outside the home;
- Among Sikhs – gift giving;
- Uganda amongst the Gisu – keeping cool and expressing creativity;
- Tahiti – manliness has no significance.

Less attention has been paid by analysts to the representation of males in the media, perhaps because males have not been seen as a disadvantaged group. The analysis examined here is from a book which uses findings from the world of psychoanalysis as the basis for investigation.

'Masculinity tries to stay invisible by passing itself off as normal and universal' according to Antony Easthope in ***What a Man's Gotta Do*** (Paladin 1986). In doing so this inevitably makes the feminine seem abnormal. The rise of feminist and gay movements has led to an examination of the nature of masculinity, but this has often led to it being defined mainly as a source of oppression.

Easthope argues that a more accurate understanding of masculinity can be achieved by thinking of it as a continual negotiation between the male and female characteristics that are present in every male, a ***divided sexuality*** that the myth of masculinity is always trying to deny. But the feminine in male nature can never be suppressed, he argues.

As an example of the conflict, Easthope cites Dennis the Menace and Walter the Softy from the ***Beano*** comic. In effect they are complementary opposites, a couple. They are neighbours who play together and they are defined against each other: 'Walter has brushed hair and wears glasses. Dennis's mop stands up in phallic spikes.... Walter's friends have names like Bertie Blenkinsop while Dennis's are called Curly and Pie Face. Dennis and his friends actively invent schemes. Walter and the softies play nursery rhyme games. Dennis hates school and tries to get out of it. Walter passes exams.'

This pairing, says Easthope, shows ***what is meant to be masculine and what is seen as feminine***. It is masculine to have a gravelly voice, to be strong, not to have to wear protective clothes in cold weather, to do outdoor labouring work, to rebel against parents and avoid contact with them, to be able to eat highly spiced meals.

It is effeminate to have a pleasant voice, to be physically weak, to have to wear warm clothing in inclement weather, to do domestic jobs, to do as parents say and accept being cuddled, to eat mild food.

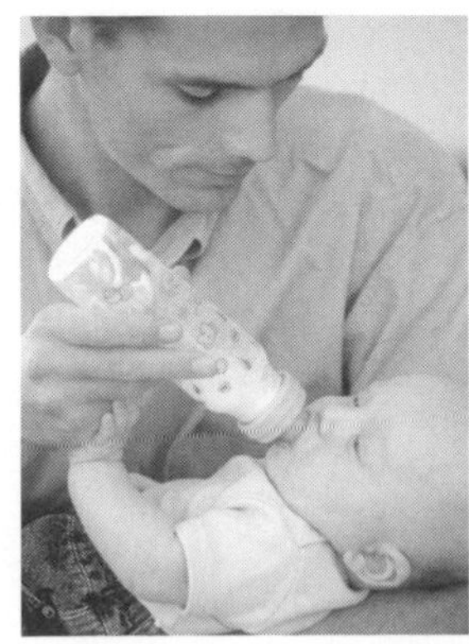

Dennis the Menace and Walter the Softy from the *Beano* comic

Dennis will progress from being a menace to being a ***hard man*** and his masculine identity depends on expelling all traces of femininity. But the female in male nature can never be suppressed. Though Dennis is the ideal that the male reader believes he identifies with, there also has to be a ***secret identification*** with Walter. Walter is a built-in necessity without which the fun can't happen. His femininity is the cause of the story which the reader enjoys.

Eastman uses findings from the world of psychoanalysis to identify four themes in the representation of masculinity. These are:

- fear of castration
- the triumph of the masculine ego
- fathers and sons
- sublimated intimacies of male bonding.

Eastman gives examples of these four themes from war films (***The Deer Hunter*** USA 1978), sport (***North Dallas Forty*** USA 1979) and a beer advertisement on television (Greenall Whitley). In war and sport the four themes translate into images of:

- defeat
- combat
- victory
- comradeship.

The subconscious ***fear of castration*** becomes the ***fear of death or dismemberment*** in battle. The example Eastman gives is the deadly game of Russian roulette which the prisoners of war are obliged to play for the amusement of a Vietcong commander in ***The Deer Hunter***. In ***North Dallas Forty*** it is expressed as ***sporting injuries*** incurred in a game of American football which is compared to 'going into battle.' In the advertisement three men are being led to their deaths by hanging in a Mexican town, representing a scene from an old Western.

The triumph of the masculine ego is depicted in scenes of ***combat***. It is the desire of the male for ***mastery***. This can be achieved by superior knowledge or by mastery of the body as in *The Deer Hunter* when Mike and Steve escape by holding on to a log which floats downstream, climbing a rope ladder and clambering up to a rescue helicopter.

The son ***seeks approval*** from the father subconsciously, because in the subconscious struggle for the affections of the mother/wife the son grows to fear the father's wrath. This need for approval from an older male figure is expressed in terms of achieving ***victory***, receiving ***medals*** after success in war, ***trophies*** in sporting contests and ***pints*** in a beer advert.

The repressed feminine side of masculinity is allowed expression in certain circumstances. In war it is ***comradeship*** in times of danger, so that men are allowed to hold each other, comforting and weeping together and admitting their love. In *North Dallas Forty* pain also gives an excuse for ***intense male bonding***. 'After the game and defeat the men comfort one another. One sits weeping silently, others murmur in pairs. Elliott crouches over Delma's stretcher, talking gently to him about his body.' In the Greenall Whitley advert it is a pub in paradise when men can drink and sing and ***play games together*** with a buxom barmaid to replenish their glasses.

Activity

In small groups recall and note examples from the media of the following:

1 Males expressing fear of death, dismemberment or castration.

2 Males delighting in triumphs.

3 Males denying or being uneasy about their feminine side.

4 Males being awarded trophies, prizes or praise by older males.

5 Males delighting in male comradeship, especially tactile.

Write an essay about Easthope's theories and your own findings.

The changing representation of masculinity

In her book ***Sacred Cows*** (Harper Collins 1999), feminist writer Ros Coward shows how the representation of men changed during the last two decades of the twentieth century. She argues that these changes were partly in ***response to feminist critiques*** of media portrayals of gender. She also maintains that there are potentially serious problems because of the ways in which these representations affect poor, young, working class males.

In the 1970s feminism did not question the portrayal of men in advertising because they featured as the 'norm', portrayed in a range of activities and types. It was women who were shown in powerless roles and in limited categories.

But this changed in the 1980s. As images of women as strong and independent career people became more common, ***men were depicted as hopeless and unappetising***. They were shown as dim, uncouth, pushy and insensitive.

For example:

- The Kenco advert which showed a female executive humiliating the men around her professionally and socially.
- The Shell advert showing men being stupid enough to try to wash parts of their car in a launderette.
- The Prudential pensions advert (1993) made men appear dumb by showing a man and a woman sitting on a sofa expressing hopes for the future. The woman is ambitious and clever and wants a big yacht and to travel around the world. The man is dim and insensitive and announces 'We want to be together' in an unfashionable regional accent, while his partner registers contempt.

Attitudes which would be unacceptable towards women have become acceptable towards men. The 1998 Coca Cola advert showed ***man as a sex object***. Several female office workers await the arrival of a handsome young window cleaner with his bottles of Coca Cola. The women exchange glances which indicate what they would like to do with him. Yet to represent a woman as the object of predatory males would be unacceptable.

Traditional masculinity has become a joke. A narrow focus on life, domestic incompetence suggesting a mind geared to higher things, emotional reserve and acts of physical endurance are no longer regarded as qualities but as signs of ***incompetence***, ***insensitivity*** or ***lack of intelligence***. Ros Coward acknowledges the part that the feminist movement played in this process but she says that disparaging masculine behaviour has spread far wider than feminism. The adverts she refers to were produced mainly by men who are colluding in the ***denigration of their own sex***.

> **Once attributes of masculinity were taken for granted as the position from which to judge all characteristics which deviated from this (especially so-called feminine attributes). But the media reflect a culture where the once desirable attributes of masculinity now seem absurd, fair game for humour and sometimes disgust. On the cultural stage the message is clear: men have fallen from grace. Masculinity is no longer a position from which to judge others but a puzzling condition in its own right.**
>
> (*Sacred Cows* p 94)

One of the consequences of the ***changing attitudes to masculinity*** has been the media's ***demonising of impoverished young men***.

The *yob* or *lout* or *scum* has been portrayed as the cause of a national moral decline. 'Yob' was once a slang insult but is now used by newspapers, and indeed Home Office ministers, as a descriptive category. It includes lager louts, joyriders and football hooligans. These are mostly young, white, working class males who are portrayed as irresponsible, foul-mouthed, violent and work-shy.

We are led to believe that they hang around council estates, live on benefits and petty crime and father illegitimate children. They are often drunk and responsible for violent behaviour in the home. The yob is the ***demon of the early twenty-first century*** and is feared by the middle classes. New Labour promised to wipe such undesirables off the streets, to destroy the 'yob culture'.

The yob is sometimes portrayed as a ***primitive beast*** attacking the social fold, as in a government advertising campaign warning car owners to lock their cars that showed the thieves as a pack of howling hyenas.

Middle class anxiety can be seen in opinion pieces in newspapers like this from Andrew Neil in The ***Times***, 28 May 1995: 'The underclass is not a degree of poverty.... It is a type of poverty: It covers those who no longer share the norms and aspirations of society. It is a ticking time bomb we do not know how to diffuse. It is at the root of our yob culture, the coarsening of our society, and most of the upsurge in crime.'

Ros Coward argues that many of the ***unpleasant aspects of masculinity*** deserve to be mocked but says when this condemnation is linked to the disadvantaged in society then the outcome is more disturbing. It leads to the belief, reflected in political action, that a ***particular class of men are the problem and women are the answer***, either by 'civilising' men or by getting on without them.

But the yob is, in fact, a myth, according to Coward. She draws parallels with social attitudes to young males just before the First World War. There was then a middle class fear of an unruly underclass of unemployable young men. However, when the war started and there was a real shortage of labour, then the 'yobs of yesteryear' were seen not as an army of degenerate unemployables, but as 'the under-employed who disappeared into the military and the wartime workforce. A myth died, just as the myth of yobbism would if impoverished young men of contemporary Britain were given genuine opportunities'.

Coward argues that the 'yob' does not exist. He is never the boy you know, always the one you don't know. 'As in all ***bigoted mythologies***, the yob is the alien and bad creature against whom the familiar and the good are culturally defined; the "them" which defines the "us".' This is a classic example of stereotyping.

Activity

In small groups recall and note examples from the media of the following:

1 Men portrayed as incompetent or foolish.

2 Men being the problem and women the answer.

3 Men as sex objects.

4 Men as louts.

Different groups could look at different media forms/genres for a week, say TV soap operas, teenage magazines, TV advertising, music videos or computer games, and then exchange information and ideas with the rest of the class.

After a class discussion, write an essay on 'Contemporary media portray men mainly as fools, problems or sex objects: discuss with examples'.

Activity

Read the following article and then carry out the research suggested.

There is a disparity between the images of masculinity which men think women admire and those which women actually do admire. Men tend to think that women do not want wimpish, insipid 'new men', capable of cooking coq au vin and changing a baby's nappy. They want the tough, silent, physically aggressive male – Bruce Willis rather than Hugh Grant, Vinnie Jones not Ralph Fiennes.

Men place great emphasis on the importance of being in control of their emotions, their physical safety and their social status. They bring that control into their personal lives and persuade themselves that women really secretly want to be controlled.

Because women often do defer to men's desire to drive, select the movie, choose the holiday, many men conclude that this means women like handing over control. But women tend to want men who can acknowledge their own weaknesses, who can express their tenderness and affection, men who place a value on love, family and personal relationships and less on power, possessions, control and achievement. They do not want a new man in the image of a woman; rather an old man who wants not to control women but to liberate himself, not to dominate women but to cherish and protect them.

(Adapted from Anthony Clare, *On Men: Masculinity in Crisis*, Chatto and Windus 2000, with permission.)

Test out Clare's generalisations by compiling a list of current male film, television and pop stars and interviewing a range of females about the characteristics they admire or dislike in them.

Stereotypes

The word 'stereotype' is a kaleidoscopic term. Shake the box and it changes its meaning. The word originally was used in the printing industry to indicate an identical copy made by a copying machine. It has come to mean, according to the ***Oxford English Dictionary***: 'A preconceived, standardised and oversimplified impression of the characteristics which typify a person, situation etc., often shared by all members of a society or certain social groups.'

According to Encyclopaedia.com it is negative: 'a prejudicial notion or set of notions a person uses to define members of a...social group outside one's own direct experience. ...[It] is a simple and ***erroneous*** idea, gained second hand that negatively affects one's ability to understand members of other social group and is resistant to change.' (My italics.)

O. E. Klapp in ***Heroes, Villains and Fools*** (quoted in Richard Dyer, *Stars* BFI 1998) agrees with the negative aspect of this definition. He contrasts stereotypes with his own category of '***social types***'. These describe a collective norm of role behaviour formed and used by a social group. For example, there is the 'good Joe', epitomised by John Wayne, who is characterised as friendly, a good sport, with a dislike of bullies and snobs and authoritarians and having sympathy for the underdog. Klapp sees such social typing as '***positive and useful*** as opposed to stereotypes which are ***wrong and harmful*** because they deal with people from outside one's cultural world'. (My italics.)

O' Sullivan in ***Studying The Media: An Introduction*** (Arnold 1994) would not agree with this. Stereotypes, according to him, are '***not always false*** and can be supported by empirical evidence'. (My italics.) He cites positive stereotypes such as 'The French are good cooks'.

According to Branston and Stafford (***The Media Student's Book***, Routledge 1996) the term is derogatory – much more than the word 'type' – and they maintain that 'stereotypes are ***not actual people***, but widely circulated ideas or assumptions about particular groups'. (My italics.)

On the other hand Mick Bowes in ***Understanding Television*** (eds Goodwin and Whannel, Routledge 1990) defines stereotypes as '***characters*** who conform to patterns of behaviour that are easily recognised and understood'. (My italics.)

The concept of stereotypes is closely linked with *categorising*. But it is more accurately a ***fixed idea*** that goes with a category. For example, the category 'Negro' can be simply a neutral, factual, non-evaluative concept. Stereotype enters if the category is accompanied with ***judgements*** of the Negro as musical, lazy, superstitious or whatever. A stereotype is not a category, but places a judgement on a category. It ***prevents people thinking clearly*** about the category.

Putting things into categories is important, however. It would be neither possible nor desirable to react to everything and everyone as if it were a unique entity. Though events and persons in all their detail are unique, unless we discover patterns and recurrences we cannot project ahead or anticipate the future. To make accurate predictions is necessary for our survival. We form categories to anticipate future encounters. The predictions may not always be accurate, but as long as we modify them in the light of experience then there should be no problem.

Sometimes the words 'stereotype' or 'stereotypical' are used to ***criticise characters*** in media texts which are not complex. And they are almost always used pejoratively, as in:

> 'These women are satisfying because their diversity makes them seem real. We are not looking just for heroines, but for allowing women to be complex and many sided as people of either sex can possibly be. Looking for ways to portray opposites that are contained within any one person can help create real portrayals. It's also the best way to avoid stereotypes.' (Linda Seger, How to Evaluate Media Images of Women: www.medialit.org/Reading Room)

So stereotypes are ***simplified characters***, sometimes referred to as 'one-dimensional', or 'flat characters', or 'stock characters'. But these should not always be dismissed because of their lack of complexity. Sometimes simply drawn characters can have an important function.

In this anonymous popular song from the Depression days of the 1930s, for instance, we are introduced to one William Brown.

A nice young man was William Brown,
He worked for a wage in a northern town.
He worked from six till eight at night,
Turning a wheel from left to right.

Keep that wheel a turning,
Keep that wheel a turning,
Keep that wheel a turning,
And do a little more each day.

The boss one day to William came:
He said, 'Look here, young what's-yer-name!
We're not content with what you do,
So try a little harder or it's out with you.'

So William turned and he made her run
Three times round in the place of one.
He turned so hard he soon was made
The Lord High Turner of the trade.

William turned with the same sweet smile;
The goods he made grew such a pile.
He filled the room and the room next door,
And overflowed to the basement floor.

The nation heard the wondrous tale:
The news appeared in the Sketch and Mail,
The railways ran excursions down,
All for to see young William Brown.

But sad the sequel is to tell:
He turned out more than the boss could sell,
The market slumped and the price went down,
Seven more days and they sacked young Brown.

Now it does not matter here that we know little about William, his home life, his hobbies, his appearance, his educational background, his family, the contradictions in his character. The ***simplicity*** of his portrayal allows people to identify with him and respond to the point of the song, which is to show the vulnerability of the employee in a free market economy.

Precisely what he does at work is not important, so it is not specified and then anyone who has performed some dull routine task at someone else's behest can identify with the situation. We can empathise with William because most of us have been cajoled into working harder by authority figures who struggle to remember our names.

People can respond to the irony of working so efficiently that we do ourselves out of a job and appreciate the ephemeral nature of fame. Whether you call William Brown a one-dimensional or clichéd character or a stereotype, he is just what is needed in this song.

Martin Barker (***Comics: Ideology, Power and Critics***, Manchester University Press 1989 pp 206–210) thinks that the stereotyping 'industry' objects to any categorising. It objects to categories which are ***false***: 'So a great deal of media representation of women is condemned for reinforcing the (false) stereotype that women want sex at any time.... Or again that the proportion of black or women characters in the media is greatly out of line with their proportion in the population.'

But stereotypers also complain when portrayals are true. 'Here, a good deal of media representation is condemned for showing women in the home, providing services to men – though of course it is in fact true that many do. Or again, black people are overwhelmingly shown living in poor conditions, in ghetto areas...even though this is (regrettably) true.'

Those who search out and condemn stereotypes are inclined to assume a very ***passive audience***. This is often linked with class according to Barker. He maintains that a variety of studies have shown that working class people are more prone to categorical thinking than 'educated, middle class people'. But he argues that working class people are 'in general more accurately aware that the social world is really divided into categories. If they have a 'stereotype' of managers, or employers, as 'exploitative', 'greedy', 'selfish', etc, that is not a false generalisation. It is an accurate summary of their experience of the inherent tendencies that arise from occupying a concrete social position. It is not a statement about the personality of an individual, but a claim about what follows from occupying a definite position in a class society.'

Barker goes on to suggest that the ***concept of stereotype is useless as a way of analysing media texts***. 'It leads to an arbitrary reading of texts which tells us only about the worries of the analyst.'

Activity

Read these three extracts and write an essay on the usefulness or otherwise of stereotyping. Refer to the extracts and express your own observations and judgements.

1 The Eternal Feminine

The stereotype is the Eternal Feminine. She is the sexual object looked for by both men and women. All she has to do is exist. She does not have to be successful because she is a reward for the achievements of others. Her virtue is assumed because she is lovely to look at. Without meaning to she can drive men to becoming mad or fighting wars. The more trouble she causes the more she is valued, for the more demand she inspires the more the possession of her means. There are strict limits to the variations of her stereotype, because nothing must stop her being a sex object. If she wears leather she must not be able to ride a motorbike; she can wear rubber but must not be an expert diver.

Because she signifies spending power and is a spender she is used to sell goods through advertising. She can be seen sitting astride the mudguard of a new car, lying at a man's feet stroking his new socks, holding a petrol pump in a challenging pose or dancing through woods in all the splendour of a new shampoo. She is always young and hairless with a smooth body. She is never seen as being humorous or intelligent or curious, but may display smouldering lust or idiot happiness.

The image of woman is everywhere, smiling interminably whether she is selling apple pies or washing machines, cheap chocolates or a stick-on bandage.

I am sick of this pretence. I don't want to pretend to be ever young, or that I am unintelligent. I am sick of the Powder Room. I am sick of pretending that some empty headed male's pompous assertions have my undivided attention. I am sick of going to films and plays when someone else wants to, and sick of having no opinions of my own about either. I am a woman not a castrate.

(Adapted from Germaine Greer, *The Female Eunuch*, Flamingo 1999, first published 1971.)

2 Women Are The New Men

Reversing sexist stereotypes had a point 20 years ago when women were trying to challenge masculine domination when everything to do with women was looked down on. But things have changed. There is no longer a system of male oppression. Men have become especially vulnerable to unemployment, homelessness and depression. Young people grow up taking female equality and even potency for granted.

But instead of rethinking old stereotypes women have become triumphalist about themselves and their values. Men are blamed for every negative aspect of society and women are regarded as the answer. A summary of recent research findings reported in *Focus* concluded that: 'Women will take over the world. Females are both psychologically and physically stronger.'

According to New Age thinking, women are more caring and understand natural, healing forces, while men are to blame for the destructiveness of technology and science, while opinion-forming journalists are criticising men more savagely, as in Janet Daley's *Telegraph* piece in which she maintains: 'Young boys will degenerate quite naturally into barbarism without adult supervision. Had half (or even some) of the lost children in William Golding's novel been female, the terrible denouement of *Lord of the Flies* would not have been credible.'

Images in the popular media in the 1990s have been depicting 'girls on top' with cool, glamorous women humiliating dim or uncouth men.

This 'womanism', which attributes all humanity's negative aspects to men, could be seen as harmless fun and a way of correcting centuries of the degrading of women. But it has harmful effects, particularly on that most vulnerable of society's groups, poor unemployed young men, those whom the media often describes as yobs, louts and scum. But instead of trying to understand the social conditions that lead to muggings, joyriding and violent crimes, womanism blames masculinity. Young men have become scapegoats in a society no longer comfortable with masculinity.

Womanism is especially dangerous when it asserts that women should be given more power simply because they are women, because they will be more constructive than men.

Girl power as promoted by the Spice Girls is asserted as a label for anything involving girls asserting themselves in 'unfeminine' ways. This 'challenging of the stereotypes' can cover many sins. Some challenges could still be useful but it can also lead to double standards. For instance, girls' assertive sexuality is taken as bravado whereas boys' assertiveness is dangerous.

(Adapted from Ros Coward, Women are the new men, *Guardian* 1/7/99.)

3 Burchill on Castle

Barbara Castle recently said: 'One of the biggest dangers women face today are men-haters. I love men. If there's a great deal of love you can get a great many things done. You don't have to be a man-hater to be a successful woman. In fact all it can do is to impede your progress.'

Just think about what she says for a while. Look at that first sentence. When it's early in the morning and you can't get a taxi and you hear footsteps behind you in the street do you think 'Oh my God it's one of those Man-haters! They are one of the biggest dangers that women face. Any minute now she's going to grab me from behind and...STICK A FALSE MOUSTACHE ON ME! Quick I've got to find a man!

And that second sentence. Barbara Castle has probably bossed more men into an early grave than a whole nation of lesbians. But as she's got older she wants to appear more cuddly and feminine and resorts to these sad man-pleasing tactics. And it's a shame that she seems to now imply that man-haters are really lesbians and therefore not 'qualified' to talk about the mysterious beauty of, say, men beating their wives.

Sorry to say it but when women go on about man-haters and dykes you wonder if it's just about repressed feelings, and if they don't fancy a bit of dyke action themselves.

Actually the highest proportion of man-haters are to be found in the man-pleasing sector of society such as prostitutes and lap dancers who see them as no more than walking wallets.

When the news is all about men being oppressed, murdered and raped by women, when a female Taliban confines men to their homes, when African women emasculate boys and say it's 'tradition', when two men a week are killed by their female partners, when boys are molested and strangled and left to die in a ditch by female attackers, come to me then and complain about man-haters, Barbara. Until then just remember that every day in every way in every culture men are hating women to death and getting away with it.

(Julie Burchill, *Guardian* G2 18/1/01.)

Activity

Gender in TV sitcoms

1 Work in small groups to pool your knowledge of situation comedies. Describe examples of and discuss the following:

The roles which men and women perform in the home. For example, which parent is more influential in bringing up children?

The roles which men and women perform at work. For example, are working women nearly always shown in 'service' occupations and men in 'controlling' occupations?

Personality. For example, are females more likely to be portrayed as submissive, weak, dependent and more concerned with making relationships?

How far are men portrayed as dominant, powerful, independent and more concerned with achievement?

In recent sitcoms are there examples of female characters being featured in leading roles, exhibiting independence, achievement, career success and potency?

2 Based on your discussion and note taking, write an essay discussing whether contemporary sitcoms display the following characteristics.

TV gender roles in sitcoms: recurrent characteristics

- Female characters are fewer in number and less central to the plot.

- Marriage and parenthood are considered less important in a man's life than in a woman's.
- Television portrays the traditional division of labour in marriage (e.g. women iron, men do DIY).
- Employed women are shown in traditionally female occupations as subordinates to men and with little status or power.
- When television women hold high-prestige positions they play less important roles and their work activities are not central to the plot.
- TV women are more personally and less professionally oriented than TV men.
- Female characters are more passive than male ones.
- Female characters are usually depicted in domestic settings.
- They are more concerned than are men about family and personal matters outside the home as well as inside.
- Where working wives are depicted, their working life is incidental to the story.
- Women shown as being successful professionally are also depicted as having unsuccessful social or private lives.

Stereotype spotting

Some critics become obsessed with spotting stereotypes and pointing them out to a less observant viewer so that their 'powerful influence' can be undermined. The language they use suggests that there are some very clever media professionals working on our feeble minds to preserve the dreaded 'status quo'. Everything they do is subtle or hidden. Here is an example from Travis Dougherty's 'Do television sitcoms enforce stereotypes?' taken from the internet.

'In the majority of sitcoms today the race and gender relations are blurred due to the conscious efforts of those controlling the shows to achieve political correctness. I have chosen two shows which illustrate how these gender and ethnic definitions are being subtly integrated into the television sitcom. The first programme, ***Grace Under Fire***, is the story of a single mother and her children. In one episode, African–American men are portrayed as blue collar workers. Although they are portrayed as clean and well-kept men, the fact remains that the African–American has been stereotyped into the role of the labourer. What does this suggest is the role of the Caucasian? I would say it suggests that the Caucasian is not relegated to the realm of physical work and that the African–American is. This structures our identification abilities and leads to racist tendencies.'

There are several tendencies here which are not uncommon amongst stereotype searchers. One is the assumption that media producers are attempting to *control our minds*.

The second is that they do this ***surreptitiously***.

The third is to *generalise from limited evidence* – the programme shows us black men doing labouring jobs, therefore it is implying that all black men are labourers.

The fourth is the *implied stereotype* – therefore white men can't or shouldn't be labourers, which seems to credit the producers with some very subtle and devious intentions.

The fifth is the assumption that the audience is ***gullible*** and will become more racist.

Activity

Small group discussion.

How far do you agree with the writer's views in this extract from the same article?

> "In another program [sic], *Spin City*, the distinctions between gender and ethnicity are blurred to the extent that not only females may be constructed as secretaries, but now anyone with feminine traits. This can be seen in the character of the African–American, homosexual secretary. In an environment where the female is almost exclusively portrayed in the role of an assistant, to insert a male with feminine qualities does not remove the gender stereotype.
>
> When we as viewers are presented with a male as secretary, we feel that the network is doing its part to break down the stereotype. This is not the case though. By characterising the secretary as having distinctly feminine qualities, what is actually shown to the trained watcher is that the female or feminine should always be second best to the typically masculine character of the boss. Although the employer is not always a male, they [sic] very often take on masculine traits and characteristics. What does this suggest about the power of femininity? It might suggest that the feminine will always be subjected to the will of the masculine. This too structures the ambitions and expectations of the viewers in ways which are often not beneficial to their ideas of self.
>
> Through the use of these very subtle mechanisms, the television serves as a powerful identification tool in our society. Through its hidden practices, it serves to further the status quo. Therefore when incorporating these programs into ourselves, it is imperative to understand the subtle messages we are being given in order to truly end the stereotype identification of the Other and begin to identify them as individuals as we should hope they would us."

Extension activities

1 Study the way values and attitudes change over time by looking at sitcoms from different decades.

Trace the way women in sitcoms were always shown in domestic settings (*Till Death Do Us Part*) to their being shown as low-paid workers (*The Rag Trade, Are You Being Served?*) then, as feminism began to take effect, bosses (*Cheers* and *Fawlty Towers*) and professionals (*Ally McBeal*).

Consider whether women are often the sensible, stable characters surrounded by silly irresponsible men (Alf Garnet's wife, the mother in *Bread*, Sybil Fawlty, Dorothy and Debs in *Men Behaving Badly*, Homer's wife, Marge, in *The Simpsons* and Mrs Meldrew in *One Foot in the Grave*).

2 Are the characters in sitcoms individuals or stereotypes?

You could describe and analyse characters such as:

- Del in *Only Fools and Horses* – is he just a loveable scoundrel?
- Barbara in *The Royle Family* – is she just a harassed, stressed mother figure?
- Basil Fawlty in *Fawlty Towers* – is he just a pompous but ineffective authority figure?

Social class in film fiction

INTRODUCTION

This chapter looks at how to analyse film fiction in terms of issues of representation and audience. Narrative and genre issues have already been addressed in chapters 2 and 3. This chapter focuses on three American films: *American Beauty* (USA 1999), *Titanic* (USA 1997) and *Small Time Crooks* (USA 2000) and on the topic of social class. The methods of analysis suggested can be applied to other films.

Key questions

Here is a checklist of questions to ask as you analyse films in terms of their representation of social class. They are meant to guide your thinking rather than become a rigid formula and some of them may not apply to particular films.

What values and beliefs do the main characters have?

Examples of values:

- that working hard is better than being lazy,
- that married people should be loyal to each other,
- that stealing is wrong,
- that sharing is better than selfishness.

How do the characters relate to their communities?

Do they rebel, reform, subvert, accept, challenge, join in or escape?

How do they relate to their families?

Do individual roles of mother, father, son, daughter, adult, adolescent, child, infant, etc, have any significance?

How is the audience positioned?

This usually depends on whose point of view the story is told from. It is easier for the audience to identify with the storyteller's point of view.

How is status or social class portrayed?

How important, for instance, are the adults' occupations and income, the type and location of family home, the furnishings, the family's transportation, etc? How far does the film encourage the audience to value, envy or despise these things?

How relevant to the characters (in films about America) is the concept of the American Dream?

This is the notion that any individual can attain power through wealth and that there are no class barriers to progress, a belief in the dignity of the common individual, a trust in democracy as the guarantee of freedom and in the quality and the importance of hard work.

Is the size of the town and its location important?

The American small town is often portrayed as acutely class-conscious, with its inhabitants gossiping, judging by appearances, and having a reactionary commitment to fading values and customs. It can be seen as representative of an extended but perverted family. Examples of American small-town portrayals can be found in (all USA) *Edward Scissorhands* (1990), *Groundhog Day* (1993), *Halloween* (1978), *The Ice Storm* (1997), *What's Eating Gilbert Grape?* (1993), *Twin Peaks* (1989) and *Blue Velvet* (1986). A comparison with the same theme from a different culture can be made with *Cinema Paradiso* (1988 Italy).

How is the portrayal of class connected with historical facts?

For instance, the 1940s saw a gradual erosion of America's cultural confidence in the nuclear family – that is, a small family of parents and children rather than an extended family of grandparents, aunts, uncles and cousins living in close proximity.

Millions of men were abroad fighting in the Second World War, while women were required to join the workforce. The films of the time reflected the changing role of women in wartime and post-war America. For example, *Double Indemnity* (1944) and *Mildred Pierce* (1946) show heroines rebelling against a suffocating middle-class lifestyle, tedious husbands and tacky homes.

Background information

Class systems

Before you begin to analyse social class in American films you need to be clear what you mean by class and know something about how the American system is different from the British.

- Class can sometimes have a *political meaning*, as in Marxism, which identifies a capitalist class that owns and controls land and businesses, and a working class who sell their labour. The theory sees these two classes in inevitable conflict.

- Another sort of classification has an ***economic and business significance*** and is of particular use to the media industry. It is the classification of people according to their occupation and earning power. This information is of use to advertisers who want to sell products to certain groups of people. The Institute of Practitioners in Advertising use this categorisation:
  - A Higher management, professional
  - B Intermediate managerial
  - C1 Supervisory or clerical, junior managerial
  - C2 Skilled manual
  - D Semi-skilled and unskilled manual
  - E State pensioners, widows, long-term unemployed.
- *Self-classification*. We can be assigned to classes by sociologists and researchers in an objective way based on jobs and incomes, ages and the way we spend our leisure time, but when it comes to assigning ourselves or others to classes emotions and beliefs become involved.

The terms people use in describing class often have emotive connotations, so that middle-class people can resent the implication in the term 'working class' that they are ***not*** 'workers', though they see themselves as working hard. Sometimes people are ashamed of the class they are part of and will try to 'aspire' to being middle class instead of working class, for instance.

This can lead to people using different terms to describe particular classes, as with some working-class people in the early twentieth century using the term 'productive class' to describe themselves but calling the upper classes the 'idle rich'. Then again some people who considered themselves to be higher class or aristocrats looked down on the 'lower orders'.

- Some people prefer ***simple classification***, arguing that there are really only two classes, the rich and the poor, or even that society has become classless.
- Others categorise people in more ***complex*** ways according to income, wealth, education, accent, dress, occupation and lifestyle and how different economic conditions influence these.

Social class in the USA

In terms of American society it is important to realise that there are some basic differences in notions of class from those of British people.

- One of the most significant aspects of America as opposed to Europe is the idea of ***new beginnings***. The first European settlers who began what we know of today as American society were people escaping religious intolerance. America was seen as a new world, a potential new Eden in the west. The Atlantic was a frontier and beyond it lay a brave new world where people could start again.
- The Puritan settlers, who had left Britain because they were persecuted for their beliefs, could practise their religion as they saw fit. They believed that they could restore Christianity to the health which it had lost in the Old World. In America, they were convinced, the human race had a divinely granted second chance at ***redemption***.

- Other groups had their own version of a new start. Many simply wanted a chance to become rich, a chance which had eluded them in Europe. Some were escaped convicts who felt reprieved. Others saw the New World as a garden of sensual delights. What they all had in common was the belief that America meant a ***fresh start***.
- The Constitution recognised that America was a ***coalition of minorities*** which had to be protected against each other's bigotries. It provided the basis for what came to be known as the ***American Dream*** by declaring that the Union of states should 'establish Justice, insure domestic Tranquillity, provide for the common defence, promote the general Welfare, and secure the Blessings of Liberty to ourselves and our Posterity'.
- America became the *land of opportunity* where it did not matter what your background or breeding was, where you could become wealthy and successful because of your own efforts. America was a land where you could forget the old evils of Europe and where there was a continually moving frontier.
- As the expansion of the settlers continued westward there were ever-renewing opportunities, a ***perennial rebirth***. There was in Americans during this period of expansion a continuing feeling of escape from the restrictions of the past, a freshness and a scorn of older society with its rigid class divisions.
- This ***frontier mentality*** fostered individualism, self-reliance, democracy, faith in man, a liking for discovery and the courage to break new ground. It involved taming the landscape, exploiting resources, testing a man's character, and confronting enemies. In short the frontier dream was the American Dream. America was and perhaps still is a country where 'anything is possible'.
- Part of the Dream has been the assumption that Americans can solve any problem. They tend to have a ***'can-do' mentality***, a disposition to 'get on with it', be optimists and have a desire to develop their talents to the utmost.
- But some argue that the ***Dream became an illusion***. Its philosophy spurred some people to build huge businesses and become extremely wealthy, but this capitalist success created conditions which paradoxically destroyed the Dream for workers, who became cogs in an industrial process.
- American attitudes to ***welfare and poverty*** have differed from European attitudes and the differences can be linked to the beliefs which were part of the American Dream. In the early 1930s, when European countries had well developed welfare schemes, the USA had no old-age pensions, no unemployment insurance, no family allowances and no health insurance.
- This was partly due to prevailing American middle-class attitudes that the ***poor were undeserving***, that they were poor because they were lazy or over-sexed or shiftless. There was a strong belief in the Protestant ***work ethic*** – the belief that nothing is worth having unless it involves effort, pain and difficulty. It followed that to give people benefits or welfare would lead to a moral degeneration. To dole out relief would destroy the human spirit and there would be a spiritual disintegration which would weaken the national fibre.

Case study

'Reading' *American Beauty* (USA 1999)

SYNOPSIS

Lester Burnham, his wife Carolyn and their daughter, Jane, are a well-off American family who hate one another. They shout and bicker, complain and criticise. Lester is in a tedious job he hates and is locked in a loveless, sexless marriage. His daughter despises him and wants him dead.

Carolyn works as an estate agent, is desperate for success and uncompromisingly materialistic.

Complications arise when the frustrated Lester lusts after Jane's best school friend, Angela, who portrays herself as sexually experienced.

Jane falls for Rick Fitts, the boy next door, while Carolyn has a wild fling with real estate 'king' Buddy Kane.

Lester, inspired by the youthful Rick, starts smoking pot and gives up his job (after blackmailing the boss into giving a handsome severance cheque). He also improves his physique in order to impress Angela.

Rick turns out to be a drug dealer, a secret he manages to keep from his ex-marine disciplinarian father. Rick's mother is a zombie-like character, presumably 'crushed' by her overbearing husband, who turns out to be a closet homosexual.

Lester tries to make love to Angela, only to find that her alleged promiscuity is a sham and she is a virgin

Jane and Rick plan to run away to New York and live on Rick's earnings from drug dealing.

Colonel Fitts, presumably ashamed of his overtures to Lester, shoots him dead.

INTERPRETATIONS

There are many ways of reading (or interpreting) *American Beauty*. These will vary according to many factors, such as the social and national background of the viewer, his/her media experience, the conditions of viewing and so on.

The film's director Sam Mendes has indicated some of his own readings in the notes accompanying the DVD of the film:

DIRECTOR'S VIEW

> 'The strange thing was that at each reading the script seemed to be something else. It was a highly inventive black comedy. It

CASE STUDY CASE STUDY CASE STUDY CASE STUDY CASE STUDY CASE STUDY CASE STUDY CASE STUDY

> was a mystery story with a genuine final twist. It was a kaleidoscopic journey through American suburbia.... It was a series of love stories. It was about imprisonment in the cages we all make for ourselves and our hoped-for escape. It was about loneliness. It was about beauty.. It was funny. It was angry.... It was sad.'

Mendes has usefully mentioned the characteristics of contemporary American society which are relevant to his film:

> 'In the end though, it remains an astonishment that a movie featuring relations between older men and younger women in the era of Clinton and casual drug taking, homosexuals in the military, teenage sexuality, the post-Columbine obsession with what's really going on in the house next door to you, and the great love that exists in even the most combative of families...could have been embraced and understood as it has been.'

VIEWS FROM THE NET

If we look at reviews of the film on the internet it would certainly appear that many people saw the film as a critique of American middle-class suburban life:

- '...a journey into the troubled heart of American suburbia';
- 'interweaving tales of whacked out suburban families with major sexual issues';
- 'a scathing tragicomic indictment of suburban materialism, conformity and ennui';
- 'it shows American middle class ideology as pervasive, dehumanising and ultimately destructive';
- 'poisoned 90s materialism and me-centred living'.

Kevin Spacey as Lester Burnham in *American Beauty*

Activity

Make your own interpretation of *American Beauty*

These points may be of use.

- Look at the *main character,* Lester Burnham, played by Kevin Spacey. He is the storyteller near the beginning, leading the audience into the film and we tend to see the sequence of events from his point of view or hear his voice-overs, though we are also given the impersonal narrator's view of some events.

The sequence near the beginning with Lester introducing himself and his environment is worth close study because it conveys so much about the basic conflicts (oppositions) and themes of the film.

How does the fact that his is a voice from beyond the grave affect your response?

- Look closely at the *settings* which are used. The fact that the environment Lester introduces us to is unnamed may be significant. A named environment would allow the audience to say, 'Well that only happens in so-and-so.' An unnamed environment means that it could happen in any place like this.

What does the aerial shot of Lester's environment suggest about the kind of place it is? Look at the sorts of houses you see and the gardens they have and the general impression of spaciousness. The dwellings are large, detached and well maintained. We have the impression of wealth and respectability. Does the fact that the town is not named indicate that it is meant to represent many American affluent middle-class suburbs? How do you respond to this sort of place – are you envious, curious, do you despise it or are you neutral?

Look at the Burnham's garden with its immaculate red roses and neat perimeter fence. What does it suggest about pride in appearance and a preoccupation with order, symmetry and tidiness? What links are there to notions of control and repression?

- *How does the main character react to this environment?* He could be comfortable with it, be proud of it, cherish it. But what do the first images we see of Lester suggest? Is he strong or weak? What is suggested by the overhead shot of him lying spread-eagled on his bed? Are the images of him in the shower or behind the window of his house or in the back of his wife's car meant to suggest he is trapped and insignificant? What impression of him do you gain as he trips and spills the contents of his suitcase as he sets out for work? What impression of him is given by his own words?

'My wife and daughter think I'm a gigantic loser, and they are right.'

'I'm dead already.'

'I've lost something.'

'I feel sedated'.

How does all this make you feel towards him? Do you feel sorry for him or dislike him? Are you influenced at all by the casting? Do you have any prior responses to the actor, Kevin Spacey?

- *How does Lester become a rebel?* What sort of job does he give up and what does he become? How does he subvert the American Dream in terms of not working to 'better himself' and acquire wealth? How does he subvert traditional family values by pursuing his daughter's best friend from school? What is the effect of making him start to smoke dope, which he buys from the boy next door? What about the way he blackmails his bosses into giving him a handsome pay-off? Does any of this make you change your own responses to him?

- *How do you react* to a hero who gives up his job, is cruel to his family and pursues an immature girl who is young enough to be his daughter? How does Lester change as a person through the course of the film?

- Comment on these aspects of Lester's character:

his weakness;
his frustrated sexual life;
the fact that his daughter despises him and wishes he were dead;
his pathetic yearning for his youth when he smoked pot and partied;
the way he tries to recapture his youth by working out, pursuing his daughter's best friend, who is still at school, buying a red Pontiac Firebird, playing loud rock music and 'flipping burgers'.

- Look at the *other main characters*.

Describe *Carolyn Burnham*'s job and her attitude to it. She is Lester's wife, played by Annette Bening. Consider how she has to be economical with the truth in order to sell homes, to use the language of advertising, so that a garden swimming pool becomes a 'lagoon' which a prospective buyer dismisses as a 'cement hole'. She feels she has to use phrases like 'it's your dream come true'.

How far do you agree with Lester's opinion that Carolyn is a 'bloodless, money grabbing freak'?

How far do you sympathise with Carolyn's own views of herself:

> 'I am selling an image and part of my job is living that image.'
>
> 'One must project an image of success at all times.'

How far do you feel sorry for her because she is anxious, deeply sad and alone?

Some critics have commented on the misogynist attitudes of the film's gay writer and you may want to think about Carolyn's portrayal in these terms.

Annette Bening as Carolyn Burnham in *American Beauty*

How true is it that Lester's *daughter Jane* (Thora Birch) is 'moody, mopey and grungey'? Why does she hate her family? How far do you sympathise with her when she takes the first opportunity to escape her environment by accepting Ricky's offer of running away to New York and living off his earnings as a drug dealer?

The middle class *family who move in next door* to the Burnhams are no less dysfunctional. The father is a retired Marine, Colonel Fitts (Chris Cooper). Is it fair to describe him as sadistic, overbearingly authoritarian, prejudiced and unfeeling? Why has he lost touch with his son Ricky? What repressed feelings lead to tragedy at the end of the film? How far is he to blame for his wife being little more than a zombie? What does it tell us about Mrs Fitts that, when her son says he is leaving home, she simply says 'OK. Wear a raincoat.'?

- How does the film portray or *represent middle-class families*? How far is it true that the film seems to be saying that whatever material possessions these people may have and however successful they appear from afar, they are really deeply unhappy and *twisted family groups*?
- Look at the *settings* of the film and consider how important they are in reinforcing the representation of this American suburb as a cold, unhappy and dangerous environment.
- Look at the *colours* in the living areas of the Burnham household. Do they suggest restraint and design consciousness, but also a lack of warmth and affection? Does it seem to be a house for show rather than one to live in comfortably? What does the absence of clutter in the dining room and the kitchen and Carolyn's concern that Lester does not spill his beer on the expensive Italian silk of the sofa tell you about the couple's relationship and Carolyn's values?

  The general *clinical coldness* of the interior scenes is frequently contrasted with small splashes of red as in the bowl of roses on the dining table. What significance does this red motif, which recurs so many times, have?
- In what ways is the Fitts' house similar to the Burnham's? Think about the colonel's office where he displays his collection of guns and some Nazi memorabilia. Notice again how there are little touches of red, as in the heart on the oven glove hanging in the kitchen. The house is very tidy and the film director seems to be suggesting that excessive tidiness goes with the unfeeling harshness of each family.

Thora Birch as daughter Jane in *American Beauty*

- How far is it true that the film is portraying affluent suburban middle-class life as dehumanising and cold, with outward show concealing emotional emptiness and destructive conflict? How far do you interpret it as portraying materialism versus personal fulfilment?

Extension activities

Describe how the film indicates visually that people are trapped.

Describe examples of people not seeing things as they really are but through some distorting intermediary such as a mirror.

How does the film show that no one is what they seem to be?

Activity

Watch the film *Titanic* and use the following method as the basis for your analysis of the representation of social class in the film.

Step 1

Write a *synopsis* of the film, that is a brief summary of the story. This should show:

- how a poor young man, Jack Dawson, manages to be on the maiden voyage of Titanic;
- the relationship between Rose DeWitt Bukater and Cal Hockley;
- the financial situation of Rose's mother and how this affects Rose;
- Rose's feelings about Cal and the starchy class he belongs to;
- how Jack saves Rose;
- what attracts Rose to Jack;
- how Cal tries to influence and control Rose;
- how Rose is torn between her genuine love of Jack and her sense of duty to her mother;
- how Rose and Jack grow closer and more intimate;
- how there is a cat and mouse series of events as the couple try to evade the increasingly jealous Cal and his minder Spicer Lovejoy;
- how the Titanic hits an iceberg and begins to sink;
- how there is a huge loss of life because of the inadequate safety arrangements;
- how the first-class passengers are given preference in the lifeboats while the third-class passengers are locked in their quarters;
- how Jack helps Rose to survive though he himself dies after the ship sinks;
- how Cal also survives but Rose refuses to acknowledge him and the two stay apart.

Step 2 Critique

Rose and Jack (Winslet and DiCaprio) in *Titanic*

Consider the roles that the main characters play in the narrative.

- Explain what sort of *hero* figure Jack Dawson is.
- Show how he is a penniless but talented artist.
- Explain how he managed to get a ticket for the voyage.
- Show how he is unresentful about his poverty: 'When you've got nothing, you've got nothing to lose.'
- Consider how he wins Rose over through his free spirit, passion and zest for life.
- Contrast him with the *villain*, Cal Hockley, who is rich but rude, arrogant and possessive.

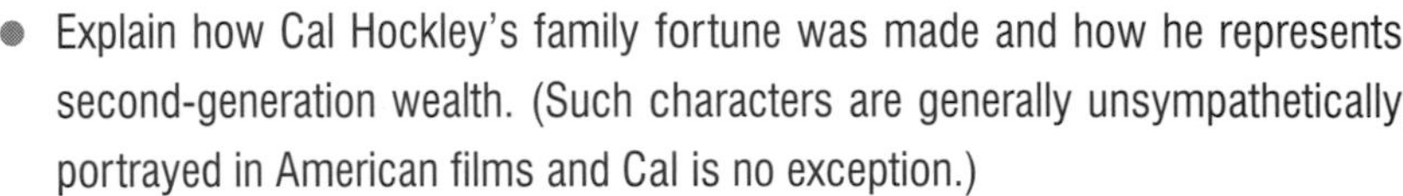

- Explain how Cal Hockley's family fortune was made and how he represents second-generation wealth. (Such characters are generally unsympathetically portrayed in American films and Cal is no exception.)
- Does he have any redeeming qualities?
- Show how he treats Rose as one of his possessions and talks to her as if she were his servant: 'You will never behave like that again Rose. Do you understand?'
- Think about what it says about his character and attitudes when he tries to get Rose to open her heart to him by giving her the present of an extremely valuable diamond necklace.
- Show how Cal's financial power sets him apart from the throng right from the beginning of the film when he arrives in a luxurious automobile, itself a rarity in 1912 when the film is set, and with another vehicle laden with possessions. Show too how he uses money to bribe officials.
- The *heroine* is Rose DeWitt Bukaker who has become engaged to Hockley presumably because her mother encouraged her. Show how her mother, though very much a part of the upper-class society on the ship, is in fact penniless. 'You know the money's gone. Do you want to see me working as a seamstress?'
- Explain how her survival in this social group depends on Rose marrying Hockley.
- Show how Rose, on the other hand, detests the man and scorns the social class to which she belongs. 'Outwardly I was everything a well brought up girl should be,' she declares. Within, however, she is empty: 'To me it was like a slave ship.'
- Show how Rose rebels against her class when she imagines her future life in it: 'The same narrow people, the same mindless chatter. I felt like I was standing on a precipice.'
- Explain why Rose runs away from the group she is with and intends to throw herself from the ship, but is saved by Jack.
- Show how this act of heroism brings the two together and triggers the clash of class cultures which forms much of the story.

Step 3 Comparison of two key sequences

- Examine closely two sequences which emphasise *class conflict:* (a) first when Jack joins the elite at dinner and then (b) when Rose is whisked off to steerage to enjoy a 'real party'.
- Show how Jack's friendship with Mrs Brown portrays a friendlier face of the upper classes.
- Explain how she is rather scorned by the other women in first class who regard her as vulgar because she is 'new money'.
- Show how Mrs Brown sees through their snobbery and teaches Jack how to survive their company: 'Remember they love money, so just pretend that you own a gold mine and you're in the club.'
- Explain how Jack learns the importance of dress, how to manage the vast array of cutlery at a multi-course meal and even hold his own in conversation, despite attempts by Rose's mother to humiliate him.
- Why does Jack decline to have brandy and cigars with the men and what does he do instead?
- Compare the upper-class environment with the steerage part of the ship where, in much humbler and more chaotic surroundings, there is a ceilidh in progress.
- Show how here, instead of the formal dress and stiff manners of the first-class dining room, there is exuberance and liveliness with wild dance music and laughter.
- What effect does this atmosphere have on Rose? How does she behave?
- You could compare the camera work and the pace of editing and show how they contribute to the contrast between the two scenes.
- Show how at the ceilidh the camera work dwells less on the surroundings than on the people, with more use of close-ups than in the dining room scenes.
- Show how quicker cutting suggests energy and excitement and how the slower pace of editing in the dining room scenes suggests control and discipline rather than vitality.
- What is the purpose of the fantasy sequence at the end of the film where Rose imagines climbing the stairs to meet Jack underneath the clock outside the first-class dining room? This is a reprise of their secret meeting before Jack takes her to the party in the third-class accommodation earlier in the film. In this sequence, however, the two classes are intermingled and they stand and applaud as Rose, in her formal evening wear, embraces Jack in his casual attire.
- How far do you think that the message is that, when it comes to love, class is unimportant and perhaps too that classlessness is better than class division?

Step 4 The American Dream

- What has Jack Dawson's character to do with the *American Dream* (see above)?
- Explain how he comes from the mid-west, Wisconsin in fact, but then travelled further west to spend much of his early life doing jobs on the Californian coast, fishing for squid off Monterey and working as an artist in Los Angeles.
- Why does his unfettered lifestyle appeal to Rose: 'Why can't I be like you Jack – just head for the horizon whenever I feel like it?'
- Explain how Jack tries to persuade Rose to break from the straitjacket of her social class and how he praises the kind of adventurous lifestyle of the pioneers and adventurers so beloved in the frontier mentality.

- How does his teaching Rose to spit have a rebellious significance?
- Show how this is used in the story when Rose finally rejects Cal during the sinking sequences.
- What is the significance of Jack persuading Rose to learn how to ride a horse like a cowboy, not side-saddle like a lady?
- Link this to the scene at the very end of the film when we see a photograph of Rose riding a horse in this style. 'He saved me in every way that a person can be saved,' she says in her narration.

Step 5 The sinking of the ship

- Show how social class was very significant when it came to survival.
- Show how the first-class passengers were given preference to places in lifeboats and how the third-class passengers were locked in by the stewards so that they could not escape.
- Show how Mrs Brown does her best to persuade the crew of the lifeboat to go back and try to save some of the people in the water and how it is a lower-class crewman (English) who shouts her down and refuses.
- Consider whether the behaviour of the English stewards and servants is portrayed as cowardly, cruel and crass.
- Explain how they are always willing to accept a bribe, become fawningly subservient to people with good tipping power and are buffoons, cowards or bullies when treating the lower-class passengers.
- Show how noble or responsible behaviour from the crew is associated with Celtic accents, such as the Welsh crew member who takes the one boat back which rescues Rose.
- Show how the superior officers such as Captain Smith are portrayed as complacent and ineffectual, more concerned with protocol than practicalities. 'Goddamn English doing everything by the book,' as Cal complains.

Extension activities

Write about:

- The symbolic significance of the aged Rose throwing her incredibly valuable diamond into the sea.
- Why Jack was seen as a 'dangerous insect' invading the upper-class space.
- The significance of music, especially Irish music, in the film.

Activity

Analyse *Small Time Crooks* using the framework suggested here.

Step 1

Write a synopsis of the story. This should include the following:

- Information about Ray Winkler (Woody Allen) and his wife Frenchy (Tracey Ullman). What jobs did they do in the past? What is the state of their relationship at the beginning of the film?
- Why is Ray interested in Frenchy's savings? What is his plan and his dream?
- Describe Ray's helpers.

- Why does Frenchy start making cookies and what happens to the business?
- What goes wrong with the bank robbery?
- Explain why Frenchy wants to join the cultural elite. What evidence was there of her ambitions in the earlier part of the film?
- How does David (Hugh Grant) try to 'educate' Frenchy?
- How do you react to the cultural events which Frenchy experiences?
- How on the surface the upper classes appear to accept Frenchy because she is very rich but privately, as she discovers by accident, they despise and mock her.
- How Ray grows apart from Frenchy as he does not want to change his social class or his way of life.
- How Ray spends most of his time with fellow lowbrow and eccentric May (Elaine May), pining for his days as a low-life failure.
- How corruption and cheating exist at all levels of society, and Frenchy loses her wealth when her accountants embezzle her funds big time and flee the country.
- How the suave David turns out to be an exploiting deceiver and Frenchy does a little robbing of her own to get enough money for her and Ray, now reunited, to fly off to Florida and be themselves.

Step 2

Write a critique.

- Show how, for Ray, there are only two classes, the rich and the poor. He would like to be rich but the only ambition he expresses is to move from New York to Florida.
- Contrast this attitude with Frenchy's. She starts off by saying, 'We're poor but we're happy' and does not want to become rich. However, there are signs that she admires the expensive lifestyles which she sees others living in television programmes. For instance, when we first see her she is enviously watching a programme about Princess Diana. In another scene she is watching a television programme called 'Rich and Famous' and is in awe of someone who has 200 pairs of shoes. She says to Ray, 'Wouldn't it be wonderful to be Patron of the Arts? Opening night at the opera, doesn't that sound great?'
- Explain how, when the couple become rich and have the means to mix with a different social class, Ray is ill at ease with this class and rejects it.
- Show how Frenchy tries to 'improve herself' and be part of it. Explain how these differences in attitudes cause conflict between them which eventually leads to a split.
- Consider how the social divisions represented in the film involve several cultural oppositions, for example what people eat/drink and where:

  Ray wants a cheeseburger while Frenchy exhorts him to eat truffles.

  'Truffles got no flavour Frenchy.'

  'They're subtle. Only pigs can find 'em.'

  Ray goes to a Chinese restaurant and delights in 'the MSG and the grease' while Frenchy is in an elegant restaurant learning how to appreciate the difference between a Burgundy and a Bordeaux.

Ray (Woody Allen) and his incompetent crooks

- Examine the different interior settings carefully and assess their significance. Show how Frenchy believes she has a flair for decoration and proudly shows off a new rug which 'lights up'.
- What do the excessive adornments of her apartment and office tell you about her taste? 'The sheer flawless vulgarity of it all. It's the definition of bad taste,' as one guest says.
- Show how Ray tries to appreciate her taste and has an idea that antiques are important but is out of his depth, believing that one is either a 'Renaissance or a Magna Carta or something'. Another is a 'Louis XIVth or XVth. Well definitely a top Louis.' Frenchy says: 'It ain't dough it's knowing the finer things of life. Class is something you can't fake and you can't buy.'
- Consider Frenchy's taste in clothes. Like her taste in decoration, Frenchy's taste in clothes is over-the-top. Some of her costumes, such as the lacy flouncy creation she wears at her dinner party, perhaps recall one of her previous jobs as an exotic dancer. Later she thinks that David has taught her how to be 'low key' though her dress is still flamboyant. She remarks that Ray thinks it is 'dullsville'.
- What do Ray's clothes tell you about him? How fair is Frenchy's dismissive: 'He likes to watch TV in his underwear sucking a Bud'?
- Study the high-brow cultural experiences in some detail. Show how Ray and Frenchy react differently. Ray prefers visiting dog tracks and baseball matches while Frenchy wants to go to Europe and visit museums and galleries 'as part of my cultural development'.
- Show how Ray and Frenchy are reunited when they lose their money and Frenchy realises that the people she admired were really hypocrites and swindlers. Show how she has done her own little bit of swindling, however, by stealing back the expensive diamond encrusted cigarette case from David, suggesting perhaps that money does matter as long as we are true to ourselves.
- Consider how the film is about life's absurdities and frustrations. Is it pessimistic about human nature with people at different social levels being untrustworthy and deceitful? How likeable are the main characters? Are Ray, Frenchy and May all dreamers who want a better life? Even though they often appear foolish and absurd in their quests, can the audience still identify with them and warm to them?

SECTION B **Chapter 11**

Celebrity in the tabloid press

INTRODUCTION

This chapter defines what is meant by the term 'celebrities' and goes on to show how to study representation of celebrity with particular reference to the tabloid press. For a definition of 'tabloid press' see p 70 in the chapter on British Newspapers.

It shows how celebrities are fashioned by the media industries and examines the role of Public Relations (PR) professionals in particular. It then raises the question of celebrities as both ordinary and special before looking at the role of the audience in constructing and accepting celebrities.

This is a guide to the kinds of stories the tabloid press print about celebrities and an analysis of the ways those stories are treated. This unit also looks at the Royal Family as a particular kind of celebrity and finally considers the issue of privacy and public interest.

What are celebrities?

An interesting way into this question is to look at the film ***Chicago*** (USA 2002) and discuss its meanings in class. The musical takes a ruthless look at those who pursue fame at any price and at the audiences and the media who 'consume' celebrities. According to Box Office online reviews (www.boxoff.com) the theme of the film is 'life is all show business in one way or another and...showbiz is a great, brassy and gilded lie'. ***Chicago*** is a film, it continues, 'in which murder, hypocrisy, celebrity and deceit are served up and sent up'.

Celebrities are people who are widely known and, usually, liked. The word 'celebrity' means more or less the same as 'star', though whereas all stars are celebrities, not all celebrities are stars. Stars are usually from groups such as pop singers and musicians, film actors, sportsmen and sportswomen, models or television personalities. These can be termed celebrities but so can people who are famous for being famous, the very wealthy, royalty, soap opera characters, criminals and politicians.

Celebrities can represent a kind of capital. If they are famous enough they hold a monopoly. So whoever owns the contract for a particular celebrity is in effect the owner of a monopoly product. Star names associated with a film draw great audiences not only because of their personal magnetism but also because they represent certain types of entertainment and because they assure production efforts far above average.

The star or celebrity could be seen by the investors in film or by TV producers as something that can be marketed and advertised. He or she can be identified with a certain genre (John Wayne and the Western) or a particular personality (e.g. the manic and dangerous Jack Nicholson). These qualities are easier to manage than having to judge the quality of a script or predict the suitability of a celebrity to a particular role.

Activity

Work as a class or group over a period of time. Choose a celebrity and collect images of that person used to sell or endorse products. Prepare a display which suggests reasons why the celebrity has been used to promote each product and give your opinions about the effectiveness of the promotions.

The promotion of celebrities

An enormous amount of money, time and effort is expended by media producers in order to establish and promote celebrities. The way this works in the film industry is described by Thomas Harris in 'The Building of Popular Images' quoted in Richard Dyer's ***Stars*** (BFI 1998 p 46):

There is 'a preliminary build-up starting months even years before the star is seen on the screen. Frequent devices used...are a 'discovery' usually concocted by the studio publicists, a series of glamour pictures sent to all the print media, a rumoured romance with another star already well known to the public, or a rumoured starring role in a major film. The publicity finds a primary outlet in syndicated Hollywood gossip columns and movie fan magazines. When the actor or actress is actually cast in a film, the studio assigns a 'unit man' to 'plant' items about the personality in these places as well as national magazines and Sunday newspaper supplements'.

The influence of PR (Public Relations)

An illustration of this process in relation to newspapers can be seen in the following account of the work of a public relations person.

It shows how there is a close relationship between the press and celebrities. They need each other. Newspapers know that their readers want gossip about famous people and people who want publicity and fame know that the newspapers want information. So there is an informal business relationship between the two. This involves PR specialists. These people have the job of feeding information and pictures to the press. The kind of work such people do is revealed in this account from a PR man, Ian Johnson, representing ITV's *Popstars* programme which created the group Hear'Say.

Case study

PROMOTING HEAR'SAY

This is an account of the publicity surrounding the final formation of the manufactured band Hear'Say. The final five members of the group had been decided but the public were not to be told this until a particular episode of the programme *Popstars* was shown. The PR representative is having to keep the press supplied with stories but preventing them from revealing the names of the successful performers.

MONDAY DECEMBER 4

LWT's entertainment chief, Nigel Lythgoe, has spent the summer searching the country for wannabe pop talent with former Spice Girls PR Nicki Chapman and Polydor A & R director Paul Adam. The results of their search are known only to a few people and I have to sign a confidentiality agreement before I'm even allowed to see pictures of the chosen five. We have to keep them under wraps for a couple of months until they are revealed midway through the series. A hard task but one which the LWT's security arrangements should take care of. Not for long. I take a call from a freelance journalist who knows their names and a lot more about the band's members. It won't be long before the whole of the press knows. We need to keep the publicity pot boiling without giving too much away. With billboards across the country proclaiming 'Nigel Pick Me' what better distraction for the newspapers than 'Nasty Nigel'.

MONDAY JANUARY 15

The show is on air and causing a media sensation. Nasty Nigel is a household name because of his auditioning techniques. His celebrity status becomes apparent when *Top Of The Pops* magazine demands that he reviews the month's singles.

TUESDAY JANUARY 16

I am woken up at 7.30 am by Kiss FM which gives me ten seconds' notice before putting me live on air. Either I take them to meet the band or they reveal the band's address.

WEDNESDAY JANUARY 17

Such is the show's appeal that even the losers are cover stories. Heat magazine wants Big Claire from Glasgow and Darius, 'the pain in the arias'. But there is a problem. Claire's bosses at Kwik-Fit won't let her have a longer lunch break. We say we'll pay for the lost income but they do not accept. We agree to take pictures in her works canteen with her work mates looking on. Fame costs and here's where you start paying.

FRIDAY JANUARY 19

Someone is spilling the beans. Too many tabloids know where the band are living, where they come from and who they are sleeping with. Most worrying is that they know about Kim's situation. I offer a steady stream of 'exclusive' stories to keep the names out of the papers until we reveal the band on screen. The tabloids agree – a revealed band does not sell papers, a real-life soap opera does.

SATURDAY JANUARY 20

The *Sunday People* is intending to break ranks. I desperately try to persuade the editor to keep the *Popstars* secret but fail.

SUNDAY JANUARY 21

The band are upset.

MONDAY JANUARY 22

Many journalists now know the final line-up and are using this as ammunition. We must provide a steady stream of tabloid fodder to keep them at bay. The *Sun* demands six double-page spreads in a week. Nigel, Darius and Claire step forward to fill the void.

TUESDAY JANUARY 23

Kiss FM want to interview the band and are willing to go to any lengths to get one. They know of my home address, where my parents live, which university I went to and details of a particularly embarrassing teenage medical complaint which even my mother does not know about.

FRIDAY JANUARY 26

Sunday Mirror journalists interrupt a meeting of ITV bosses to introduce a woman who beat Nigel in a tap dancing contest 40 years ago. There is a tearful reunion.

SATURDAY MARCH 3

The show is going stellar and the *Popstars* also-rans want a share of the cake. We get them on the guest list at the latest celeb hangout, the Red Cube. Jordan and her celebrity breasts contact the office and demand to be fixed up with Darius. Dane Bowers, her ex, has been critical of him in the press and she can smell revenge mixed with tabloid headlines. *Popstars* failures now rank above D-list footballers and Big Brother contestants.

MONDAY MARCH 5

Finally the five are officially revealed and it is time to show them off at a press conference at Heathrow. They sing, they charm, they head off to shoot their first five magazine covers and I breathe a sigh of relief.

(Adapted from the *Media Guardian*, 19/3/01, reproduced with permission)

Activity

Summarise Ian Johnson's problems, the solutions he came up with and their relative success.

Activity

Apply what John Patterson says in The Moronic Inferno (below) about the rubbishy reporting of the Kidman/Cruise split to the piece adapted from the *Sun* pages 4 and 5, 6 February 2001.

- Is there any news, in respect of something being fresh information?
- What are the named sources of the information and how many sources are unnamed?
- How much is history or gossip?

The Moronic Inferno by John Patterson

(Adapted from the *Guardian* G2 16/2/01)

The media reaction to the announcement of Tom Cruise and Nicole Kidman's divorce was horribly predictable.

There were old rumours, unfounded, about their alleged sexual problems. There was scrutiny of the couple's links to the Church of Scientology, but there was nothing that was really news. Most of it was infected by the AIDS virus of modern entertainment journalism: the unattributed source.

All that journalists had to work from was a brief press statement which was in essence: 'Divorce. Scheduling Pressures. Amicable. Great Pity.' From that statement there grew a vast stream of rubbishy reporting.

What was happening was the kind of news management applied by Ronald Reagan in the early 1980s: say nothing, never explain, never apologise. What happens then is that you get a surge of news people anxious to interview you to get information even if it is managed and massaged. The sceptics who like to be partly honest will leave you alone.

The consequence is artificial news coverage prone to spin doctoring and lying, cravenly admiring of its subjects and based on cosy but corrupt relationships between newsmakers.

Journalists are invited to Hollywood junkets run by the film industry. They are flown in in large numbers, put up in hotels and fed and watered. They are then allowed to meet directors and stars for 15 minutes at a time. They ask easy questions at the level of 'What's it like working with a great star like so-and-so?' and get these kinds of answer: 'What an amazing, talented, generous, humanitarian artist.'

When I tried to ask more searching questions I was removed from an interview and have not attended junkets since.

But media coverage is more likely to be given by journalists who make a living on the junket circuit, who need to keep friendly, non-critical relationships with the studio publicists and who are providing the editors with exactly the kind of glorified PR they seek.

The *Sun* story (adapted)

They seemed to be the perfect celebrity duo. Two of Hollywood's top stars who declared they had been happily married for ten years.

Just six months ago 38-year-old Cruise said that he and Nicole were forever. 'Since we married we've stayed totally in love.'

Their adopted children went everywhere with them as they seemed to be the perfect loving family. The couple even showed their closeness on screen when they acted out steamy scenes in the film *Eyes Wide Shut*.

But yesterday Cruise and 33-year-old redhead Nicole, both devoted Scientologists, announced they were splitting.

A statement from their publicist said: 'Tom Cruise and Nicole Kidman have regretfully decided to separate.'

Cruise will move out of their £10 million mansion in Los Angeles. Kidman will stay there with the children.

It is thought the couple will share custody of the children eventually.

The split has shocked Hollywood insiders. One said: 'Tom and Nicole always seemed happy together. This announcement is like a bolt from the blue.'

Tom Cruise met Nicole when the pair starred in the movie *Days of Thunder*. Tom said then that when he was with Nicole it was as if they were one being.

He was already separated from *Lost in Space* star Mimi, who said that the fact that they could not have children had put a strain on their marriage. 'Living with Tom was like living with a monk,' she added.

Tom is Hollywood's top male earner, earning £50 million from *Mission Impossible 2* alone.

Nicole got rave reviews when she stripped off on the West End stage in the play *The Blue Room*.

It is not known where Tom will live but he has houses in Hawaii, Australia and New York.

If the couple divorce, Nicole is unlikely to get hands on much of Cruise's £200 million fortune, according to celebrity lawyer Raoul Felder. He said Tom would have made her sign a pre-nuptial agreement barring her from claiming a half-share.

Celebrities are 'ordinary'

Celebrities are often described as being ordinary, despite their special qualities or talents. They are often portrayed as living expensive lifestyles but underneath being just like the rest of us.

This kind of reporting is parodied in this extract from a *Viz Annual* 1994, page 89.

'I STILL USE PUBLIC LAVATORIES' Says ***Bullseye's*** TV comic Jim.

Millionaire game show king Jim Bowen may have made his fortune as host of the highly popular darts show ***Bullseye*** – but he's still prepared to use public lavatories.

Comic Jim, whose showbiz career began with appearances on TV's ***The Comedians***, has climbed to the pinnacle of the entertainment ladder. And the one-time schoolteacher now drives a glittering Rolls Royce and wears £40 shoes when he's not swimming in the luxurious heated pool at his sumptuous Lancashire home.

Yet Jim, 62, still has his feet firmly on the ground and is, under certain circumstances, still prepared to use public lavatories.

'My wife and I often go shopping – we've worked for our money and we're not afraid to spend it. On one occasion I needed to use the lavatory when we were out shopping. I didn't think twice about using the public loo nearby.'

But that's typical of Jim, 65, who has very much steered his own course throughout a spectacularly successful showbiz career.

TV stardom has not meant many changes for Jim. Now the proud owner of an old motorbike, he is not ashamed of his wealth. 'I've worked hard for my money, and I'm not afraid to spend it,' he told us. And yet, at 66, Rolls Royce and £40 shoe owning former schoolteacher Jim, 59, is still prepared to use a public lavatory.

Taking a break from his meteoric showbiz career to sip champagne by his luxury pool, Jim kicks off his £40 shoes. But even as he dips a toe in the luxury water, Jim's feet remain firmly on the ground. 'I wouldn't think twice about using a public lavatory,' he told us.

(*Viz Annual* 1994, reproduced with permission)

Activity

Write a spoof celebrity piece similar to the above.

Work in pairs with an interviewer and a 'celebrity'.

The celebrity should invent details of what has made him/her famous and details about how 'ordinary' they still are.

The interviewer finds this information and then writes it up as in the 'I still use public lavatories' style.

The roles can then be reversed.

Alternatively, write a spoof report about a real contemporary star who insists he/she is just ordinary.

Audience interpretations

The manipulation, management and construction of celebrities is not a complete explanation of the celebrity phenomenon. The audience plays its part. Celebrity images are offered, but not always accepted. For those which are, the following processes seem to be happening, according to Andrew Tudor (***Image and Influence***, Allen and Unwin 1974 p 80):

- There is an ***emotional affinity***. This means an empathy between the celebrity, the kinds of stories about the celebrity and the personality of the individual member of the audience.
- There is ***self-identification***. This happens when there is so much involvement that the member of the audience feels as if he or she were actually the celebrity himself/herself.
- There is ***imitation*** where the celebrity becomes a role model for the member of the audience, usually young, influencing behaviour and appearance.
- There is ***projection***. In this situation the member of the audience does more than just mimic the outward appearance and mannerisms of the celebrity, but makes life judgements and decisions based on what they think the celebrity would do in particular situations.

Activity

Interview five people about their favourite celebrity and find out which of the above categories most accurately describes their attitudes.

Ask questions such as:

- Which famous person do you most admire?
- What qualities do they have that you particularly like?
- Can you recall any stories about the person?
- Has the person ever influenced your decisions, attitudes, actions or appearance?

Subcultures

The importance of audience interpretation is shown in the way *different subcultures* can read or interpret celebrities in different ways.

In *Heavenly Bodies* (Richard Dyer, Macmillan 1987, pp 169–177), for instance, Richard Dyer examines the gay interpretations of Judy Garland's image. Garland's PR image stood for happy family values in a heterosexual culture but her 'normal' image seemed to be contradicted by an unhappy private life. Perhaps, therefore, her image was only an act. She also dressed in particular ways, mixing conventionally male and female attire which suggested that the difference between masculinity and femininity was not something deep-seated but was superficial. Judy Garland did not represent a gay lifestyle, but her contradictions and cross-dressing questioned dominant ideas of sexuality and made her amenable to gay readings.

John Fiske in his essay British Cultural Studies and Television, printed in *Channels of Discourse Reassembled* (ed. R Allen, Routledge 1992) shows how a mass-produced text can only be made into a popular text when it has been *transformed* into various meanings by various subcultures. He illustrates this process with the example of Madonna.

Madonna meanings

To some extent Madonna has been a major phenomenon in popular culture because of the effectiveness of her publicity machine, but not all her fans are easily manipulated by PR spin. They can actively choose to *imitate Madonna* rather than anyone else and for this to happen they must be able to make meanings which connect with their own social experience. If that experience has been of powerlessness and subordination, then Madonna must in some way be a role model for *female resistance* to male power and domination. She helps young girls in a male-dominated society, where women had long learned that they had to be attractive to men and submissive, to keep the *bravado and exhibitionism* that they feel and not let it be knocked out of them when they reach womanhood.

Madonna was seen by many young females as an *empowering figure*. She represented a powerful female figure in control of her own body. Her sexuality offered a *challenge to dominant definitions of femininity and masculinity*. She invited females to get in touch with their own sexuality and identity. This was expressed by her admirers in terms such as: 'She's sexy but she doesn't need men.... She's kind of there all by herself' or 'She gives us ideas. It's like women's lib, not being afraid of what guys think'.

Fiske argues that Madonna's adolescent fans find in her meanings of femininity that have broken free from the virgin/whore, angel/devil representations that were dominant in a patriarchal society. She is *independent*, she is herself. Fiske illustrates the way Madonna comes to represent a sort of feminist rebellion with reference to her video *Material Girl*:

'Madonna's image is based in part on that of Marilyn Monroe, the great sex symbol of an earlier generation. But the differences between the two 'blonde bombshells' are more instructive than the similarities. In the video *Material Girl*, Madonna goes through a dance routine with tuxedo clad young men in a parody of Monroe's number Diamonds are a Girl's Best Friend from *Gentlemen Prefer Blondes*. During the number she collects jewellery from the men as she sings the refrain, 'Cause we're living in a material world, and I am a material girl'. But despite her whore-like gathering of riches from men and her singing that only boys with money have any chance with her (which is close to Monroe's performance in Diamonds are a Girl's Best Friend) she toys with the boys, showing that jewellery has bought them no power over her, but instead that extracting it is an expression of her power over them'.

Tabloid celebrity stories

Activity

Research this topic by tracking celebrity stories in a number of papers over a few weeks to see what patterns emerge.

The following checklist is to help you start your research and is not meant to be a complete categorisation.

When you have done your research present your findings as a display or as a web page. The kinds of story which you are likely to find are:

1 Who's going out with whom?

The papers are especially interested in love triangles as in this *Sun* (22/5/01) story:

> 'Amanda Holden and Neil Morrissey nuzzled, hugged and smooched in front of stunned celebrity clubbers in an encounter which is bound to infuriate her hubby Les Dennis.'

Even denials make stories. This appeared on the front page of the *Daily Star* as a lead story: 'Furious Boyzone star Keith Duffy last night denied that he and *Celebrity Big Brother* babe Claire Sweeney were anything more than pals.'

Even the sex life of cartoon characters can make the news: 'Cartoon tearaway Bart Simpson is about to lose his virginity.'

Splits also make news. The importance attached to them can be seen in the front page of the *Sun* (see p149) on the day that Nicole Kidman and Tom Cruise announced their estrangement.

2 How the famous spend their money

The tabloids seem fascinated with how much people earn, how expensive their houses are, what kind of vehicles they drive and how they spend their leisure time. So, in a story about how Chris Evans gave away £46 million to charity, the *News of the World* has pictures of Evans's 'mansion' in Belgravia, of his red Ferrari, of him out with a girlfriend and on a 'bender' with Danny Baker and Paul Gascoigne.

Stories about spending seem to fall into two categories, one suggesting how wonderful it is to have wealth and the other about wastefulness and decadence.

3 Appearance

Stories such as Angelina Jolie having to increase the size of her breasts before taking on the role of Lara Croft in a new film are prominent in some newspapers which have a tendency to print soft porn pictures of females.

It is not unusual for trivial 'appearance' stories to make front pages, especially if they are accompanied by revealing pictures. This appeared on page 1 of the *Daily Star* (21/11/00):

> 'Here's a sneak preview of what Britney Spears fans are desperate to get their maulers on.
> The teen pop sensation shows off her sexy new image on the cover of her next single Stronger, flashing her pierced belly button.'

The clothes celebrities wear, especially at ceremonies like the Oscars, can receive considerable attention and analysis.

4 Any brush with the law or officialdom

'Gail Porter faces being banned by the BBC after boasting about being drunk while presenting a children's TV programme'. *Sunday Mirror* (4/2/01).

5 Any threat they suffer

'Film star Antonio Banderas refused to stay in hiding last night after receiving death threats from Basque terror groups'. *Star* (22/3/01).

6 Any health problem or minor injury

'Speed film star Sandra Bullock loves being needled – she's spending £1,200 a day on acupuncture. The Hollywood beauty is followed everywhere on the set of her new movie Miss Congeniality by two personal acupuncturists'. *Star* (22/3/01).

Caroline Aherne, 'who has battled a drink problem and sought treatment at the Priory Clinic following a suicide attempt in July 1998, has decided not to write another series'. *Sunday Mirror* (2/4/01).

7 Awards they receive

'Jennifer Aniston, John Goodman and Mel Gibson slipped into character when they picked up gongs at a back-slapping awards bash. Waif Jennifer looked like it was taking all her strength just to hold her glass thingy, action man Mel looked like he was going to open fire with his and lardy John tried to eat his'. *Star* (9/1/01).

8 Their downfall or failures

The *News of the World*, possibly peeved because they were denied access to the ceremony, treated Madonna's marriage to Guy Ritchie as a disaster, with the front page headline 'Bride and Gloom' accompanying pictures of the two looking sad and the sarcastic caption underneath Madonna, 'The radiant bride: Madonna shows a fashionable slump' (24/12/00).

This category includes pop group splits as in: 'Sporty Mel C last night said she had left the Spice Girls...then tried to hush up her shock confession'.

9 Anything to do with relations of famous people

This appeared in the *Daily Star*: 'The student who lied his way on to *Blind Date* with the cousin of newlywed Catherine Zeta-Jones is a scheming love cheat.' Star (21/11/00).

10 Presents they give or receive

'Lucky Mariah Carey has been given a £1 million speedboat by her lover, Luis Muguel'. *Star* (22/3/01).

Britney Spears has shown her undying love for N-Sync fiancé Justin Timberlake by splashing out £20,000 on a diamond encrusted watch. And, I can exclusively reveal, she has had it engraved with the words, 'To my Justin, love you always, Britney'. *News of the World* (24/12/00).

NEWS OF THE WORLD

A MERRY CHRISTMAS TO ALL OUR READERS

DECEMBER 24, 2000 FOR SARAH: Pages 8 & 9 Price 60p

EXCLUSIVE

SANTA CHRIS GIVES AWAY

PAGES 12 & 13

THE HAPPY GROOM: Ritchie on way to honeymoon with his beloved

Bride and Gloom

EXCLUSIVE

BY **LOUISE OSWALD** & **LEE HARPIN**

AFTER the finest wedding money can buy and a party dripping with stars, these are Madonna's best attempts at honeymoon photos.

She and hubby Guy Ritchie have obviously taken such care with pictures that will stay with them for ever.

Not for them the smiles to show the world they're in love. Oh no, Mr and Mrs Ritchie do it the celebrity way . . . tight-lipped and glum, sitting as far apart as possible in the back of a Range Rover, glowering at fans who trudged away disappointed.

A local said: "I heard baby Rocco kept them up all night." Earlier, the couple were also believed to have rowed over Guy's love of game shooting.

Today Guy, 32, is expected to try carp fishing with Sting. That should be easy enough. He and the missus already look experts at carping.

FULL STORY: Pages 4 & 5

THE RADIANT BRIDE: Madonna shows fans a fashionable slump

11 Characters from soap operas treated as if they were real people

This is how the *Sun* reported Ian Beale's wedding on 22 March 2001. There was a front page picture of the wedding party with a headline 'Ian gets wed' and the promise of more pictures inside. There is a middle page spread with more wedding photographs and the story.

'WEDDING BEALES

Whirlwind fling ends in marriage for TV Ian and Laura.

This is the moment *Eastenders*' crafty Ian Beale gets married for the third time – despite saying 'Never again'.

Bankrupt Ian – played by Adam Woodyatt, 32 – proposes to nanny Laura Dunn after she inherits a pile of money when her grandmother dies.'

How are these stories treated?

These are the key questions when you analyse how the tabloid press report celebrity stories:

- What things are emphasised and what things are omitted?
- How do the carefully chosen visual images communicate both obvious and subtle messages?
- What language is the newspaper using and how does it convey judgements, values and beliefs, either implicitly or explicitly?

Case study

CASE STUDY CASE STUDY CASE STUDY CASE STUDY CASE STUDY

This is an analysis of a story from the *Daily Star*, 9 January 2001. It is a double-page spread with several pictures, probably from the newspaper's own library, concerning Sheryl Gascoigne, ex-wife of soccer star Paul Gascoigne.

There is a shot of Sheryl and Paul on holiday on a beach. It is the kind of picture which suggests that the couple do not want to be photographed, which gives readers the impression that they are getting some kind of illicit snoop into someone's privacy. Sheryl has her hand on Paul's shoulder and it seems as if she is trying to restrain him, perhaps from attacking the photographer.

There is also a large fashion picture of Sheryl modelling a designer dress. It is a low-angle shot which makes her look powerful as well as attractive.

Smaller pictures show a confident Sheryl posing with Cindy Crawford, a sad Sheryl after she had been injured by her husband, and a caring Sheryl holding her son's hand while Paul looks wary and tense in the background. There is also a picture of her 'luxury' home.

The images are intended to reinforce the positive image of Sheryl portrayed in the story. They suggest that Sheryl was once victimised but has recovered and does not need men any longer, that she is still glamorous, well-off and successful, but at the same time a caring mother who gives time to her children.

The story was written by Debbie Pogue after what appears to have been a press conference organised by the Metropolitan Police to launch a campaign against domestic violence. Though it reports what Sheryl says, there is no indication that an interview took place, so it is probable that the writer attended the press conference and took notes.

This would seem to be in accord with the unquestioning tone of the story. It takes Sheryl Gascoigne's point of view and version of events without challenge. The ideology (the values and beliefs which are 'taken for granted') seems to be that women are caring, resilient, brave victims with great powers of recovery. They can be caring mothers, become successful professionals, be glamorous and forgive the men who torment them. Men on the other hand, personified by Paul Gascoigne, are cruel, jealous, violent, childish and irresponsible. Men are the problem, women are the solution.

Debbie Pogue emphasises physical appearance and wealth in her treatment of the story:

> 'Dazzling Cheryl',
> 'the stunning 35 year old mother of three',
> 'the pretty blonde',
> she lives in a '£300,000 Hertfordshire home',
> she had a £700,000 divorce settlement and £120,000 a year settlement for life and cars worth £85,000.

Her credentials as a celebrity are established. Now Pogue has to establish her as a celebrity worth emulating because of her female qualities.

Here is a downtrodden wife who 'suffered mental and physical abuse' which would make most women want to hide away and lose their self-esteem. But Sheryl is 'courageous' for telling the world about her suffering. She is now 'the public voice against domestic violence'. She is so strong that she even lets her ex-husband back into the house from time to time. She was such a wonderful woman that even when she was being mentally abused she still tried to keep the peace and 'make sure the children are OK and he's OK'.

Sheryl was also strong enough to resist Paul's jealousy when she insisted on modelling at a show even though 'he was completely off the wall'. But she also has tender female qualities. She can be generous: 'More than anything, I would love to see him come good and come clean. It's my mothering instincts.'

Here is a slightly abridged version of the article on pages 22 and 23 *Daily Star* 9/1/01

'For eight years she suffered mental and physical abuse at the hands of Paul Gascoigne.

How Sheryl Gascoigne picked up the pieces after a nightmare marriage

BRUISED, BUT NOT BEATEN

STILL PALS: Sheryl and Gazza go on holiday with their son

BACK TO WORK: With fellow model Cindy Crawford

GOOD DEAL: Sheryl got to keep their luxury home

BATTERED: Sheryl after the Gleneagles attack

CARING: She says Gazza is a great father to Regan

DAZZLING: Sheryl loves working as a model and TV star, but likes spending time with her kids even more

FOR eight years, she suffered mental and physical abuse at the hands of Paul Gascoigne.

By DEBBIE POGUE

That's enough to destroy every shred of self-esteem and would make most women want to hide from the world. But not Sheryl Gascoigne.

Since taking the courageous decision to tell the world how she suffered before and during her marriage to the former England footie ace, life has never looked better for the stunning 35-year-old mother-of-three.

As well as her public voice against domestic violence, she is now a successful model and TV presenter.

"Life is so much better," she admits. "Things are brilliant. I'm free."

That freedom has seen her model for celebrated designer Isabel Kristensen, become the face of Joy jewellery and front a number of successful telly shows.

Despite the years of pain, she even spends time with Everton player Gazza and welcomes him into the £300,000 Hertfordshire home they used to share.

Freedom

And she is the first to applaud him for being a good dad to their five-year-old son Regan and her two children from her first marriage, Bianca, 14 and 10-year-old Mason.

"Paul supports us," she says. "I can never ever knock him for that. Since the divorce, that gives me and the children the freedom to enjoy our lives more."

The generous settlement Gazza made in February last year gave Sheryl £700,000 plus £120,000 a year for life to help her look after Regan. She also kept cars worth a reported £85,000.

But while she has been rebuilding her professional life, there has been no one to replace Gazza.

"I miss romance, I miss physical contact, I miss sex," she said recently. "I'd like to meet somebody. I don't want to be on my own."

But the pretty blonde admitted she was not ready to re-marry. "I'm not ready to have a full-time relationship, but I'm quite happy to go out."

Yesterday, launching a Metropolitan Police campaign against domestic violence in London, she admitted that although they were now friends, she was still a little frightened of her ex-husband.

"I probably still am, if the truth be known," she confessed. "You can't be with someone for that long and have them do that.

"I don't think it will change, but I hope for his sake he does and he can maintain a relationship."

Recalling her moments of terror at the hands of the soccer star, she said: "I never told anyone how bad it was. There are things I still don't tell.

Peace

"I feel much better than I have been but I can't imagine the mental abuse ever going away. It's such a gradual process – that's what abusers do.

"I was very much in love with him. You remember incidents, but you are so busy trying to keep the peace and trying to live and make sure the children are OK and he's OK. You're too busy surviving to think what's really going on. You always think you're the one that can change them. You think it's your fault."

It was the famous photo of Sheryl with a battered face and dislocated fingers following a bust-up at the Gleneagles Hotel in Scotland which gave her the courage to get out of the destructive relationship.

"I just thought, 'If I've got any ounce of respect for myself left in me, I have to walk away'. I left and drove home with my arm in a sling.

"There was no contact at all. And by the time he was saying he was going to get help, that was it."

Even after she'd left him, Gazza tried to interfere with her life.

Designer Kristenssen, who created Sheryl's fairytale wedding dress in 1996, asked her to model at a show – and Gazza went berserk.

"He was off the wall completely," said Sheryl. "I was the biggest trollop in the world to him because I modelled. I'd always been offered lots of work. It's by association – I'm not stupid, I know that. And he wouldn't let me forget that anyway.

"It was difficult, but I did it. It was a first step."

Sheryl sees her appearance on Trevor McDonald's Tonight as the biggest turning point in her life.

Scared

"It's easier because people know why I always looked so miserable," she said afterwards. "I was scared to look up, let alone talk to someone. I never stood up for myself before. I was always part of an image put out to make Paul look better.

"But I hope now I've been able to be myself and people will see I'm not as horrible as they thought."

Yet she insists she has no regrets about her marriage to Gazza. The couple are frequently seen shopping or holidaying together with their son.

"I love him deeply, I care deeply," she said yesterday. "More than anything, I would love to see him come good and come clean. It's my mothering instincts.

"The person I met and fell for was charming and very funny. He made me feel it was me and him against the world. It was exciting, and there was chemistry there. His personality was unique. But that changed.

"Yet, you know, I think I've got everything. I'm happy with my children, I'm happy with my life.

"I hate people who wallow in self-pity. Why regret something? You can't change it.

"I'm on a high at the moment and life looks good for me. After all these years, I'm feeling very happy and very positive."

That's enough to destroy every shred of self-esteem and would make most women want to hide from the world. But not Sheryl Gascoigne.

Since taking the courageous decision to tell the world how she suffered before and during her marriage to the former England footie ace, life has never looked better for the stunning 35-year-old mother of three.

As well as her public voice against domestic violence, she is now a successful model and TV presenter.

...Despite the years of pain, she even spends time with Everton player Gazza and welcomes him into the £300,000 Hertfordshire home they used to share.

And she is the first to applaud him for being a good dad to their five-year-old son Regan and her two children from her first marriage, Bianca, 14, and 10-year-old Mason.

....The generous settlement Gazza made in February last year gave Sheryl £700,000 plus £120,000 a year for life to help her look after Regan. She also kept cars worth a reported £85,000.

....Yesterday, launching a Metropolitan Police campaign against domestic violence...she admitted that although they were now friends, she was still a little frightened of her ex-husband.

....Recalling her moments of terror at the hands of the soccer star, she said: 'I never told anyone how bad it was. There are things I still don't tell. ...I was very much in love with him. You remember incidents, but you are so busy trying to keep the peace and trying to live and make sure the children are OK and he's OK. You're too busy surviving to think what's really going on.'

....It was the famous photo of Sheryl with a battered face and dislocated fingers following a bust-up in the Gleneagles hotel in Scotland which gave her the courage to get out of the destructive relationship.

'I just thought, if I've got any ounce of respect for myself left in me I have to walk away. I left and drove home with my arm in a sling.'

....Even after she left him Gazza tried to interfere in her life.

Designer Kristenssen asked her to model at a show and Gazza went berserk.

'He was off the wall completely,' said Sheryl. 'I was the biggest trollop in the world to him because I modelled.'

....Yet she insists that she has no regrets about her marriage to Gazza.

....'I love him deeply. I care deeply.... More than anything, I would love to see him come good and come clean. It's my mothering instincts.'

The Royal Family as celebrities

Britain's Royal Family are treated as celebrities by the tabloid press in the UK. The public are as familiar with the latest developments in the family as they are with those in soap operas such as *Coronation Street* or *Eastenders*. They are informed about romances, weddings, births and deaths, conflicts and rivalries.

Just as the soap opera with its access to millions of homes in Britain developed a form of story telling which could go on indefinitely, so parts of the media treat the Royal Family as a ***family melodrama***, a long-running story of an extremely wealthy and privileged group of people. The topics of the narratives of soaps and the Royals are similar: the unity of the family, wealth/poverty, sexual partnerships, family responsibilities, deceit and loyalty, alliances with outsiders/rivals/people from different social groups.

Almost all our knowledge of the Royal Family is based on media stories, not direct knowledge, and is consequently partly fictional. There is, of course, a real-life family, but we are only allowed to know them through the mediation of the storytellers – that is, reporters, producers, editors, press officers and so on. They determine what is significant and what is not.

Prince Charles falls off his horse while out hunting and breaks his shoulder. The *Sun* devotes 40 paragraphs to the incident under the headline 'ONE IS A PLONKER – Charles in sling again after he falls off his horse'. It fleshes out a double-page spread with pictures of the Queen driving a car without wearing a seat belt and riding a horse without wearing a hard hat under the headline 'QUEEN'S SAFETY RAP'. The *Sun* staff judges that these are details that its readers want to know about and its market research will reveal whether this is the case.

The tone of the *Sun's* reporting is gently censorious. Some reporting of royal stories can be reverential and deferential but the *Sun* adopts a tone which treats royalty as if it were familiar with them. It is as if they were like partridges – dumb creatures to be kept in good health so that they can be shot down for sport.

Such a disrespectful attitude is not exclusive to the *Sun*. Here's Linda Lee-Potter of the *Daily Mail*: 'Princess Margaret is vivid proof that we end up with the appearance we deserve. Her anger and self-absorption are unmistakable. She looks what she is which is a bitter, unhappy, selfish old woman.' (Quoted in the *Editor* 5/1/01.)

This perennial interest in the royals is because, even though they have elevated status, their conflicts and problems are those which all families share. These are evident as ***oppositions***: rebel/conformist, promiscuous/faithful, good mother/ bad mother, good son or daughter/bad son or daughter, nobility/commoner, rightful heir/rival claim.

The royals have to become ***characters in the media's narrative structure***. When Lady Diana came along she became the beautiful princess and Princess Anne became not the 'good sport' but the ugly sister, arrogant, bitchy, ungainly. Whereas the Queen was the good mother, dutiful and tactful, her sister Margaret was portrayed as the decadent and undeserving side of wealth. Andrew, 'Randy Andy', became the Casanova character, Edward the effeminate, unfortunate runt of the family.

ONE IS A PLONKER

Charles in sling again after he falls off horse

By CHARLES RAE, JOHN SCOTT and CLODAGH HARTLEY

PRINCE Charles was nursing a broken shoulder yesterday after being thrown from a horse — as a pal revealed: "He is feeling a bit of a plonker."

Embarrassed Charles, 52 – who crashed to the ground while fox-hunting – went to church near his home in Highgrove, Gloucs, sporting a sling on his left arm.

The injury comes just three years after he broke a rib falling from a horse and ten years after the famous polo tumble which left him crocked with a broken arm for ten months.

Witnesses winced as Charles – riding with the Meynell Hunt in Derbyshire – was sent sprawling.

But he did not even realise he had bust another bone for 3½ hours as he climbed back in the saddle and rejoined the pursuit.

One onlooker said: "The Prince was bowling along like a good 'un when his horse made a mistake at a comparatively small fence.

"You always think 'ouch' when you see somebody fall while out hunting and this was no exception.

Joking

"But he just dusted himself down and carried on.

"The first we all knew that he had broken his shoulder was when we heard it on the radio and TV."

A barmaid told how Charles even called in for a 45-minute drink with fellow riders after Saturday's hunt.

The woman, who works at the Cock Inn in Muggington, said: "He was thoroughly relaxed and very friendly – chatting and joking.

"There was no mention of him having fallen from his horse or that he was carrying any kind of injury."

After Charles left he was taken to the Queen's Medical Centre in Nottingham by his detective.

The Prince feared he had dislocated his shoulder – but X-rays revealed a broken acromion bone.

His shoulder was strapped up and he was told it would take six weeks to heal on its own.

Hunt master Johnny Greenall said: "I had no idea the Prince had broken his shoulder.

"It must have been a very painful injury but he did not show it. He is a very tough man."

After leaving hospital, Charles returned to Highgrove where he had dinner with eldest son William, 18 – who himself had been out riding with the Beaufort Hunt in Gloucestershire.

A spokesman for Charles said: "The injury is uncomfortable but not too serious.

"It is all part and parcel of riding that there will be a few tumbles.

"There is no question of the Prince giving up riding and he will not have to cancel any engagements – private or public – because of his shoulder.

"The Prince himself decided on a check-up because he thought he had just dislocated his shoulder."

Orthopaedic expert Dr Carol Cooper said: "Charles's broken bone is part of the shoulder blade and symptoms are very like a dislocated shoulder.

"But suddenly it's painful and you cannot use your shoulder. There will be a little bit of swelling and pain.

"It's not as serious as other breaks. He will be in a sling for about six weeks but should not need any surgery."

Charles has ridden regularly with the Meynell for the past decade – joining the hunt at least once a month during the current season.

The Prince was out in the lead with three other riders when he came to grief at a 3½ft wooden fence.

Sling back . . . Charles in 1990

Potatoes

The horse landed on its feet but Charles was pitched from the saddle on farmland near the Derbyshire village of Mercaston.

Those who saw him fall said soft ground after the recent bad weather saved him from more serious injury.

An eyewitness said: "It was not simply a case of the Prince just falling off like a sack of potatoes – it was the result of a bad stumble by the horse.

"The kennel huntsman – who was behind Charles when he came down – caught his horse which had run on about 20 yards.

"By the time the mount had been returned to the Prince he was already on his feet.

"Charles confessed he thought he had hurt his shoulder but insisted the injury was not serious enough to stop him hunting.

"He then carried on for 3½ hours and must have jumped at least a dozen obstacles far larger and more difficult.

"The Prince is obviously a tough nut who loves the thrill of hunting. He is also still a very good rider."

"The old adage that it is always best to get straight back on as soon as you fall off still holds good today."

Limo-seen . . . Queen and Queen Mother arrive at church in Sandringham, Norfolk, in a chauffeur-driven motor yesterday

Margaret 'getting stronger'

Princess . . . suspected stroke

By CHARLES RAE
Royal Correspondent

PRINCESS Margaret is slowly recovering from her suspected minor stroke, the Queen told well-wishers yesterday.

Her Majesty gave out the royal bulletin on her ailing sister after she attended church at Sandringham in Norfolk.

Pensioner Mary Relph asked the Queen about 70-year-old Margaret as she emerged from St Mary Magdelene Church with the Duke of Edinburgh and Queen Mum.

Better

Mary, of Shouldham, Norfolk, said: "I asked how the Princess was and the Queen told me she was getting better."

Rector of Sandringham, the Rev George Hall, said prayers for the Royal Family in church as usual. But no specific prayers were offered for the Princess.

Margaret has been ill in bed on the royal estate since before Christmas.

A Buckingham Palace spokesman said: "Tests conducted against the background of her previous stroke in February 1998, suggest she may recently have had a further minor stroke."

Margaret, who has had part of a lung removed, suffered her first stroke while on the Caribbean holiday isle of Mustique.

QUEEN'S SAFETY RAP

By JOHN TROUP

SAFETY campaigners rapped the Queen yesterday after she drove without a seatbelt — and then went horse-riding without a hard hat.

Her Majesty took her Land Rover 300 yards on a public road near Sandringham.

Later, during the hour-long ride on her Norfolk estate, the Queen was protected only by a scarf and the hood of her blue waxed jacket.

Jane Eason, of the Royal Society for the Prevention of Accidents of which the Queen is patron, said: "We hope she sets a better example."

Meanwhile, a trailer ploughed into three cars outside Sandringham Church yesterday moments before the Queen and Queen Mum arrived.

Belt up . . . Queen flouted law on public road

Hat's stupid . . . she has only a scarf and hood

From the *Sun* 8/1/01

The *roles are continually changing*. Charles, before his marriage to Lady Diana, was portrayed as a royal romancer. He then had to be the faithful and devoted husband to the child bride. As the marriage weakened, he then became the long-suffering husband and shy Di, in the words of the ***Sunday Times***, 23 January 1983, became 'the diet obsessed anorexic Di, then hen-pecking, scolding Di, and now the little madam or fiend or spoilt brat according to whom you read'. When she died she was a heroic martyr and the 'people's princess', ordinary but special.

One of the problems of this fictionalising of the royals and the narrative emphasis on the family melodrama is that it ignores political and economic questions about privilege. The way in which the story is told means that we never have to deal with the Royal Family as a political institution; we only have to think about human behaviour, human emotions, and choices restricted to the family.

Activity

What aspects of the Royal Family's lives are currently interesting the media? Find examples of the attitudes described above and, after studying them, write an essay on representations of the Royal Family.

This should focus on (i) the roles of the people concerned as determined by the media, (ii) the thematic oppositions (e.g. aristocrats/commoners), (iii) the tone and style of the reporting, (iv) differences among tabloid papers and (v) differences between tabloid papers and broadsheets.

Activity

Read the following article and answer the questions on it.

Caution: big name ahead

By Lynn Barber

Sunday January 27 2002

The *Observer*

Lucky old Talk magazine in the States has someone called a 'celebrity wrangler' whose job is to lasso the celebs for interview. I love the image of this sweating cowboy coming into editor Tina Brown's office with a tightly roped, wriggling bundle over his shoulders: 'Got that Kate Winslet for you, boss – where do you want her?' 'Oh put her on the front cover – brush her up a bit first.' Alas, we don't have celebrity wranglers in Britain, more fool us – we still haven't recognised the pursuit and capture of celebs as the highly skilled, full-time job it is. All we do is grumble: it's so difficult catching celebs and, even when we bag one, they make such impossible demands.

The commonest demand is for copy approval – which means they want to see the article before publication and delete anything they don't like. In other words, power of censorship. Then there is picture approval – same idea, where the celebs get to choose which photos can be published and which can't. Robert Redford's press office used to put out 'instructions to picture editors' about where his photographs should be retouched – 'the wrinkled area between his lower lip and chin', 'the veins on his nose', 'the area around the throat and neck'.

Then there is 'writer approval' – the chosen weapon of top Hollywood PR Pat Kingsley. She simply bans any writers who ever write anything nasty about one of her clients from ever interviewing any of her clients again. I got the black spot from

Kingsley years ago when I interviewed Nick Nolte for *Vanity Fair*. He didn't like the tone of my questions and Kingsley pulled the plug, before I'd even written a word. Of course, *Vanity Fair* could have defied her and published my interview anyway – but then where would it have got its future cover stars? (Kingsley's power increased further still last year when her company PMK merged with Huvane Baum Halls, previously a rival outfit in entertainment publicity. The resulting merger now means that one firm controls access to many of the A-list in Hollywood and Britain, including Tom Cruise, Tom Hanks, Gwyneth Paltrow and Jude Law.)

Undoubtedly the celeb wars have got worse in the 20 years I've been a participant, and the reason is not far to seek. Nowadays, there are far more media outlets chasing essentially the same number of stars. You only have to look at the newsstands – the number of magazines with a celeb on the cover seems to increase month by month, never mind year by year. Journalists today are buyers in a sellers' market and a market which gets tougher all the time.

Back in the mists of time when I started, PRs were a pretty dozy bunch on the whole – either clapped-out old hacks who were too sozzled even for Fleet Street, or dimbo girlfriends who thought they liked meeting creative people. They were often very hazy about lead times (the gap between going to press and publication) and barely seemed to know the difference between a daily newspaper and a monthly magazine. That's all changed. Today's PRs are focused, professional, dedicated – frankly terrifying.

They are hired, not by the individual celebs, but by whoever is putting out their product – publishers in the case of books, film studios in the case of actors, record companies in the case of CDs. Their job is to get maximum publicity just before the product launch, so that every single member of the public will know that product X is coming out on, say, 10 February. Occasionally they actually seem to achieve their goal of saturation coverage – look at *Pearl Harbor* last year. The publicity blitz was everything the producers can have dreamed of – it was only the reviews that let them down. Thank God for reviews.

Celebrities now learn from the cradle that there is no point in doing 'wasted publicity', by which they mean interviews that are not attached to selling a product. In the old days, celebs might give an interview just for the hell of it, but not now – they've been taught it looks vain, pathetic, to talk to the press when they have nothing particular to sell. Moreover, PRs insist they talk only about this product, the one they are supposed to be promoting at the moment. This sometimes leads to odd situations in interviews. It's quite common to find yourself interviewing a film actor who has only the dimmest memory of the film he is supposed to be talking about. Films quite often get stuck in the pipeline for two years or more – and meanwhile the actor has made a much better film which he is dying to talk about, but the film company PR sitting in on the interview gives him dirty looks if he ever so much as mentions it.

The whole business is incredibly complicated – the pre-interview negotiations often take much longer than the interview itself. All newspapers and magazines subscribe to 'arts diaries' which list all the films, plays, books, records coming out in the next few months, and give the contact numbers of the PRs handling them. So you go down the list with your editor, choosing the people you think would be worth interviewing, and put in requests with the relevant PRs. The PRs never give immediate answers but say they'll add your name to the list – I suspect so they can augment the list by ringing round your rivals saying, 'The *Observer* wants to interview X, are you keen?'

Eventually they get back to you and say, 'Yes, you might be able to interview X – it depends.' This is where the real negotiating begins. The PR wants to know whether we can guarantee it will be the cover story. 'Maybe if it's an exceptionally good interview – how long have we got?' 'An hour.' 'An hour for the interview and another hour for photographs?' 'No, an hour altogether.' 'No way, forget it.' 'All right, I'll get back to you.' The PR comes back a day or two later saying, 'Well, we can give you two hours, provided it's the cover story.' This is a very tight call. No editor wants to guarantee a cover, in case the interview is a dud, or in case something better comes up. On the other hand, X is a big star and the film sounds as though it might even be good. So on this occasion we say, 'Yes, go for it.' 'Fine,' says the PR, naming the date, the time, the place for the interview and arranging for you to see a private screening of the film beforehand.

At the last minute – always at the last minute – the PR casually adds, 'And, of course, he won't answer any personal questions.' 'What?! What are we going to talk about then?' 'The work' is the inevitable, deadly answer, which actually just means the plug. So then you have to make the decision – is it worth going ahead? Of course you always do, in the hope that you can swing the interview from the work to the life – and sometimes you can and sometimes you can't. The trouble is, you never actually know till you arrive what people mean by 'no personal questions'. Usually they just mean no questions about their rocky marriage, or a recent affair, but sometimes they actually mean no personal questions. I remember Keith Floyd refused to tell me where he bought his shoes because that was 'personal'. And Harriet Harman refused to tell me when she first got interested in politics because 'I am chronically not interested in navel gazing'.

I remember aeons ago I had to interview an actor called Timothy Dalton who was temporarily hot because he was playing James Bond (where is he now?) and the PR was amazed afterwards that he'd told me he liked fishing. 'He told you that? He told you he liked fishing? Wow!' Then there are actors like Rupert Everett who used to have an exciting personal life but suddenly banish it when they make a hit in Hollywood. But conversely I've had plenty of people say 'No personal questions' and then chatter away perfectly happily about their childhood, or their rehab, or their PMT or whatever. In my experience, the only really taboo subject is money.

Sometimes PRs unwittingly give you a clue as to the story – 'Whatever you do, don't ask about her sister.' 'Of course,' you say gravely, while mentally shrieking, 'Her sister? What about her sister?' You go haring back to the cuttings to find whether her sister is an axe murderess – what it usually means is that the sister has made some disobliging comments about the star. But sometimes it's odder than that. Tina Brown recently claimed that a PR rang her at *Talk* magazine demanding a letter 'with assurances that nowhere in our story about a particular star will we include the detail that the celebrity "bleaches her asshole"'. Of course, being Tina Brown, she didn't reveal who the star was – so now I can't look at a picture of a celeb without wondering, 'Does she bleach her asshole?'

But after all the pre-interview negotiation, what it actually boils down to is two people in a room together, often for no more than an hour. There is no time for breaking the ice, getting to know one another slowly, decently, like normal human beings. The clock in my head is ticking so loudly I'm surprised the interviewee can't hear it. That is why I'm always rather gobsmacked when people like my mother say, 'Oh it must be so nice meeting all those famous people.' Well, of course, it is, sort of – but it's a bit like saying to the school tennis captain, 'It must be so nice playing against Pete Sampras'.

The absolute pits, for everyone concerned, are the hotel circuses where a Hollywood star is flown into London for a couple of days to do 'European publicity'. They are dumped in a suite at the Dorchester (if they are grand) or the Halcyon or the Covent Garden Hotel and expected to talk non-stop from dawn to dusk to a succession of journalists who are wheeled past them at bewildering speed. Consequently, the stars are often semi-deranged by the time you meet them; they answer questions you haven't asked; they tell the ends of anecdotes but not the beginnings; they repeat themselves endlessly. Once or twice, with Audrey Hepburn years ago and with Lynn Redgrave more recently, I've felt I was watching someone spiralling into madness. And outside, in the anteroom with the cooling coffee pots and the scummy orange juice, the journalists circle like hungry jackals, feeding each other disinformation – 'You know she's really a lesbian' – and making up fictitious websites – 'Didn't you see all the stuff on puff.com?' – to put their rivals off their stroke. Journalists are good mates most of the time, but not in the minutes before an interview. I remember Andrew Billen of *The Evening Standard*, a former colleague and normally a good friend, coming downstairs after interviewing Barbara Windsor, seeing me waiting in the lobby and sitting down for a gossip. Only after about 20 minutes did he say, 'Oh by the way, she said to tell you to go straight up'. Bastard!

Everyone hates hotel circuses, so why do we do them? Because our editors tell us to – because, I'm afraid, the name of a big star on the cover helps sell magazines and newspapers, even the *Observer*. So until readers rebel, PRs have it all their own way. Moreover, I don't see any hope of this situation improving – on the contrary, I fully expect it to get worse. The PRs will push for whatever they can get away with and it's going to be harder and harder for newspapers to hold the line against giving copy approval and/or paying for interviews.

But I do see hope from a different quarter – the readers. In the last decade, readers seem to have had a crash course in understanding news management and the way PRs work. I think it started with the Royal Family, specifically the Wales's divorce. The dazzling revelation that even the palace could tell porkies left the broadsheets looking silly, the tabloids triumphant. The broadsheets were then bitter enough to expose how they'd been lied to. The same thing happened with Labour spin – journalists who'd fallen victim to it retaliated by reporting the back-room machinations. Of course, politicians complained that this made the public cynical, but maybe they were right to be cynical? I prefer the term 'informed'. So with the whole celeb circus: I don't think journalists should collude with PRs in keeping it secret; I think, on the contrary, the more they can expose it, the better they are serving their readers.

1 Explain how celebrities can censor interviews.

2 How do PR people try to control what is written about celebrities by 'writer control'?

3 What according to Lynn Barber is the main job of PR professionals?

4 Explain why pre-interview 'negotiations' are important.

5 Why are 'hotel circuses' the 'absolute pits'?

6 What hopes does Barber express about 'the readers'?

Issues of privacy

The celebrities

While celebrities court publicity, they do not always welcome attention. They may resent intrusion into their privacy. They may not like photographers taking pictures of them and their friends and family when they are off guard. Thus BBC's newsreader Anna Ford objected to the publication of pictures of her on a beach in Majorca with her new companion, former astronaut David Scott, and her children, in what she thought was a relaxing family getaway and a stress-free half-term break.

Anna Ford wrote a newspaper article criticising the Press Complaints Commission for failing to uphold her complaint against the ***Daily Mail*** and ***OK*** magazine for printing the pictures. She said: 'I intensely dislike the way in which tabloids now seem to be able to get away with the most unsettling intrusions into private lives. Everyone is entitled to respect for his or her private life. We all need to enjoy peace, quiet and solitude.'

Michael Douglas and Catherine Zeta-Jones sued ***Hello!*** magazine for damages after a photographer took unauthorised pictures of their wedding in New York. And, in a separate action, model Naomi Campbell sued the ***Daily Mirror*** for printing photographs of her attending a Narcotics Anonymous therapy group in London.

These three cases all relied on the European Human Rights Act, which came into force in 2000 and offered celebrities a powerful legal weapon against the press.

The media

Editors, however, believe that limits on their powers have a harmful side. Privacy laws, they argue, would have stopped the important investigation into the harmful effects of the drug Thalidomide, investigations into the activities of foreign spies, the publication of the toe-sucking pictures of the Duchess of York, which led to revelations about her extravagant lifestyle, and revelations about Peter Mandelson's secret home loan.

There are two conflicting rights in this debate. Article 8 of the Human Rights Act says that everyone has the right to respect for their private and family life, their home and their correspondence, while Article 10 says that everyone has the right to freedom of expression, freedom to hold opinions and to receive and impart information and ideas without interference from public authorities.

The question involves whether celebrities can have things all their own way, media attention only on their terms, or whether the public's desire for information about the rich and famous should be catered for. As the head of a celebrity agency put it: 'These days it does not matter if you read the news like Anna Ford or pose in sequinned nipple tassels like the Spice Girls, people will want to see pictures of you and read about you. We remind all our clients that there are plenty of jobs going in the Post Office and they can have an anonymous life if they want it, but if they play the public game the switch is set to ON all the time. Sure you can ask for privacy and decency. Will you get it? No. If you dance with the devil, you get pricked by the horns.'

(Adapted from Privacy and the Media by John Arlidge, *Observer* 4/3/01, with permission.)

Activity

In small groups discuss what you would do if you were adjudicating on the following privacy case.

Two women have sold their stories to a Sunday paper about their relationships with a famous professional footballer. They argue that their stories are important because he used the influence of his fame and wealth to seduce them. They had no idea that he was married and had two children. They want to warn other women about him.

The Sunday paper's editor says that the stories are 'in the public interest'. She also believes that any interference with the media's right to report must be carefully justified. Otherwise the media will not be able to do their job. She also said that footballers are role models for young people and undesirable behaviour on their part can set an unfortunate example.

The footballer argues that these salacious stories cannot possibly be in the public interest. The women concerned are just after the money. The Sunday paper in question is notorious for printing stuff about sex. He is entitled to a private life. The Human Rights Act says that everyone has the right to respect for their private and family life, their home and their correspondence.

You may want to refer to some of these guidelines to journalists from the Press Complaints Commission:

- Don't write material that is inaccurate or misleading.
- Make sure you distinguish between comment and fact.
- Don't intrude into people's private lives.
- Don't pretend you are not a journalist in order to obtain information, unless it is in the public interest and the material can't be obtained in any other way.
- Don't write anything pejorative about a person's race, colour, religion or sex.

SECTION B **Chapter 12**

Consumerism in lifestyle magazines

INTRODUCTION

This chapter shows you how to investigate the representation of a topic (in this case 'consumerism') in a particular media form (in this case magazines). It describes a method for analysing texts and applies it to three lifestyle magazines. The activities lead you into applying the method to current magazines of your own choosing.

> 'Consumerism: Preoccupation with consumer goods and their acquisition.'
>
> *Oxford English Dictionary*

The term 'lifestyle magazines' according to the OCR examination guidelines refers to a 'flexible category, which could encompass anything from Loaded to gardening magazines'. The guidelines suggest you should look at a range of titles, especially those with which you are unfamiliar such as ***Country Life***, ***The Oldie***, ***Motor Caravan Monthly*** and ***Women's Realm***. This will help you, they say, to 'defamiliarise the concept and focus on what consumerism, lifestyle and value mean across the whole culture'.

The guidelines also suggest that you should develop a set of criteria to examine these unfamiliar texts and then apply them to more familiar material. This chapter makes some suggestions for developing these criteria.

To break the topic up into more manageable segments you could take some consumerist themes or topics and examine how they are treated in different magazines. Here we look at the topics of ***homes*** and ***fashion***. The kinds of investigation suggested and illustrated can be applied to other consumerist topics such as food, holidays and possessions, depending on the magazines being studied.

First decide what to look for and where to find it.

What to look for:

- evidence of people buying things for show rather than need
- people showing off their possessions (conspicuous consumption)
- links between editorial content (i.e. articles) and advertising
- clues about the magazine's target audience
- ideal selves, partners, homes, families, lifestyles
- people's values and beliefs associated with having/buying possessions.

Where to find these:

- magazine covers
- editorials
- visual images and captions
- positioning of advertisements
- advertising content
- magazine articles
- letters pages
- magazine media packs and websites.

Representation of homes in lifestyle magazines

Many magazines specialise in images and articles about people's homes. In 2002 there were:

- *BBC Homes and Antiques*
- *Brides and Setting up Home*
- *Country Homes and Interiors*
- *County*
- *Good Housekeeping*
- *Homes and Gardens*
- *Homes and Ideas*
- *House and Garden*
- *House Beautiful*
- *Ideal Home*
- *Livingetc*
- *Period Living and Traditional Homes*
- *that's life!*
- *Sainsbury's The Magazine*
- *Vogue*
- *Woman and Home*.

The magazine market is constantly changing and new titles appear as old ones die, so you need to consult publications such as the annual *Writer's Handbook* (Macmillan) for an up-to-date list.

You can start your investigation into how homes are represented by looking in detail at individual magazines. Those analysed here are magazines as in this example.

1 First look at the magazine cover and describe in detail the kind of interior or exterior which is featured as in this example:

The cover of *Livingetc* in April 2003 shows a room in an old house. It is light and airy with stained, bare floorboards. The decoration is simple and neutral. The walls and ceiling are painted white. There are blinds rather than curtains at the large windows which let in lots of light. The furniture is minimalist with a low bench/seat which has storage space underneath, a bean bag and net chair. What ornaments there are are simple and neutral - a vase with dried flowers, a fruit bowl and a couple of small pictures. There are no warm colours. The room looks as though it has had a modern conversion with new stairs leading to other levels in the house. The figure climbing the stairs looks like a female wearing smart blue jeans. She is barefoot.

This is a an example of denotation - an attempt to describe objectively what the picture shows.

What about the connotation of the image?

The picture suggests a town house occupied by young middle class people, perhaps professionals, who admire traditional buildings but want to put a modern gloss on them. This is an old house stripped to its basics which represent quality and good workmanship ('they don't build them like this anymore') but then decorated and furnished to suggest understated 'class'.

It is worth thinking about what is absent from the image. There is no evidence of children, no clutter, no disorder, no colour or frivolity. It suggests that the people who live here are design conscious, concerned about appearance and meticulous about presentation. The fact that the woman is not wearing shoes suggests that she is relaxed and cool with maybe an interest in keeping fit.

2 Can you learn anything from the cover picture of the magazine about its target audience?

The image of the room is meant to appeal to the target readership. It is saying you too could have a room like this if you listen to our advice and read our ideas. It would seem to be appealing to town dwellers with a reasonable income who are not bringing up a family, have an interest in modern design and enough money to pay for expensive conversions of old houses.

3 Is there any textual evidence on the cover about the target audience?

The magazine's slogan is 'The homes magazine for modern living' so it aims at being fresh and up-to-the-minute. Each issue is themed. Its cover lines, telling you what's inside, give more clues :

(The words in bold were printed red on the magazine cover.)
Interior seduction
FLIRTY HOMES WITH FASHIONS
WITH VA-VA-VOOM!

COME PLAY WITH THE BIG BOYS
DESIGNERS GET DECORATIVE WITH SCALE

DES RES
MAKING THE MOST OF YOUR HOME'S NATURAL ASSETS

SEXY SPAS
HAPPY HOMES
URBAN TRENDS

GLAM DECORATING
COOL FINDS
WICKED STYLE

There is a strong connection here between homes and sex. The phrase WITH VA-VA-VOOM! was used as a catchphrase in a car advert featuring footballer Thiery Henry. He was filmed in a modern, trendy, minimalist house speculating on the sexual appeal of various people. VA-VA-VOOM! was a synonym for 'sexy'.

The other sexual references are: 'seduction', 'flirty', playing 'with the big boys', 'sexy spas', 'glam', 'wicked' and 'natural assets'. These seem to be references which are aimed at a young, sexually active, female audience. Again try to think about what is not emphasised. There is nothing about motherhood, marriage, home comforts, or family togetherness, all images which might be used on other women's magazines aimed at a different sort of reader.

Launch date:	1998
Circulation:	92,695
Adult readership:	299,000
Female readership:	246,000
Core readership:	ABC1 Adults aged 25-35 years, Young affluent working couples
Female/male Split:	82:18
Frequency:	Monthly
Cover price:	£3.00

Livingetc's 'brand profile'

4 Other ways you can find out about a target audience are to obtain a copy of the magazine's media pack or visit the publisher's web site. You will find the kind of information which advertisers need about the age, spending habits, social class and lifestyles of the readers.

This is the publisher's description of ***Livingetc***

Livingetc is the ultimate glossy homes magazine for relaxed modern living. Our readers have got great taste and a love of the good things in life - they're social, stylish, confident and sexy and so are their homes. ***Livingetc*** is their style reference for the 21st century - each month we thrill readers with our fast track to the must-have products, inspire them with drop dead gorgeous houses and motivate them to revamp their homes. After all, ***Livingetc*** is the magazine that made decorating sexy.

Livingetc readers are affluent, independent, young urban professionals who own property and have a high disposable income. Confident and optimistic, they are well travelled, cosmopolitan and know how to enjoy life. Bright, creative and independent, they are style driven and individual, love shopping and see their home as a reflection of their attitude and flair.

5 Articles in the ***media pages*** of the broadsheet newspapers can give you insights into editors' perceptions of their audience.

This information about *Red* magazine was obtained from the Media Guardian (Stuck in the middle by Jessica Hodgson, 14/1/02).

Red magazine. First published 1997. Competes for 'Middle Youth' market with magazines such as ***Eve***, ***Real***, ***Aura*** and ***Glamour***. Middle Youth means 25–45, an age defined by ***Bridget Jones***, ***Cold Feet*** and ***Sex in the City***. Sometimes described as the thirty-somethings market.

'Middle Youth' is 'listening to Destiny's Child while you're doing the ironing. It's cooking a gorgeous organic meal and then putting a ***Grease*** album on really loud and dancing around before your two-year-old goes to bed. 'Middle Youth' is a kind of attitude. It's women who have grown up without growing old.' (Dawn Bebe, managing director of Emap Elan's women's titles.)

Cover of Red magazine October 2003

6 The magazine's editorial also tells you what audience the magazine is

addressing and sometimes about the philosophy of the publication. This is from ***Livingetc***:

'Notice anything different about us this month? As well as the dazzlingly stylish decorating ideas, drool-worthy homes and gotta-have-'em new finds, our talented design team has been busy giving the pages of ***Livingetc*** a fresh, beautiful and thoroughly modern new look. We wanted to bring you a magazine that reflects all that ***Livingetc*** stands for: relaxed, modern style ideas, inspiration for your home you won't find anywhere else - guaranteed - and a big dose of glamour. From the gorgeous decorating ideas in Interior Seduction (p132) to the ethereal beauty of our Bloomsbury-inspired story (p58), and the damn-useful design advice on making the most of your home's best assets (p83), we have a jam-packed issue.

And what better time to launch our new look than on our 5th birthday. Yes, we're five years old and boy, we've covered a lot in that period, as our romp through the magazine's history proves (p28). That only leaves one more thing for us to do - get celebrating. Enjoy!

PS We hope you like our 50 Modern Kitchens magazine, free with this issue of *Livingetc*'

There is a cheerful informality in the mode of address. The editor wants to be your friend. She seems to be talking to you and receiving your responses.

She uses conversational phrases such as 'damn-useful', 'jam-packed' and the rather trendy 'Enjoy!' to let you know she is relaxed and friendly, a woman whose publication is lively and up-to-date.

She uses one of the commonest lifestyle words – 'style' or 'stylish. Style it seems is something people like to have, though it is very hard to define.

The emphasis is on homes being 'fresh' and 'modern' but there is also a feeling that homes should be showpieces, with vocabulary such as 'gorgeous', 'drool-worthy', 'ethereal beauty' and 'gotta have em'.

There are underlying assumptions about the spending power of the readers, with the emphasis on things being desirable rather than affordable. There is also an assumption that readers will know what 'Bloomsbury-inspired' means, which gives the text a metropolitan flavour.

The impression is that this magazine is addressing young professionals with money to spare and this is reinforced when you notice that the readers' homes featured in the magazine belong to: an artist, a production assistant and art director, a theatre producer and business woman and a garden designer and landscape architect. Remember though that the target audience will also include those people who aspire to the sorts of lifestyles depicted in the magazine.

7 Another way to gauge the target audience is to scan the *letters page* which can tell you something about the occupations, geographical locations and the concerns of some readers.

8 What do the main feature articles tell us about the readership and the values of the magazine?

In another lifestyle magazine a feature article about people and their homes introduces us to:

> Bele (who 'works in software') and Reinhard, a German architect and their 19th century house in Surrey;
> Barney Loehnis, who works for a dot com company and lives in an Edwardian house (location not mentioned) with Dom, a banker and Ambroise, a photographer;
> Neil Stuke, an actor, in his Andalusian holiday house;
> Carol (works for a design group) and John Wood (head of an advertising company) who live in a Victorian terraced house in North London.

Why these houses and why these people? The interiors are all from metropolitan southern English locations, with the exception of a middle-class holiday home in Spain. The houses are old ones which have been done up in modern designs. The people who own them are all young and well off.

These seem like the kind of people and locations which Ros Coward describes in the chapter Ideal Homes in her book ***Female Desire*** (Harper Collins 1984). She maintains that the interiors which are depicted in lifestyle magazines belong to a very small middle-class group of people and that what we are allowed to see depends very much on ***public relations organisations*** which offer to magazine editors photo opportunities and interviews with their clients who need publicity.

Ros Coward maintains that there is a group of influential people who have power over what the reading public is offered. This group is a self-appointed arbiter on questions of design, taste, style and elegance. They are journalists, designers, graphic designers, furnishers and publishers who tell us what we should think, what we should buy and what we should like. There are, she says, ***commercial pressures and economic forces*** behind the images we are presented with, though they are never easy to spot.

9 *Key words* tend to be vague, with terms such as personality, flair, style, individuality, homely, handsome, cool, softly modern, uncluttered, sense of continuity, relaxing white space, dreamily pale, eclectic. 'Style' is a key word though its meaning is never precise. The ultimate accolade is 'personal style' which is in fact a strange paradox.

10 *What is not represented?* Working-class homes for a start. If working-class homes are mentioned in magazines about people's homes, they are the subject of ridicule, material for an easy joke: 'An index of proscribed examples of bad taste will be regularly published. I promise that the following obvious candidates will have fallen to the axe, hammer or incinerator – replica Victorian telephones, onyx and gilt coffee tables...large red brandy glasses with tiny porcelain kittens clinging to the side.... Cocktail cabinets... spare toilet roll covers...doorbells chiming tunes.... Crazy paving.' (*Company* magazine – quoted in Coward, ibid).

Activity

Choose two current lifestyle magazines and analyse the way homes are represented in them using this critical framework:

- What does the *magazine cover* indicate about the magazine's *target audience*? Look at visual images of people, their homes and their possessions. What do you infer about the audience from the list of contents and the way this is expressed?
- Write to the magazines and ask for a *media pack* or look at the publisher's *website*. Find information about the magazine's target audience.
- Collect articles from the media pages of broadsheet newspapers about the magazine. The Guardian Unlimited media page website is a good source of information (www.guardianunlimited.co.uk/media).
- Study the magazine's *editorial* (editor's message) for evidence of the *audience* the magazine is addressing.
- Read the *main feature articles* and determine what they tell you about the *readership* and the *values* of the magazine.
- Analyse the language of the articles, especially the *modes of address*, to find out what assumptions are being made about the audience's age, interests and culture.
- Scan the *letters page* to find information about the occupations, geographical locations and the concerns of some readers.
- Ask what could be represented but is not. Try to work out what commercial and economic reasons there may be for these omissions. Bear in mind that magazines are often targeting audiences with specialised interests.

Activity

In the 1980s Ros Coward raised interesting questions about social class and gender power. Read the summaries of her arguments (below) and organise a class debate about how things have changed.

Write a synopsis for an essay on either (i) lifestyle magazines and social class or (ii) whether lifestyle magazines encourage attitudes which trap women in their homes.

Ros Coward's arguments

Social class

(i) Working class homes are arranged according to different criteria from middle-class homes. They do not display possessions because they are valuable but because they have some pleasurable associations, memories of holidays, families and friends. Furniture is not chosen because it fits into an overall design but because it is liked or is a 'favourite'.

(ii) The idea that home improvement is merely an expression of individuality through good taste obscures the way in which this kind of restoration is a *very real economic activity*. People who restore homes and acquire valuable possessions then create wealth which they pass on to their children who then have no rent to pay and have huge economic advantages over those who pay a huge proportion of their income on housing. Thus a new elite is created.

Gender power

(iii) Magazines which emphasise the display of homes and the absence of clutter and mess *obscure* or *ignore the role of women* in relation to domestic work.

(iv) Emphasising the notion that a home has been designed through co-operation between male and female to become a kind of display cabinet of unity obscures an important truth that *for many women home is a prison*.

(v) Women are confined in homes through limited possibilities, and bear the 'awesome responsibility for the survival of young children, or are torn by commitments to work and children'.

Representation of fashion

The ***Writer's Handbook 2002*** lists the following as Fashion and Costume magazines:

- *Attitude*
- *B Magazine*
- *Black Beauty and Hair*
- *County*
- *Dazed and Confused*
- *Elle*
- *The Face*
- *Goodlife Magazine*
- *Harpers and Queen*
- *Heat*
- *i-D Magazine*
- *Jersey Now*
- *Loaded*
- *Looks*
- *marie claire*
- *Maxim*
- *New Woman*
- *19*
- *Sainsbury's The Magazine*
- *Shout Magazine*
- *Total Style*
- *Vogue*

Case study

An analysis of Harpers and men, *Harpers and Queen's* first ever men's supplement, which was published in November 2000.

THE COVER

The cover featured an ageing pop star, Bryan Ferry, in a black velvet blazer with matching trousers. The suit cost £519. His cotton shirt, we are told inside the magazine, cost £57, his cufflinks £47 and his shoes £380. Ferry is pictured leaning on a pale blue Aston Martin at Goodwood motor racing circuit.

The messages seem to be about luxury lifestyles for middle-aged men. Black velvet suits suggest extravagant, fashion-conscious lifestyles. Bryan Ferry, according to the information inside, 'became a style icon of the Eighties' and, lest he appear too old-fashioned, has just released (November 2000) 'a dazzling new album'. The Aston Martin suggests speed, old-fashioned quality and James Bond. The motor racing circuit suggests speed, danger and excitement and a touch of glamour.

The *cover lines* tell the reader that there are three topics covered inside the magazine – fashion, sex and expensive shopping:

BRIAN FERRY BRITAIN'S COOLEST MAN IN TOP GEAR
WHAT WOMEN REALLY WANT
HEY BIG SPENDER: THE MALE SHOPAHOLICS

The supplement is an excellent example of how *content and advertising are interdependent*. Magazines like this are produced to attract an audience of readers which can be sold to advertisers. The articles and pictures are used to attract a certain readership, in this case mature, middle-aged men who are wealthy and who are likely to be interested in buying certain products.

In this case the guest editor, Sir Paul Smith, is a fashion store owner as well as a fashion journalist. After his conventional *editor's letter* which begins 'In *Harpers and Queen's* first ever men's supplement, we tackle life's great questions: what to eat, what to wear, and, most importantly, how to get the girl.'

This is followed by two pages of fashion *photographs* which are really *adverts* for Smith's clothes. This is followed by what purports to be an interview with Sir Paul about the woman who has designed his chain of shops.

The rest of the magazine *links features and advertising* closely. Sometimes it is hard to distinguish between the journalism and the advertising. There are two articles about being well dressed. One, 'Fop Watch', is about five successful businessmen who are noted for their dress sense. The other is about the pop singer Bryan Ferry.

'Fop Watch' is about clothes as an indicator of *success* or *social status*. It suggests that there are certain rules and standards which only the really sophisticated can know. It also suggests that *ostentatious spending and display are admirable*. These characteristics are linked with professional success:

Fop watch picture from Harper's and Queen

' "I consider myself a good salesman, and therefore a good shopper." So says Arnaud Bamberger, the face in front of and the brains behind Cartier's success in the UK. Bamberger owes his success to the fact that he is...a fearless socialiser and shopper. Whether shooting with the Sangsters, talking vintage cars with the Earl of March, or watching a few chukkas of polo with the Queen, Bamberger is always impeccably turned out.'

The implied message is that if you want to be a successful businessman and mix with the social elite you have to dress well and spend extravagantly. In the rest of the article there are brand names and the names of shops where Bamberger buys his clothing.

The reader is positioned to admire excess, as in the mention of Bamberger spending at least £20,000 a year on clothes and accessories. Then there is this:

'Take that watch, a classic from the Fifties. Sober yet beautiful, it is just one of a collection of 25 Cartier watches that he has assembled over as many years....

'I buy one a year; it is a rule that I have set myself.... I obviously have a strong love for the old styles, such as the one I am wearing today, but I also have most of the current models of Tank and Pasha.' He opens a drawer and pulls out a fistful, scattering them over the desk.'

The excess is emphasised in another part of the article about Jean Pierre Martel, Spain's top decorator:

'Martel's wardrobe is divided across three European countries and four cities. In France he has 52 suits, 120 shirts, and 75 pairs of shoes. In London he keeps 45 suits, 110 shirts, and 85 pairs of shoes. In Valencia, where he has a furniture factory, he also has an emergency capsule wardrobe of 22 suits, 60 shirts, and 100 pairs of shoes. But most of his wardrobe is to be found in Marbella, where he keeps 120 suits, 180 shirts, and 235 pairs of shoes.'

Over the page is another *feature* 'Daddy Cool'. It is about singer Bryan Ferry. It is a combination of a lightweight interview and a fashion shoot, with the pop singer modelling a variety of clothes from expensive fashion shops. There are six full-page photographs of Ferry wearing an assortment of fashions including 'a Paisley-print scarf' costing £105, a 'long cashmere coat' (£1,050), 'shoes from the Tattoo collection' (£380) and a 'Helmut Lang jacket' (£560). Those readers who can afford such items are directed to a list of stockists.

CASE STUDY CASE STUDY CASE STUDY CASE STUDY CASE STUDY CASE STUDY CASE STUDY CASE STUDY CASE STUDY CASE STUDY CASE STUDY

The choice of Ferry as a *celebrity* to endorse these fashions suggests that the magazine is aimed at the 40+ market, as he 'fronted the most glamorous band of the Seventies'. He is also chosen because he is apparently sophisticated and sexy: '[He] wrote some of the most sophisticated songs of our time, and possesses the enviable ability to excite unbridled desire in women and ungrudging respect in men.'

As well as the article and its pictures being more or less an advertisement for particular clothes and accessories, it is followed by a double-page advert for a gentlemen's clothes shop called Hacketts of London. Its *advertising copy* makes interesting reading.

> 'Hackett's new casual kit makes it easy for you to dress down.
>
> Smart-casual, casual, relaxed, dress down...the message is ambiguous, yet the way forward is clear. The gentleman's uniform has been dismantled: it's not just the chalk stripe that defines the office kit, nor are button-down shirts with chinos the only weekend alternative. The boundaries between work-wear and leisure-wear have been slowly eroded, and men now face an agonising decision each morning when they choose how best to dress for the day ahead.'

Stage one – make the reader *aware of problems or weaknesses*. The dilemma has been identified. The reader has been told he has a problem. Fashion is changing and he does not know what he should be wearing.

Stage two – offer a *solution*.....

> 'Hackett, the British brand for any occasion, has developed an exclusive range of business casual-wear that fills the void between the traditional suit and weekend attire. It also releases you from the daily headache of choosing the correct clothes. Hackett smart-casual is an intelligent new combination of informal suits or smart wool jackets teamed with relaxed shirts and trousers. The look is confident, stylish, and individual – perfect in and out of the office.'

Stage three – promise a *reward*....

'Whichever outfit you decide upon, the Hackett smart-casual kit will make you the envy of the office.'

> The implications here are that experts (by implication Hacketts) can help men out of a dilemma of not knowing what to wear at work. You can trust their designs because they know about fashion. The phrase 'correct clothes' suggests that there is a right and wrong way of dressing. But the 'right' clothes can also 'make you the envy of the office', so they are about vanity, about being noticed and admired. The adjectives in the piece tell the reader the desirable qualities a well-dressed man should have: 'intelligent', 'relaxed', 'confident', 'stylish' and 'individual'.

Activity

Study the fashion sections of several lifestyle magazines. Look for and collect examples (pictures and text) of the following:

i) Endorsement of a fashion by a famous designer.

ii) The modelling of clothes by successful people.

iii) Distancing from what are seen as non-stylish people.

iv) The need to seem cool and to be envied and attractive.
For example, 'Natasha, daughter of actor Michael Caine, has worn Armani for years.... Husband Tim [owner of Fluid juice bars] shares her passion, but this super cool couple aren't about to start co-ordinating their outfits. 'We don't do Posh and Becks,' says Natasha.' (*Red* magazine)

v) Links between fashion and home.
For example, 'Interiors have never been more fashionable, with style gurus such as Paul Smith and Jasper Conran turning their talents to the home.'

'Fashion folk are extending their stylish vision, stretching beyond clothes to encompass homeware.' (*Red* magazine)

vi) Fears of being unfashionable.
For example, again from *Red* magazine: 'It takes time and skill to concoct a home that reflects personality and quirks without a hint of predictable, prescription chic; yawning gaps that ache for the right finishing touch; or inappropriate gifts too large to be hidden away and too obvious to be given away.'

Use this research as a basis for a group or class discussion about:

- the consumption of clothes is good and is linked with being successful and envied;
- lifestyle magazines encourage readers to see clothing not as functional but as a social statement about wealth, good taste and class;
- lifestyle magazines value conspicuous consumption highly.

Audience

Introduction

The concept of 'audience' is crucial to media studies. It is partly about the way media institutions and producers research and target audiences and partly about how those audiences receive and consume media texts.

Audiences are the people who read newspapers and magazines, the viewers who watch television programmes, cinema goers, listeners to radio, internet users – all the consumers of media products. They are essential to the process of communication and they are subject to a wide range of social, economic, political and environmental influences.

This chapter looks at how media producers spend a good deal of effort and money trying to measure and evaluate audiences. It examines how far media products *reflect* actions and opinions rather than *creating* them, how far audiences *believe* what the media shows them and how they respond to complex texts.

The chapter also looks at *reception theory*. It shows how the concept of the active audience has replaced the passive model.

It introduces information about the media's *effects*, especially on the young, and encourages debate on this issue.

It shows how researchers have begun to analyse the complex ways television has become part of daily life, how it fits into patterns of domestic relations and how its place in the home varies from culture to culture.

Finally it encourages you to conduct your own research into different attitudes to watching television in your own home.

Media producers and audiences

All media producers shape their products to fit what they believe to be the needs of the audience. This means trying to understand the level of receptiveness of the audience – can they understand, are they engaged in the text? It also means ensuring that messages are delivered in the appropriate medium at the right time to the right place.

The audience can be seen as both a ***public*** which needs to be informed and as a ***market***. The former attitude is characteristic of a ***public service*** approach to communication where the emphasis is on information, knowledge, education and enlightenment. The latter is characteristic of a ***commercial*** approach, which sees the media as a way of gaining audience attention in order to sell the consumer goods and services. The difference is simple but profound: media aimed at audience as public sees its purpose as being to serve whereas the audience as market approach means trying to ***sell***. How producers or researchers think of an audience implies what is expected from them and consequently what is provided for them.

Media producers usually have a ***target market***. That is, they have a clear idea of who they are communicating with, though it is worth remembering that some assumptions are based on over-simplifications. This could mean knowing things like:

- where they live, e.g. a local radio station broadcasting to a limited geographical area;
- how old they are, e.g. *Saga Magazine* which is read by the over-50s;
- what gender they are, e.g. women's magazines;
- how they spend their leisure time, e.g. readers of golf magazines;
- what time they tune in, e.g. soap operas scheduled at prime time viewing;
- how they spend their money, e.g. the publishers of ***Beano*** know what proportion of their readers are keen on trendy trainers;
- where they spend their holidays, e.g. the advertising department of the ***Sun*** newspaper know a high proportion of their readers choose Spain.

Audience measurement

A good deal of effort and money is spent trying to measure and evaluate audiences. There are two categories of measurement – ***quantitative*** and ***qualitative***. The former is about how many watch, read, listen, and the latter is about what people think and feel about the media product. Both methods have their problems as well as their advantages.

For example ***BARB***, the Broadcasters' Audience Research Board, continuously measures TV audiences by having monitors in 5,100 homes. It also has a Television Opinion Panel which conducts a weekly survey of reactions from 3,000 viewers. BARB is a research body which publishes its findings in an annual report. The organisation was set up in 1981 and is a limited company owned by BBC, ITV, Channel 4, Channel 5 and BSkyB.

Previously ITV and BBC had measured audiences independently but their figures never agreed. Viewing figures are important because they affect how as much as £3 billion of ***advertising revenue*** is allocated. Commercial broadcasters need accurate figures on which to base the rates they charge advertisers. If they overcharge on the basis of old data, advertisers can demand a refund later in the year.

In January 2002 there was a furore because, according to BARB, there appeared to be an unexplained drop of 25% in viewers watching commercial television. One possible explanation was that new measuring equipment was being installed and not all of the cross-section of viewers were hooked up. The composition of the sample audience had also been changed to include more young people and more people from the south-east of England.

One member of the cross-section being monitored is supposed to represent 10,000 viewers, so when the Worthington Cup semi-final between Sheffield Wednesday and Blackburn Rovers rated 105,000 viewers for the ITV Sport Channel this was determined by the viewing choices of only ten people in the cross-section. With such small numbers involved it was not surprising that the

Sci Fi digital channel was shocked to learn that the size of its audience had varied by a staggering and highly improbable 240% in a fortnight.

Qualitative findings about people's opinions can be useful, but they can also be ignored. Various researchers have found that mass communicators tend to have a low opinion of their audience. (See Burns, 'Public Service and Private World' in ***The Sociology of Mass Media Communicators*** ed Halmos, University of Keele 1969). There is a prevalent attitude among media professionals that they know better than their 'customers' what is good for them. A cynical view that mass audiences are stupid, incompetent and unappreciative prevails. (See P. Schlesinger in ***Putting Reality Together: BBC News***, Constable 1978.)

An arrogant attitude to their audience seems to be particularly common among women's magazine editors, oddly enough. (See M. Ferguson, ***Forever Feminine; Women's Magazines and the Cult of Femininity***, Heinemann 1983.)

Mallory (Juliette Lewis) and Mickey (Woody Harrelson) in *Natural Born Killers*

Effects

How do media texts influence audiences?

People assume that mass media have an effect on audiences, otherwise there would be no calls for censorship of violent films or pornography, bans on cigarette advertising or complaints about unfair political coverage.

Some people argue, for instance, that films like ***Natural Born Killers*** (1994 USA) inspire real-life murders, or that right wing newspapers persuade people to vote for right-wing political parties, but it may be that films and papers only r***eflect actions*** and opinions rather than ***creating*** them.

That dilemma was at the heart of the debate in February 2003 when the World Health Organization produced a report that blamed Bollywood films for glamorising smoking. It reported that three out of four Indian films showed their stars smoking cigarettes. It then maintained that teenagers who watch Bollywood characters smoking were three times as likely to do so themselves. It also said that if young people see their screen idols light up on screen they are 16 times more likely to think positively about smoking. A spokesperson for the Indian film industry responded that the blame for any increase in young people smoking lay with the tobacco manufacturing companies. 'The easiest people to blame are the movie stars. How long can people blame the virtual world for their real problems?'

BOLLYWOOD BLAMED FOR TEENAGE SMOKING

Activity

Collect cuttings from current newspapers about a 'media effects' controversy. Read the stories and the following information and organise a class debate about the need or otherwise for stricter censorship of the media.

Discussion points

- In 1964, Hans Eysenk claimed that 'the best way to destroy civilisation was to pour out more and more violent fantasies through the media'.
- In the same year a researcher suggested that televised Belfast street riots did more harm to young children than gun battles in Westerns.
- Again in 1964, a police chief warned youngsters of the perils of imitating Kung Fu film star Bruce Lee.
- In 1984 newspapers criticised the violence in the television programme *The A Team* and the bad language of re-runs of *Till Death Us Do Part* for their influence on young children's behaviour.
- In 1992 the cartoon *Beavis and Butt-Head* was blamed for the death of a two-year-old in Ohio. She was killed in a fire started by her five-year-old brother after he had allegedly watched the programme. The programme was criticised for being 'Sesame Street for psychopaths' and 'pure social poison, glorifying losers, violence and criminality'.
- In 1993 the video *Child's Play 3* was blamed by some newspapers for influencing the behaviour of two ten-year-olds who murdered and tortured a two-year-old boy, Jamie Bulger. The video was subsequently removed from video shops throughout the UK.

Still from Beavis and Butt-Head

- In 1999 after the Columbine High School shootings in Ohio, USA, when two students shot some fellow students and teachers, there were calls not only for gun control but for more regulation of videos and computer games, which had supposedly influenced the killers.
- The Bulger case led to the Newson discussion paper 'Video Violence and the Proection of Children'. According to Bazalgette and Buckingham the debate echoed 'those which have been made throughout history in relation to successive "new" media, such as theatre, the press, popular literature, cinema, radio, and television'. (Bazalgette and Buckingham, *In Front of the Children* BFI 1995).
- The Newson paper concluded that 'watching specific acts of violence on the media has resulted in mimicry by children and adolescents of behaviour that they would otherwise, literally, have found unimaginable'. It concluded that, as some parents clearly cannot be trusted to restrict their children's viewing habits, society must therefore take on the necessary responsibility in protecting children from material through active censorship.
- 'Images sink into the great quagmire of the unconscious where they work away unseen.... I am disturbed by the video revolution. The idea that someone can freeze a frame, rewind and play a scene over and over again unleashes the possibility of sexual perversions that I do not even like to think about.' (Rosalind Miles, *The Children We Deserve* Harper Collins 1994.)
- It is possible that people seeing violent acts on television can be turned against violence because of its unpleasantness.

- People rarely say that they themselves have been made more violent, over-sexed, materialistic, or racially intolerant by watching television programmes.
- Most children, though not all, can make sophisticated judgements about the programmes they watch.
- 'American research has shown that violence occurs much more often on television than in the real external world, and that this in turn leads heavy viewers "of this distorted world" to become even more fearful of crime.' (Bob Mullan, *Consuming Television* Blackwell 1997.)
- Working-class individuals are more likely to blame social and economic factors for crime, whereas middle-class individuals are more likely to blame lack of discipline in the home or the effects of television on unsupervised minds.
- Nothing has no effect.

How far do audiences believe what the media shows them?

Belief depends on *circumstances* and *expectations*. When we see an adventure film like Indiana Jones and three people escape from a doomed aeroplane in an inflatable dinghy which toboggans down a snow-covered mountainside before going over a precipice and plunging hundreds of metres into some rapids, we are prepared to believe that they survive. That is the kind of stunt we've come to expect from action/adventure films and we know that what we seem to see didn't really happen that way. As long as it looks real then we accept it in the context of film going. If the same series of events were relayed to us by a stranger who said he saw it all happen, or even if we read it in a newspaper we would be inclined to be more sceptical.

Indy and companions after their incredible escape

The medium and the audience expectations of it affect the degree of credibility. On television, real-life programmes are reckoned to be more credible than news stories, party political broadcasts are believed more than the *Sun* newspaper's reporting. Readers of broadsheet papers tend to trust papers more than television whereas the opposite applies to readers of tabloid papers. Because something is biased does not necessarily mean it has influence.

Surveys that show that readers of the ***Telegraph*** are more likely to vote Conservative (71%) than readers of the *Mirror* (19%) might seem to show that right-leaning and left-leaning papers influence the way their readers vote. Alternatively they might also indicate the way left- and right-leaning people choose their papers. Research by Curtice and Semetko (Does it matter what the papers say? in ***Labour's Last Chance? The 1992 Election and Beyond*** by A Heath *et al*. Dartmouth 1994) seems to indicate that 'many electors still appear to view newspaper reports (and watch television news) through a partisan filter that enables them to ignore politically uncongenial messages'. What seems to happen is that people tend to read newspapers whose prejudices coincide with their own.

Early ideas about the audience and the mass media offered a view of the world composed of fragmented individuals who were subject to powerful propaganda messages – the so-called ***hypodermic needle model***. Hypodermic means 'under the skin' and the model is basically a metaphor about media power over audiences. The assumption is that the mass media have a direct effect upon audiences by 'injecting' information into the consciousness of the masses.

This approach has often been challenged – most recently by the theory of the '***active***' audience. This theory postulates that meaning is not simply transmitted and received and that effects are not easy to measure. Meaning is not a transparent feature of a text but the product of ***interpretation by viewers and readers***. Texts have to be made to produce meaning. The media supply resources out of which people fashion their own view of the world.

So groups or individuals 'actively' construct their own interpretations and meaning of the world. The implication is that the media do not have any effects on audiences because people interpret the media's messages in many different ways and according to their own prejudices. Some people believe and accept the message, others reject or criticise what is being said.

Greg Philo in ***Seeing and Believing*** (Routledge 1990) found:'A key result of our research was to show how people used their own direct experience or alternative sources of knowledge to evaluate media messages. A corollary of this was that if there was no direct experience or other knowledge of an issue, then the power of the message would increase.'

Philo also reported that:

> 'In our work on the Gulf War of 1991, we noted the low level of public knowledge when it began and how media outlets were in a strong position to "instruct" their audiences. The *Daily Mirror* for example has a whole front page listing (literally) who were the "Heroes" and who was the "Villain".
> We normally found that, if people had direct experience of an issue and that this conflicted with the media account, then they would reject the media message.'
> (Philo and McLaughlin 1995, 'The British media and the Gulf War', in Philo, G (ed) *Glasgow Media Group Reader* Volume 2, Routledge.)

The researchers do report an exception to this rule.

> 'An exception to this was where a great anxiety or fear had been generated by media coverage. When we studied TV and press reporting of mental illness, we found that it focussed on violent incidents. People who worked in the area of mental health and who had professional experience tended to discount this media view and pointed out that only a tiny minority of people with mental health problems were potentially violent. Yet we found some cases where the fear generated by media accounts actually overwhelmed direct experience. In the following case a young woman described how she had worked alongside elderly people in a hospital. These people were in no way dangerous or violent yet she was afraid of them because of what she had seen on television:
> "The actual people I met weren't violent – that I think they are violent, that comes from television, from plays and things. That's the strange thing, the people were mainly geriatric – it wasn't the people you hear of on television. Not all of them were old, some of them were younger. Not all of them were violent – but I remember being scared of them, because it was a mental hospital – it's not a very good attitude to have but it is the way things come across on TV, and films – you know, mental axe murderers and plays and things – the people I met weren't like that, but that is what I associate them with."' (Quoted in Philo, G. (ed.) 1996, *Media and Mental Distress* Longman.)

Activity

The effects of video games on young people
Read 'Unfair Play' by Zoe Williams (*Guardian* 31/12/02) and answer the questions on it.

Worried that its killjoy reputation might be flagging after the season of goodwill, the government is seeing in the new year with legislation expressly designed to stop the young enjoying themselves. Video games, long a province of boundless freedom, in which children as young as three could learn the value of shooting Germans, are soon to be subject to the same age classification as films.

For such sad sacks who don't have a PlayStation, here's the problem – the tone of video games has moved on somewhat since all you had to do was shoot Chubby and not necessarily malign invaders from space. In Grand Theft Auto, your core aims are to steal cars, trash them, beat prostitutes to death and then set upon the sailors who are unaccountably stalking the highways of generic America and may or may not be homosexual. ... Hooligans: Storm Over Europe is an imaginative construction of what would happen if Millwall supporters could fill in forms to the satisfaction of the passport office. If you were going to extract a moral universe from all this, you would come up with a) private property is meaningless, b) people in tight clothes are either gay or whorish, c) the gay and whorish should be exterminated, d) Germans are born mad, and e) maiming, killing and driving recklessly are activities worth pursuing for their own sake....

You can see why it would be better if these messages weren't thrust upon the impressionable but the truth is, of course, that PlayStations are mostly played by 30-year-olds whose moral universes are already formed.

That said, children do play these games too, so it's odd that they have escaped censorship for so long. I suspect this is a technical issue rather than an oversight. In the early 1990s, when I used to enjoy nothing more than a game of Die Fuhrer, Die, the figures on the screen looked like lumps of dough in uniform; they would no more inspire you to kill

Germans than eating toast would inspire you to eat Germans. Now the graphics are so good most of the characters could match Bruce Willis for humanity. Taking into account the fact that games are more actively involving than films, they should rightly be subjected to the same if not stricter rules.

But in fact, it is a mistake to equate games with films. The latter are, regardless of merit, operating under a banner of art. Even though no credible case has ever been made for violence in fiction begetting violence in fact, we have still accepted that children shouldn't see make-believe rendering of sex or death lest it infect their view of the real world. In games, by contrast, children have traditionally been allowed to do whatever they like. They play with soldiers and have them kill each other. Sometimes they gather cuddly anthropomorphised items and give them pretend tea; other times, huge massacres occur when Lego meets a dinosaur. I don't know what avenue of social intercourse they are exploring...but imaginative genocide seems to be a childhood constant. Computer games may have hardline conservative and/or obsessively anti-German messages, but then so can grandparents.

If there's one case to be made against games it's that they turn ardent players flabby of mind and body because of all that time they should have spent interacting and exercising, they've wasted in front of the telly. On this basis the first thing that should be banned should be the really witless games, like The Sims, where you don't need reflexes since there isn't even an enemy. Then get rid of *Big Brother*, and all other reality shows; these skew young minds because they really do create a sick value system.

We are blundering after the wrong target, directed by a lazy certainty that there's nothing worse than violence. In fact loads of things are worse than violent fantasy – growing up wanting to be Kylie Minogue is more likely to send you crackers than growing up with the idea that, while we enjoy close cultural and trade links with real Germans, computer ones still have hearts of blackest evil....

(*Guardian* 31/12/02, reproduced with permission)

1 What does Zoe Williams think children should be protected against?

2 Why does she think that video games have escaped censorship for so long?

3 Why does she think that video games should not be regulated ?

4 What three things would you ban and why?

Audience behaviour

Scholars have recently begun to analyse the complex ways television has become part of daily life, how it fits into patterns of domestic relations and how its place in the home varies from culture to culture. They are interested in such things as how viewing is a social process affected by material circumstances, social class and gender.

An example of such research is David Morley's ***Family Television*** (Routledge 1986), which describes the relationship between television and family life. He observed and interviewed eighteen south London families. He found that, for ***fathers***, television viewing was a night-time respite and escape. They preferred to watch programmes attentively and not to be interrupted.

Mothers, on the other hand, whose workday lasted well into the evening, had a more distracted mode of watching television. In fact some women even reported feeling guilty if they did sit down and watch some programme attentively. For women, television was a means of encouraging rather than stifling family talk. These different attitudes and behaviour patterns sometimes provoked conflict.

Dorothy Hobson is another researcher interested in the relationship between gender and television viewing (Soap operas at work in ***Remote Control: Television, Audiences and Social Power*** ed Ellen Seiter *et al*., Routledge 1989). She found that soap operas provided a focus for ***socialising*** among female office workers. The women shared, revised, challenged and continually reformed their understanding of plots and character relationships in soap operas.

Other researchers have found that television becomes part of our daily lives at a very early age, with some children as young as ten months already being fascinated by ***Teletubbies*** and that as early as sixteen months babies are able to turn on the television by instruction or at will.

Activity

Observe and make notes on different attitudes to watching television in your own home.

Consider things such as how attentively people watch, who uses the remote control most and what conversations about the programmes take place.

Also make notes on peer group conversations about programmes. What aspects of programmes are discussed and in how much detail?

Try to observe and make notes on television viewing by very young children. Find out what interests them, what their attention span is and ask questions to determine what they think is happening in particular programmes.

Share your findings with other people and then write an essay about how people watch and use television, noting gender and age differences where possible.

Institutions

INTRODUCTION

The term 'institutions' covers:

- the ownership of media companies
- production and distribution processes
- technological developments
- issues of censorship and control
- how all these affect the media texts themselves.

This chapter looks at different sorts of ownership and their consequences, with particular reference to the newspaper industry.

It encourages debate about public service broadcasting.

It looks at how media organisations are funded and how they are regulated before showing you how to investigate the ways in which new technologies affect the production and consumption of media products.

Types of ownership

Most media belong to three sorts of *ownership*:

- *Commercial companies*, which can be public or private, large conglomerates or small independents, owned by media tycoons who want to have influence.
- *Private, non-profit bodies*, which could be neutral trusts designed to safeguard independence, as with the ***Guardian*** newspaper, bodies with a special cultural or social task, political parties, religious organisations, etc.
- *State/public ownership* – this can be in many different forms such as direct state control or independent public organisations funded by a 'tax', as with the BBC.

Commercial companies are often owned by media ***tycoons*** who take an interest in editorial policy and use their power. Here, for example, are two descriptions of media tycoon Rupert Murdoch, owner of News Corporation, a huge, global media enterprise, which emphasise his power.

> 'He smashes unions. He squares politicians. He keeps in with national leaders, offering them news-space and book contracts (Thatcher and the Speaker of the House of Representatives Newt Gingrich to name but two). Everywhere he lobbies. He attacks regulations that threaten him, or tries to sidestep them.... The world stands gaping; national leaders feel a little smaller in his presence. His power is intense.'
>
> (Andrew Marr, BBC political editor, *Ruling Britannia* Penguin 1995)

Rupert Murdoch

> **'When you work for Rupert Murdoch you do not work for a company chairman or chief executive: you work for a Sun King. You are not a director or manager or an editor: you are a courtier at the court of the Sun King.'**
>
> (Andrew Neil, formerly an editor of a Murdoch newspaper paper, *Full Disclosure* Macmillan 1996: quoted in *Mass Media, Politics and Democracy* by John Street, Palgrave 2001)

How such power is used and what effect it has on audiences is a central issue in media studies. Some people see Murdoch as a demon, others as a commercial genius. Some people assume that he wields political power, influences what his papers say, what voters think and what governments do.

In February 2003, when there were massive peace rallies all over the western world in protest about the impending attack on Iraq, Rupert Murdoch's newspapers, without exception, took a pro-war stance. At the time, Murdoch's News Corp owned more than 175 titles on three continents, dominating the newspaper markets in Britain, Australia and New Zealand. According to Roy Greenslade, writing in the Media Guardian (page 2, 17/2/03), an exhaustive survey of all Murdoch's newspapers found every one coming out in favour of war against Saddam Hussain. 'It doesn't need a semiologist to see that the leader-writers are trying to break down public opinion,' Greenslade said.

Others think that Murdoch has no political agenda, but just wants to make his operations commercially successful. Whichever point of view is right, it is true that his papers worldwide have tended to support right-wing policies. Yet his papers have not always espoused right-wing attitudes. The ***Sun*** in its early days opposed capital punishment, apartheid, racism and the Vietnam War. In 1970 the Murdoch press backed Labour in Australia and the UK. In 1972 it supported the striking British miners. In 1997 it supported Tony Blair.

What has been consistent is a support for people who are anti-establishment, people like Andrew Neil who opposed traditional power and were products of a meritocracy.

Greater power can be exerted where one person or organisation owns different media in the same geographical area. This is called ***cross-media ownership***. The kind of thing which can happen was illustrated with the banning of a book written by the ex-governor of Hong Kong, Chris Patten.

Rupert Murdoch owned the publisher, Harper Collins, and the story was that he stopped publication of Patten's book in case it damaged his interests in China. Murdoch denies this part of the story. The story was reported widely in all rival papers but was barely mentioned in the ***Times*** (owner Rupert Murdoch). Not long after, the President of China allowed the showing of the film ***Titanic*** in Chinese cinemas to the delight of 20th Century Fox (owned by Rupert Murdoch). The premiere of the film in China was positively reviewed by the ***Sun*** newspaper (owned by Rupert Murdoch).

This case illustrates the problem of one individual exerting too much power, so that different points of view are suppressed. The power that goes with ownership can be dangerous if dissenting voices have no audience.

The expansion of companies so that there is a ***concentration of ownership*** is also important. What looks like a rich diversity of brands can, in fact, all be owned by the same company. Time Warner, for instance, publishes books, makes records, produces and distributes feature films, shows television programmes through CNN News, Home Box Office, Cinemax and the Cartoon Network, makes video games and children's toys. One of the consequences of this multi-sector ownership is that, for instance, the papers can be used to publicise and sell the books and films while the films can be used to sell the records and so on.

Staffing policies and decision making in media organisations can affect the programmes made or the content of newspapers and magazines. The content and style of BBC television changed dramatically when Greg Dyke took over from John Birt. Dyke shifted serious programmes with small audiences like ***Panorama*** to BBC 2, moved the ***Nine O'clock News*** to ten o'clock and concentrated on popular entertainment programmes (crime, soap operas, quizzes and landmark programmes such as ***Blue Planet***) for BBC 1. This resulted in BBC 1 having a larger share of the market than ITV 1 for the first time ever in 2001. But some argued that mass audiences were being denied serious programmes or at least that access to such programmes was being made more difficult.

Greg Dyke

Sometimes media power can lead to ***political power***. In Italy the media mogul Silvio Berlusconi made extensive use of his media outlets during a political campaign. His Fininvest channels were filled with advertisements for his party. When he subsequently became Prime Minister he was able not only to supervise the three television channels he owned but to influence the conduct of the three state-owned channels.

Activity

Read the article by Roy Greenslade (*Media Guardian*, 16/12/02) about newspaper owners and editors and their influence on politicians and then answer the questions on it.

The article was written at a time when much of the press, led by the *Daily Mail*, were criticising Cherie Booth, the Prime Minister's wife, for allowing a convicted fraudster to help her buy some property in Bristol. She was obliged to make a public statement explaining her actions and apologising for misleading the press. During the speech she had to fight back tears when she mentioned her son being away from home. Some journalists thought the tears were not genuine.

'HOW AND WHY THE PAPERS TOOK SIDES OVER CHERIE

Spin is a four-letter word which now taints the Labour government. Some people – members of the audience on BBC's *Question Time*, radio phone-in callers, assorted columnists – seem to regard it as the epitome of evil. Media repetition of the sin of spin has convinced the public that Tony Blair and Alastair Campbell somehow invented political public relations. What everyone overlooks is the much longer, and arguably more venal, record of newspaper spinning.

But the coverage of Cheriegate offers a fascinating insight into the way in which editors indulge in the art of spinning. Note first, and most importantly, the different weight papers gave to the story. Why, for example, did the *Daily Express* and *Daily Star* virtually bury the story while the *Daily Mirror* gave it the big treatment? Why was the *Sun,* the highest selling paper that has made a selling point out of shouting louder than any other, so unusually reticent?

To understand the spin we have to look more closely at the specific agendas of owners and editors.

The *Express* and *Star* proprietor is Richard Desmond, a man who has been currying favour with Blair ever since he bought the titles two years ago. His fortune was founded on the sale of pornography and there was a potentially worrying period when he feared that he might be termed an undesirable owner of national papers.

In fact, his purchase was nodded through by a Labour minister and then, quite coincidentally of course, he donated £100,000 to the Labour Party. So did his papers go softly-softly on Cherie Booth out of loyalty? Possibly.

Then again, it might well have more to do with favours in the future rather than in the past. Imagine this scenario some time next year: Trinity-Mirror decides to sell off the *Daily* and *Sunday Mirror*, and the *People* – or, at least, the latter. A natural bidder would be Desmond who, like him or not, has shown himself to be a serious Fleet Street player.

If he was to bid for the Mirror Group papers he would, in normal circumstances, face a Competition Commission inquiry. But I think he could advance arguments which would avoid a referral – as long as the government took a very relaxed view of him.

So, given that thought, it makes sense for the calculating Desmond to have suggested to his *Express* editor, Chris Williams, to soft-pedal on Cherie. He wouldn't need to offer much advice to Peter Hill, editor of the *Star*, because his paper largely ignores politics.

But the spinning over at the *Daily Mirror* was very different. That paper has no single owner, its chief executive is serving his notice and its chairman allows the editor, Piers Morgan, to do as he likes. Morgan has been moving his paper away from Labour at an increasing rate of knots ever since Blair and Campbell successfully wooed his rival, the *Sun*. He has gradually adopted an anti-Blair line which, at times, has verged on the hysterical.

He hired one of New Labour's most bitter detractors, Paul Routledge, and – with an Iraqi war imminent – has given space to another of the government's greatest, and most effective, critics, John Pilger.

Morgan's antipathy to Labour was keenly felt by Cherie who was emboldened to suggest to Trinity-Mirror's outgoing chief executive, Philip Graf, that he needed to control his editor and supposedly suggested he lacked "a moral compass".

Morgan was stung by the rebuke and there was undeclared war between them for many months. It was noticeable, for instance, that Cherie refused to attend the *Mirror's* lunch at the Blackpool party conference. She can't bear to be in the same room with Morgan.

So Morgan leapt at Cheriegate with more enthusiasm than, given *Mirror* readers' known pro-Labour voting habits, seemed appropriate. Here was a chance to sink his teeth into a woman who, he claims, tried to get him fired. One front page, after her public statement, asked whether her tears were "real remorse or more spin to save her skin".

But what was Morgan's front page if not spin itself? He was presenting a deliberately negative view of the Prime Minister's wife to his readers because she doesn't like him.

He may justify it by saying that, irrespective of his personal animus towards her, he sincerely believes she was play-acting. His readers will never know of his underlying agenda though, will they?

By contrast, the *Sun's* largely pro-Blair stance has been obvious since early 1997. Its owner, Rupert Murdoch, has kept faith with Blair ever since, despite some government decisions going against his business interests, and there isn't the least sign of him changing his mind. His editor, David Yelland, has worn kid gloves throughout the Cherie affair.

Five years ago the *Daily Mail* and the *Mail on Sunday*, owned by the third Lord Rothermere and overseen by Sir David English, looked as if they might move into Blair's camp. But both men were soon dead and, under the fourth Lord

Rothermere and his editor-in-chief, Paul Dacre, the titles have been vehemently anti-Blair, lighting on every opportunity, no matter how trivial, to criticise the government.

I don't think there is any hidden agenda here. Dacre wears his politics on his sleeve and genuinely believes this government to be the devil incarnate. His problem is that he spins for a Tory party that no longer exists. Oh, Margaret, how they pine for you.'

(*Media Guardian* 16/12/02, reproduced with permission)

1 Why, according to Greenslade, did:

- **i)** the *Express* go 'softly-softly on Cherie Booth'?
- **ii)** the *Mirror* editor become anti-Blair?
- **iii)** the *Sun* become pro-Blair?
- **iv)** the *Mail* attack Cherie?

2 What is 'spin' and how do both politicians and newspapers use it?

Public ownership – the BBC

The British Broadcasting Corporation is an example of a state-owned (but not state-controlled) broadcasting network. It is financed largely by money from the sale of television viewing licences and is not allowed to carry advertisements. It was converted from a private company established in 1922 to a public body under royal charter in 1927. Under the charter, up for renewal in 2006, news programmes are required to be politically impartial. Though the BBC is widely admired, there are those who criticise it in principle, as in the following example.

Activity

Read the extracts from 'Time to axe the TV tax' and answer the questions on it. The article was written by Nigel Hatislow, former editor of the *Birmingham Post*. It appeared in the *UK Press Gazette*.

'TIME TO AXE THE TV TAX

Today the British Broadcasting Corporation is the mouthpiece of its political masters....

It's not surprising the BBC represents the interests of the public sector, of big government and of the tax-and-spend economy. It needs all this to justify its own existence.

But the time has surely come to put the BBC's audience out of its misery. We will never again be happy with the corporation as long as its extravagances, bias and political correctness are all paid for out of a compulsory poll tax on everyone with a television set. The BBC must be privatised.

.... We still endure a TV tax which is enforced by law on every household in the nation. It keeps going up and like so many other taxes, we get less and less for it.

Not long ago I asked a BBC executive what programmes he could recall from the past two years which were so special they could only be made by a public service broadcaster. He came up with *Walking With Dinosaurs*. But one series in two years is not sufficient to justify the compulsory nature of the tax.

The BBC was founded when broadcasting was in its infancy. The state set it up to encourage the development of radio and then television.... It was there to educate and inform as well as entertain. It was free from political bias, it was part of the nation's establishment and identity. It had a clear purpose and won nationwide affection.

Today the world has changed. There are more broadcasters than ever and the number of radio and TV channels seems to be expanding all the time. And that fails to take into account the vast array of services available on the internet.

So why, apart from it being against the law not to, do we pay the BBC's poll tax?... Its mission is only to ape the commercial channels while imposing a politically correct view of the world on the rest of us. The refusal to broadcast the celebrations for the Queen Mother's 100th birthday was proof that the BBC is no longer a unifying national force but just another company in search of an audience.

...The BBC used to be famed for sport. No more. Most of the major sporting events are to be seen anywhere but on the BBC. And the innovations introduced by commercial broadcasters show just how staid, dull and self-satisfied the BBC has become.

So why don't we flog it off? Privatisation, in one swoop or in bite-sized chunks, would raise billions of pounds – and all of the money would go straight into the pockets of its shareholders, you and me, the licence payers.

The BBC wants to compete with the commercial channels so let it. Why don't we encourage it to finance its own future through advertising, sponsorship, the marketing of its own programmes and better exploitation of its unique back catalogue? Even through subscriptions from its viewers.

It would axe the poll tax once and for all. We would no longer have to meet the cost of things like the BBC's online internet service or its digital channels which no one ever watches anyway.

...And it would mean that at last we stopped feeling outraged every time the BBC let us down by snubbing the monarchy, appointing a blatantly biased New Labour Director General and a blatantly biased New Labour political editor, or paid vast sums of money to third-rate celebrities to keep them from defecting.

After privatisation, the BBC's future would depend on the only thing that really matters – the ability to attract viewers. And from the proceeds of the privatisation, you and I could afford to go out and buy ourselves a new widescreen, digital TV in the hope that somewhere in the ether someone is broadcasting something worth watching.'

1 Why according to Hastilow is the BBC no longer needed?

2 What does he think should happen to it?

3 What advantages to the public would his proposals give?

3 After reading the following section, write a letter to the *UK Press Gazette* expressing your opinions about Hastilow's ideas.

In defence of the Beeb

Defenders of the public service principle argue freedom from strict commercial pressure to come up with popular programmes inexpensively produced allows broadcasting to be an instrument of cultural and social betterment with the emphasis on quality.

These are some of the reasons why people value the BBC:

- as it is free from commercial pressures it is able to take risks;

- it has produced landmark factual events such as *Son of God*, *Blue Planet* and *Walking With Beasts*;
- it produces a wide range of programmes that appeal to audiences of all ages;
- it helps people to connect;
- it makes people better informed;
- it offers people opportunities to acquire new skills;
- it helps people relate to their neighbours;
- it extends their horizons to the rest of the world;
- it supports and promotes British culture;
- it generates income, e.g. in 2002 the *Tweenies* had generated £32.5 million while the *Teletubbies*, seen in 120 countries, had earned £116 million.

Commercial media revenue

The main sources of revenue for commercial media are *direct sales* and *advertising*.

Both tabloid and broadsheet newspapers rely heavily on income from selling advertising space. As the broadsheets tend to have smaller circulations they depend even more than tabloids on advertising revenue. Commercial television and the free press depend overwhelmingly on their advertisers.

Advertising-based media are assessed on the number and *type of consumers* (who they are and where they live) measured as circulation, readership, reach or ratings. These figures are needed for establishing advertising rates, that is the amount of money that can be charged for space in print media and time in broadcast media. Media which are heavily dependent on advertising revenue are more vulnerable when the economy is doing badly and companies cut down on the amount they spend on advertising. This can have a spiralling effect with lower revenue meaning a reduction in the quality of the product prompting a further fall in audience numbers and a reduction in the amounts that can be charged.

The advertising can *affect the content* of the media product. Newspapers and magazines will produce specialist sections or supplements, such as motoring or travel, to tempt advertisers. Attracting advertisers may also mean changing the content or tone of the publication in order to attract the kind of readership the advertisers want. This could mean, for instance, a move away from hard news to more human interest stories. The same can be true of TV as this comment from a TV executive demonstrates:

'The dynamic is really news attracting the kind of audiences that advertisers want to buy, and the channel controllers sitting there saying "I want those kinds of advertisers, I need this kind of content. I need the news to deliver this kind of audience".' (*The Times*, 12/3/99)

To this extent *advertisers set an agenda for the media*, getting programme-makers and journalists to address some topics and not others. As a general rule the higher the dependence on advertising revenue, the less independent is the content, which gives it less credibility.

Advertisers can make their adverts look like newspaper stories. The *Daily Mirror* produced a supplement, which at first glance seemed to be conventional journalism produced in the ***Mirror*** style. A closer look showed that it was an eight page advertisement for Hoverspeed. The advertisement copy was set out with headlines, columns and lead paragraphs to look like standard reporting. But the 'stories' were:

- how to get a free day trip to France,
- how to apply for a 'Hovercard',
- what you can buy in a Hoverstore,
- some places to visit in France,
- how Belgium has 'something for all the family',
- where to stay in Belgium,
- how to book a Hoverspeed holiday.

How do you respond to advertorials like this? Do you feel duped or do you not mind? Are stealth adverts like this subversive?

Broadcast regulation

In 2002 a new framework for regulation of the broadcast media was being developed. The government proposed to create a new unified regulator called OFCOM. These were some of its objectives:

- to protect the interests of the consumer in terms of choice, price, quality of service and value for money;
- to maintain a high standard of content, a wide range of programmes and a range of opinions;
- to protect citizens by maintaining accepted standards of content, balancing the freedom of speech with the need to protect against offensive or harmful material, and ensuring fairness and privacy;
- to protect children and vulnerable people;
- to help prevent crime and public disorder;
- to attend to the special needs of people with disabilities, the elderly, those on low income and those living in rural areas.

OFCOM would be responsible for dealing with ***complaints*** about content of television and radio.

It also aimed to ensure the availability of ***accurate and impartial*** news services and to maintain a ban on political advertising.

It aimed to help people make informed choices about what they and their children see and hear and to promote media literacy.

It would also:

- regulate advertising in broadcasting media;
- keep existing controls on religious advertising and programmes;
- promote rating and filtering systems that help internet users control the content they and their children see;
- consider a reclassification system for videos, DVDs and computer games.

Activity

You and a small group of others are working for OFCOM and you have been asked to adjudicate on the following complaints. You have to come to a consensus (all agree) about whether to uphold the complaint or not. Bear in mind the 9 pm watershed before which items unsuitable for broadcasting to children should not be shown. You can decide your own penalties, but you should compare these with what OFCOM actually does.

1 On ITV 1 at 20.30 in the British Academy Awards programme the presenter made a joke which implied that all scousers (people from Liverpool) are criminals. Several people have claimed that this is racist.

2 A viewer has complained about racism in the European Under 21s Championship report shown on Five at 23.45. The commentator Jonathan Pearce said of a Nigerian player, Luyindula, "He is quicker of foot...perhaps not of thought...and can use his head when needed.'

3 On the reality programme *Big Brother* shown on Channel 4 at 22.00 two of the housemates, Kate and Johnny, had too much to drink and behaved, according to some viewers, irresponsibly. This set a bad example for young viewers and made drunkenness appear funny.

4 Viewers have complained about the bad language, the sexual references and the tasteless humour in an episode of the cartoon *South Park* – Cartman's Mom Is A Dirty Slut – shown on Channel 4 at 23.00.

In particular:

- the idea of a woman asking for an abortion when her 'baby' was eight years old
- showing a nurse with no arms
- a patient's head falling off and hitting the ground
- the suggestion that Cartman's mom would sleep with a politician in return for his voting for abortion for eight-year-olds,
- young children swearing throughout the programme.

5 Animal welfare groups have complained about the cartoon Itchy and Scratchy from *The Simpsons* (Sky One 18.00) which showed young children applauding as cartoon animals were dismembered, tortured, beheaded and blown up.

New technologies

The media industry depends on technology and is constantly changing in response to more advanced equipment. For historical examples you could consider the effects of the introduction of sound on the film industry or the effects of the advent of television on both radio and cinema.

Developments in media technology affect the ***kinds of products made*** and the ways in which audiences ***receive*** them.

In the home the movement is towards having a central system from which all media products can be operated. Each home will be able to have a network of television screens, computers, phones and radios all linked with one central source.

The scope of these developments for the ***consumer*** is shown in this 2003 advertisement for 'home cinema and multi-room audio':

> 'Take control of your entertainment
> Imagine having your own cinema in your living room, music that will follow you around the house and fingertip control of your favourite radio stations and CDs....
> All our systems can be integrated into your living environment. Flat screens can be built into your kitchen or bathroom.... You can control your lights from your armchair...surf the internet from any PC in your home and share all the peripherals such as printers and scanners. You can even store your music on hard disc servers to download directly onto your system.'

This is an example of the increasing interconnectedness or ***convergence*** of media technology in so far as it affects the way people make use of media products. The following example (Passion Plays by Meg Carter on page 204) illustrates a way in which a media producer uses convergence.

Media technology

Terrestrial (land) television

This is land-based as opposed to satellite transmission. BBC 1, BBC 2, ITV, Channel 4 and Channel 5 all depend on a network of transmitters which pass on signals from one to the other. The wavebands are Ultra High Frequency (UHF) radio waves. The main problem with this system is that the signals can be weak in hilly country and tall, expensive TV aerials may be needed to receive a good signal. One advantage is that regional programmes can be broadcast to a single region and not the rest of the national network.

Cable television

Cable television is transmitted through underground cables. You do not need an aerial to receive the signals. You need a decoder box to 'interpret' the signal.

Cable offers a wider choice of programmes than terrestrial TV. It can also be linked to a telephone system. People can only link with it if cables have been laid in their area and laying cables is expensive and time-consuming. Viewers have to pay the cable company a fixed monthly fee depending on which channels they receive.

Digital television

Digital TV has a different way of transmitting signals. The signals are more concentrated and more compressed than conventional analogue signals. This has three benefits. One is that the pictures are clearer and sharper. The second is that viewers have more control over the pictures on their screens, being able to zoom in on details or choose a camera angle in sporting events. The third is that many more programmes can be transmitted.

Interactive television

This allows people to have access to home banking and shopping services that are not connected to television schedules. Viewers have remote control boxes which allow them to deliver messages to television via telephone lines.

Satellite

Signals are transmitted via satellites which orbit the earth. They are like space relay stations that can transmit from and to stations on the ground. Before the signals are transmitted to the satellite they are encoded. Viewers need satellite dishes on their houses to receive the signals and a decoding box to translate the signals. The signal will have travelled almost 50,000 miles, but the journey will have taken a quarter of a second.

Personal Video Recorders

The PVR uses a computer hard disk to record programmes digitally, so that no tape is needed. PVRs can transform the way in which people watch TV, as they do away with viewers being tied to the broadcasters' schedules.

Convergence

Increasingly media companies control different parts of the communications process from production to distribution and reception. In the home the movement is towards having a central system from which all media products can be operated. Each home will be able to have a network of television screens, computers, phones and radios all linked with one central source.

Activity

Read Passion Plays (below) and answer these questions:

1 What different media forms and technologies has PlayStation used to increase awareness of its brand?

2 In what ways is Project Zool providing 'interaction and participation'?

3 Describe briefly an example of 'brand funded content'.

4 In what ways is it claimed that Project Zool is different from mainstream, conventional media?

5 Write a treatment for a new film for Project Zool.

Passion plays

By Meg Carter

Media Guardian
Monday 16 December 2002

A skateboarding fanatic and a Welsh language MC are among the unlikely cast of 'ordinary' people featured in a series of internet films commissioned by Sony's PlayStation 2.

A dedicated website, which goes live next month to showcase them, will create a platform for young people to express what they care about. Known as Project Zool, the initiative has involved Sony Computer Entertainment Europe (SCEE) commissioning five documentary film profiles of ordinary people with extraordinary passions. These will be seen on the Zool website. Other young people will be invited to submit short films about themselves and the best 15 will then be added to the site in the coming months. Eventually SCEE hopes to use the films within an exhibition. It has already done a deal to have the first five played during the break at concerts given by Brit Awards favourite The Streets, and may soon distribute them in indie cinemas, or sell them on to a broadcaster.

PlayStation is already a regular sponsor of grassroots sports and other activities, such as skateboarding and dragster racing. But creating content has become an increasingly important activity for the brand, says SCEE sponsorship and events manager Carl Christopher. 'To evolve as a brand you have to create content and instigate it. There's little point in merely reflecting what's going on around you. The difference is involvement. And we want to find new, different and interesting ways of getting people involved with the PlayStation brand.'

Brand-funded content is a strategy already established by BMW. Its bmw.films.com initiative has so far produced nine short films, each directed by leading Hollywood talent and accessible only via the internet. No films contain overt branding; each is united by the appearance of the actor Clive Owen and a BMW car. BMW estimates more than 13 million people have seen the first five films since their launch last year, generating a database of more than 2.4m email contacts.

Earlier this year PlayStation got involved with the second series of Channel 4's youth lifestyle show ***Passengers*** which it co-funded. It also brought out the first three editions of a fanzine called Pilchard Teeth (an anagram of PlayStation's advertising strapline: 'the third place'). Pilchard Teeth now sponsors the Clerkenwell Literary Festival. 'It's all about developing new forms of communication that go far and beyond the usual marketing routes,' says Christopher. Yet PlayStation's past activities have had one fundamental weakness: lack of interactivity. Zool is an attempt to remedy this. Interaction and participation, after all, are what PlayStation products are all about. At one level the 'real lives' theme is a natural extension of PlayStation's 'third place' line. 'The third place is all about how people create their own entertainment, and how people define themselves,' Christopher explains. 'We're featuring people who are pushing the boundaries – doing things away from the mainstream. It's not about highlighting the weird or bizarre. This isn't a freakshow – something to laugh at. But it is a platform to channel emotions and to bring out what young people today are really passionate about, and highlight this in a positive, celebratory way.'

'This is a redefinition of "reality TV",' says Sacha Teulon, co-founder of youth content provider Hotbed which produced Zool's first five films. 'We set out not to reduce youth culture to the stereotypical snapshot you see throughout established media. We wanted to present the raw, rough, vibrant reality of what it is and what we saw.' Her co-founder Kirsty Robinson adds, 'So-called reality TV offers such a polished, insular perspective on reality. This is much more honest, and wears its heart on its sleeve.'

The subjects selected for the first five films were chosen specifically because they did not fit into the London–Manchester–Leeds youth culture axis that dominates conventional media. Also featured are a traveller who regularly takes part in illegal horse races along Britain's motorways and a British breakdancer who makes it into a leading US breakdancing crew.

'We looked for people who were distinctive and true to themselves rather than wannabes eager to bask in fame and glory,' says Teulon. 'We used the old-fashioned, fly-on-the-wall approach, and participants had editorial control. It's all about people defining themselves on their own terms.' 'It's the opposite to how ***Popstars*** or ***Big Brother*** is run,' Robinson says. 'Yes, I suppose there is an opportunity to become famous, but being totally genuine will make someone of real interest.'

In return for baring their passions on air, those featured will gain access to a platform likely to raise their profile, create contacts with like-minded enthusiasts and even secure sponsorship or other commercial backing for their chosen activity. But isn't all this taking the venture rather too close to the star-making obsession already gripping TV executive boardrooms? Christopher thinks not. 'We are not setting out to be responsible for making people famous,' he insists. 'We have – and must be seen to have – more integrity. This isn't about money or fame. This is absolutely not about being manufactured, it's about being real.' And as such PlayStation's involvement as commissioner, funder and executive producer is clearly signalled throughout. 'It's not advertising. These are genuine films: and people who have seen them so far are intrigued.' Christopher adds. 'But we're not going to shy away from the fact that PlayStation is the content provider. Why should we? It's about providing the material, saying this is what it is – take it or leave it.'

People accept now that content has to come from a commercial entity, he adds: 'So long as we're not cheating, and content isn't compromised by any overt commercial message and, of course, it's entertaining – that's what really counts.'

(*Media Guardian* 16/12/02, reproduced with permission)

Switching to digital

There is an important question about replacing the analogue system of transmitting television pictures with a digital system. In 2001 only 25% of households had digital sets. By 2006 65% should have digital TV. This would still leave 35% of households which do not want digital services.

Many people do not want more channels, don't understand 'interactive', don't e-mail and don't want to shop on television. As the government will make several billion pounds from selling off analogue frequencies to mobile telephone companies, it may have to encourage that reluctant 35% by giving free digital conversion systems.

According to journalist Polly Toynbee: 'The trouble is that digital boxes and dishes have a downmarket, shell-suit image. Young, brash, vulgar, sports-pub, Sun-reading, Murdoch tainted, digital TV just does not have class.'

On the other hand the commercial and business potential of interactive digital television is enormous. This allows people to have access to home banking and shopping services that are not connected to television schedules. It was predicted by Jupiter Media Matrix that more than 32 million households in Europe will have idTV by the end of 2003 and by 2006 half the households in Europe will have it. This trend will coincide with more personal use of television with less mass broadcasting and therefore less money from conventional advertising. Television companies will then need to encourage people to use their idTV for buying things and the resulting transaction fees will replace advertising revenue.

Activity

Investigate audience responses to changing technology and write a report on your findings.

Interview people from a variety of age groups and ask them about their feelings and thoughts concerning digital broadcasting. Note whether or not they have digital equipment. In particular, find out if they respond/would respond to the vast choice of TV programmes that digital technology offers. How far do they/would they use the interactive facilities of digital broadcasting?

Useful websites for research:

BBC Online at www.bbc.co.uk
The *Guardian* and Media Guardian: www.guardianunlimited.co.uk
The *Independent*: www.independent.co.uk
The Times: www.thetimes.co.uk

Department of Culture, Media and Sport: www.culture.gov.uk
Includes reports of the working groups and select committees – particularly useful for AS/A level media studies.

The Press Complaints Commission: www.pcc.org.uk
Includes information about rulings on complaints. Useful for material about privacy and standards.

National Readership Survey: www.nrs.co.uk
Up-to-date information about circulation of newspapers and magazines.

Nation Viewers and Listeners Association: mediawatchuk.org/nvala.htm
Opinion about broadcasting standards and media morality from a pressure group.

The Independent Television Commission: www.itc.org.uk
Information about new technology.

Videos

Introduction

This chapter gives advice about how to produce your own video. It describes the different sorts of shots you need to take and how to edit them effectively. It takes you through the various planning stages, including generating ideas, commissioning a product, writing briefs, treatments and scripts. It shows you in particular how to produce an opening for a thriller.

Film and video production has its own jargon or specialist language. There is a glossary of some of these terms at the end of this chapter. Some of them will be useful when you come to write up your production log. There are some useful internet sites for film production and jargon such as www.realityfilm.com/resources/terms/chtml.

Video production

medium shot

Make sure from the start that you think about health and safety. For example, do not allow loose cables to trail around as potential tripwires. In the studio, those cables that can be fixed should be taped down near flush with the floor. Pay attention to advice you are given. For instance, if you look through a camera viewfinder at the sun you can blind yourself. As a general rule, never point a camera at the sun.

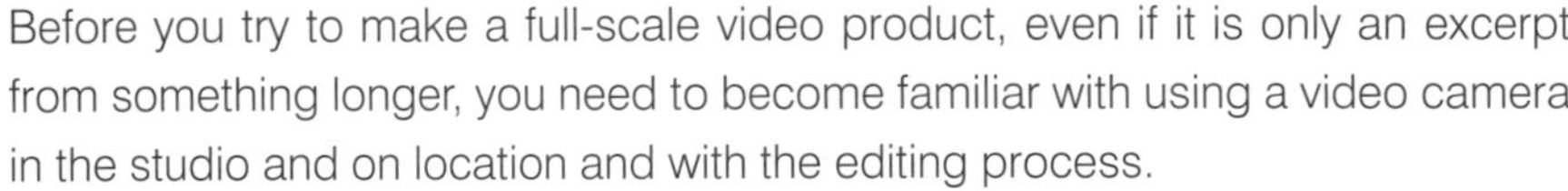

Before you try to make a full-scale video product, even if it is only an excerpt from something longer, you need to become familiar with using a video camera in the studio and on location and with the editing process.

close-up

There are three *basic shots* which you should master – the medium shot (people from the waist up), the close-up (head and shoulders) and the long shot (anything from full human figure to infinity).

In mainstream European and US film-making these shots have come to have general uses or meanings conventional to these Western popular cultures. Medium shots are often interactive, showing people in conversation, for example. Close-ups are more subjective. They often show emotion and sometimes an intense point of view or opinion. Long shots are the most objective shots in that they can be used to give an overview of a scene or establish a setting. These conventions do vary, though: close-ups have particular uses in the wildlife documentary genre, for example.

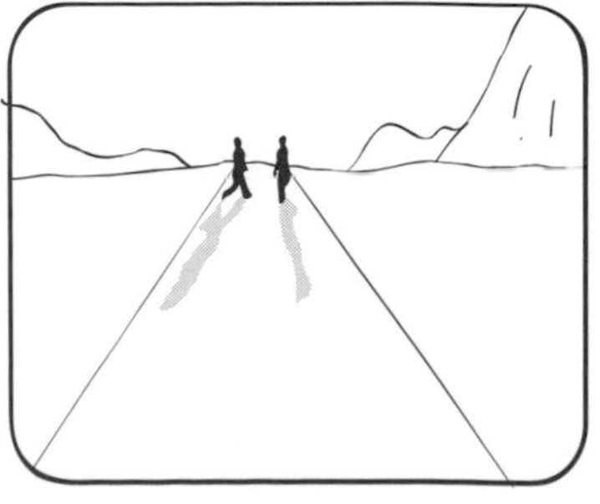

long shot

Activity

1 Practise using a still or video camera to take random examples of the three basic shots. Play the results back to a small audience and make notes on feedback about what looks good and what doesn't.

2 Develop your skills further by filming a simple narrative excerpt such as the planting or exchange of a suspicious package. Make notes on feedback.

3 Use a camcorder to record this simple narrative. It could be the opening of a thriller where you are trying to capture the audience's attention and create suspense. Use a variety of types of shot. Film some 'run-in' time at the beginning of each shot and some 'run-out' time at the end of each shot to help when you edit.

   1 Character A is looking for a book on a bookshelf.
   2 Character B dons a mask. We only see the silhouette of the head and shoulders from behind.
   3 A sits down to read the book.
   4 We see a close-up of B's feet walking along a corridor.
   5 We see A turning the pages of a book. In the background there is a door with a window.
   6 We zoom to see the blurred shape of B standing at the window.
   7 A close-up shows A engrossed in the book.
   8 A close-up of B's gloved hand opening the door handle.
   9 A turns over a page of the book deliberately and coolly.
   10 From outside the room we see the back of B as s/he enters the room.
   11 The hand-held camera follows B into the room slowly.
   12 A close-up of A's eyes.
   13 A close-up of B's eyes.
   14 A puts down book on table. Looks up.
   15 A says, 'I thought you'd never make it.'

4 View the compilation and plan a simple edit, noting where you want to come in on each shot and where you want to cut out. Perform a simple edit. After you have viewed the compilation, add some music or sound effects to it to establish the atmosphere.

Camerawork

Take care when setting up shots. Camera operators need to understand some of the DO'S and DON'TS of photography, such as being aware of everything in the viewfinder and not 'showing off' what the camera can do.

One key skill is that of being able to follow the conventions of ***framing***. Frame close-ups and medium shots tightly. Don't cut people off across joints such as elbows and ankles. Don't leave dead space in a shot, such as too much space above a person's head, unless there is a good reason for doing so. Where a person in shot is looking or walking in a certain direction, they should be positioned so that there is some space in that direction.

An ***establishing shot*** often refers to the first shot an audience sees. It tells us where something is happening. In the TV comedy ***Friends*** we often see the exterior of the apartment building where the characters live. This is shown at the

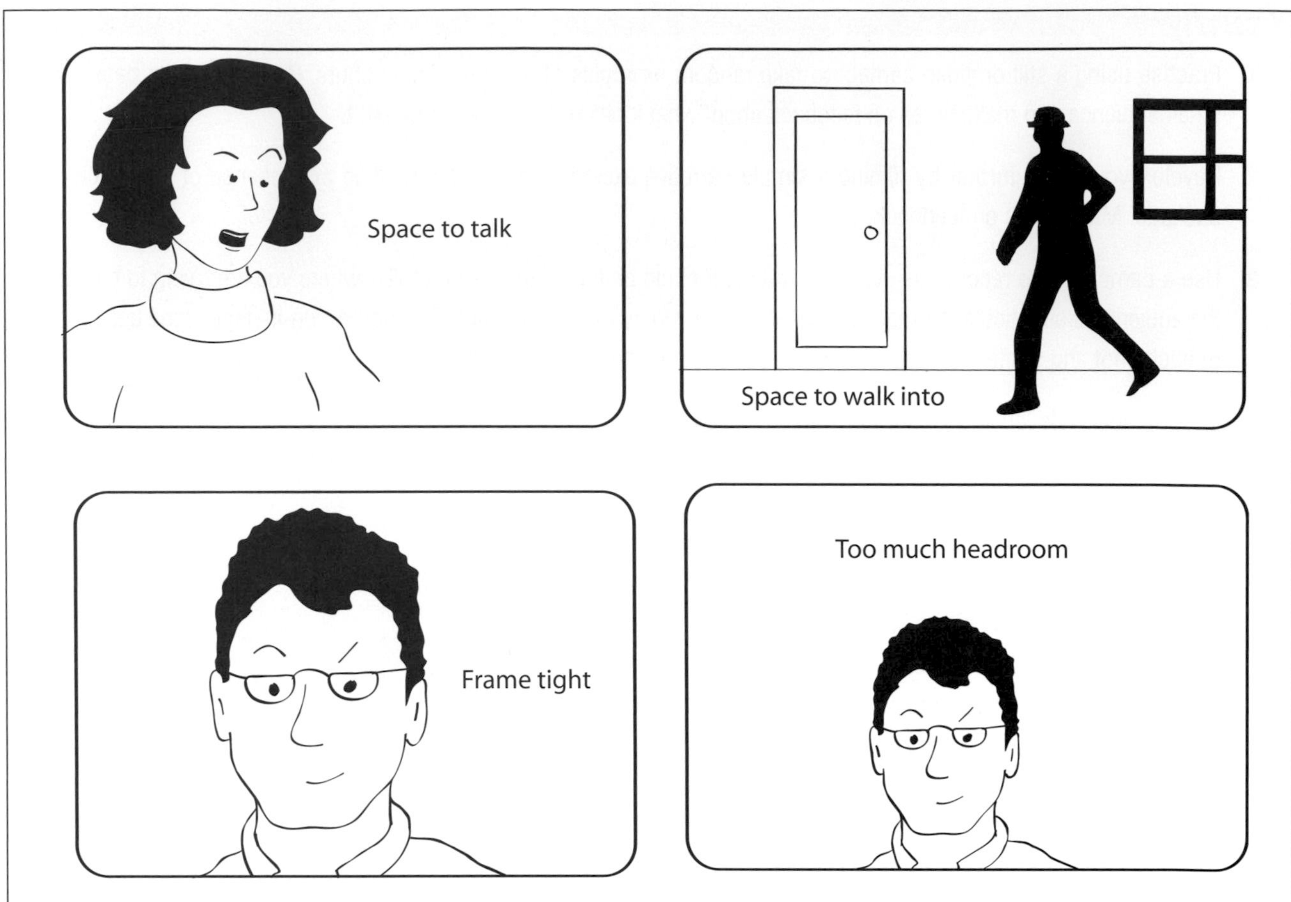

Framing a shot

beginning of the show and after we have seen a different setting, such as a hospital, to let us know we have returned to the main location of the programme. Sometimes group shots can establish the number of characters in a scene before we focus on particular individuals. Such establishing shots can be used within scenes or at the end of scenes where they act as a kind of reminder.

The ***point of view shot*** (often abbreviated to POV in shooting scripts) shows the audience what the character sees. The audience may even see the point of view before they see the character.

The aim of ***cutaways*** is to fool viewers into thinking you have two cameras. After you have filmed an interview, for instance, you can film some close-ups of the person asking the questions or nodding (they are called 'noddies') in response, some close-ups of the person listening to the questions and a long shot of the two people talking but without showing their lips. These shots can be edited into the final video to give the impression that the interview has been filmed with more than one camera. You can also take pictures of significant objects in a room or location and use these to add information or interest or simply to cover gaps and mistakes.

Panning is when the camera person stays still but moves the camera horizontally in an arc. Keep the movement smooth and use a tripod if you can.

Hold the shot for a few seconds before and after the pan to help when you edit and pan more slowly than you think is necessary. Try to finish on something interesting. Don't pan backwards and forwards as this unsettles the viewer. Pans are useful for establishing a place or following some action but they should be used sparingly.

Zooming makes things appear larger or smaller. Sometimes a slow zoom into a character's face can create tension. Again this is a technique which you should use sparingly and with a definite purpose, not just because you can do it, as if you use zooming in and out too much it irritates the audience.

Low-angle shots or 'tilt-ups' have the effect of making the person appear more dominant, while ***high-angle shots*** do the opposite, making the person appear vulnerable.

Tracking is where the person who is holding the camera moves. Professionals have tracks laid like a miniature railway and the camera is moved along the track following some action. Some tripods are fitted with optional wheels but you can improvise by attaching the tripod to a base fitted with wheels.

Equipment

Here is a checklist of desirable 'gear'.

- Video camcorder with external microphone facility, manual focus and zoom and 'white balance' option. Exam boards recommend an S-VHS system rather than a standard VHS system for better quality results when converted to digital editing.
- External microphone and headphones to allow you to check sound levels when filming.
- Tape recording equipment for background sound, to be added at the editing stage. (You can use your camera for sound-only recording.)
- Charged batteries.
- A tripod (for steady shots).
- Portable lights.
- A reflector for 'bouncing light' onto subject matter.
- A clapperboard.
- Editing equipment – either an editing suite, where you transfer material from one videocassette to another or, ideally, computer software that allows you to edit digitally. The Media 100 system is recommended for the Mac while a Matrox or Canopus video card with Adobe Premiere are sufficient with a PC.

You should make a checklist of what you have access to. In your log consider what is missing or difficult to obtain and how you can get round this. For example, where editing time is limited, it is possible to plan your filming so minutely that you can in effect 'edit in camera'.

There are many ways to improvise with limited equipment. Even the humble torch can be put to good use as a portable lighting device in appropriate circumstances. There are ways in which you can improvise tracking shots. If your tripod does not have wheels you can attach it to a base which does have wheels. Or you can sit in a chair with castors on it and get someone to push you along. Even the supermarket trolley has been used to improvise tracking shots.

You can get by with a single camera set-up. If necessary, you can achieve the effect of multiple cameras by filming a number of takes with the camera in different positions and angles. This can be very time-consuming though and poses continuity problems when you edit.

Making a video

The secret of a good video product is simply explained – preparation. Correcting a mistake on paper is always cheaper and quicker than correcting it during production. In the media industry this is understood very well. There are three stages of production: pre-production, production and post-production.

The production stage is the most expensive of these. It involves filming, the presence of paid talent and the occupation of expensive spaces such as studios or hired locations. Part of the purpose of pre-production is to reduce the time and costs of production. In other words, preparation can ensure that the time needed to make a video product is as short as possible. Planning ahead can also reduce the time spent editing, which will also reduce costs.

Generating ideas

Pre-production begins with various processes to generate, evaluate and decide upon the ideas forming the project. It is nearly always better to generate ideas separately before evaluating them and making decisions. You should record all ideas you can think up, regardless of merit or practicality. Brainstorming sessions can work well and sometimes ideas which at first seem ridiculous can contain the seeds of something very promising. Suggestions can often be combined to make even better ideas.

Here are some ways of building your own personal creativity and generating ideas:

i) Build up possibilities based on 'what-ifs'. These might generate interesting ways of transforming existing stories or texts. For example, 'What if Cinderella were a prostitute?' generated the plot of the film ***Pretty Woman*** (USA 1990).
ii) Open up your senses, particularly your eyes and ears. Film director Ridley Scott was familiar with the huge chemical works on Teesside from his art college days and they inspired his design for the decaying metropolis in *Blade Runner* (USA 1982).
Dialogue can be inspired by things overheard. The writer Alan Bennett says he often incorporates into his dialogue things overheard on buses. What sights and sounds are prominent in your memory, imagination and life?

iii) Keep a notebook by your bed. The advice 'sleep on it' is good advice where generating ideas is concerned. Ideas often come to you when you wake or even while dreaming or only half awake. However, much is forgotten if you do not write the ideas down while they are still vivid in your mind.
iv) Keep a scrapbook of unusual or thought-provoking newspaper stories or pictures.
v) Look to other people for ideas. Many a production idea has come from the experiences of the families and friends of those who work in the media. Topics of conversation, 'true stories' and urban legends can all provide the basis for investigative items or fiction narratives.

Making decisions and commissioning a product

When you come to the stage of evaluating ideas and making decisions it is important to record your decisions in a written document. Groups may need a formal meeting with a chairperson, secretary and a formal record of the meeting in the form of a circulated agenda and follow-up minutes. More individual work can be supported with a diary which can be drawn on in your final log.

Factors to consider in making decisions include:

- the limitations you are working under, particularly the directions of the exam or coursework specifications;
- the needs and accessibility of the target audience;
- the available resources;
- the budget needed;
- deadlines for completion;
- research needed.

You need to think about a real or realistic production context for what it is you want to make. Seek guidance from your teachers and the exam specification as to how 'real' the distribution of your product needs to be. The best productions often have a real production context and meet a real need.

Can you find someone to 'commission' the product? There are often opportunities in schools or colleges to plan and make video products for which there is a real need. Reflect on these issues in your log.

Production roles

If the production is for your own coursework, you will have to play the lead role in the production. In this sense you must be producer, director and writer of what is called an 'auteur' product. It is also just about possible to be your own camera operator, lighting technician, sound assistant, continuity assistant and editor. However, video productions are usually the product of group work. You are likely to need the help of others and if you enlist such help you must record honestly what they do.

Will you need to cast actors or talent to be filmed? If you do, you need to make it clear to them exactly what they have to do and what their responsibilities are. All these decisions should be recorded in your log. You may even wish to draw up 'contracts'.

Brief/treatment/script

A working plan or summary of the video product and what it will contain is known as a brief or treatment. Both are written under headings and include indications such as title, audience, genre, storyline, etc. Some producers see a brief as more concerned with strategies to make the best product, whereas they see a treatment as more concerned with subject matter and storyline.

It is a good idea to get hold of a script related to the style you wish to achieve. You can place a copy of this script with your research to act as a guide to the script conventions which you are guided by or following.

Some film and video products, such as dramatic fiction, are fully scripted, while factual based or reality TV products are part-scripted. Even live or spontaneous programmes have pre-planned shots and there are scripted introductions, questions and prompts.

Planning the shots

Once you have a script you need to begin planning the shots you will use. You will find further information about shot possibilities in the production section. It is a very good idea in the first instance to simply consider what shots will be effective without necessarily doing this in order. If your production is using a studio set you will need a ***set design and floor plan***. The positioning of your cameras on the floor plan will help you plan your shots. The floor plan shows where you will position scenery, furniture, some lighting and the cameras. The design shows what the set will look like when it is on screen.

For location shooting you need to organise a ***reconnaissance*** or 'recce'. You might need written permission to use some locations. Any filming in public places needs clearance from the police. You should take still pictures of your location from different angles to help you plan your shots. You should visit more than one location and explain in your log why you preferred one rather than another. Think about all the possible things which could go wrong and try to eliminate as many of them as possible.

You need to make a *final shot list*. This means that you should write down and number each shot you plan to take in the order you plan to take them. You might also have a shot list for the way they will be arranged in your final video.

Activity

Pre-production exercise

Produce a brief and a storyboard for a TV advertisement promoting a public service or public information campaign.

The brief should include: title, a description of the target audience and the creative purpose of the advert. The storyboard should have 15 to 20 shots with at least one close-up, medium and long shot. It should include sound as well as visuals. Display these materials and gain and record feedback from a sample target audience. Explain what improvements and changes you need to make.

(5)

SAMPLE SCRIPT LAY-OUT

NB: INT = Interior
L.S. = Long Shot
B.P. = Back Projection

31. INT OLD PEOPLE'S CLUB DAY
(THIS IS A LARGE ROOM WITH SEVERAL TABLES PILED HIGH WITH ARTICLES. CARDBOARD BOXES, PAINTINGS ETC. WITH OLD AGE PENSIONERS WORKING AT THEM

THE PRINCIPAL, MRS WEATHERBY, A HANDSOMEWOMAN OF FORTY-FIVE, IS CONDUCTING THE NEW-COMERS ROUND. SHE PUSHES MRS. HALLIDAY BESIDE A SHARP-FEATURED SMALL WOMAN

MRS. WEATHERBY: This lady is making cardboard boxes. Mrs. Williamson, show Mrs. Halliday how you do them.

MRS. HALLIDAY: We've met.

(PAN WITH MRS. WEATHERBY AS SHE GOES OVER TO GRAN AND TAKES HER ARM, LOOKING FOR SUITABLE INSTRUCTION.

SHE REACHES A ROBUST LATE-SIXTIES HANDSOME MAN, NAMED MARSHALL, SMARTLY DRESSED, SMOKING A CIGAR, ENGAGED IN A LOVE/HATE RELATIONSHIP WITH A BASKET OF RAFIA WORK.)

GRAN: Please! Do carry on (POINTS TO BASKET)

MARSHALL: I was afraid you'd say that.

GRAN: Of course, if you have a car, and plenty of spare time, you could be doing more important things.

MIX TELECINE

L.S. of an open old Rolls speeding through the country-side with four people in it: MARSHALL, GRAN, MRS. HALLIDAY AND O'MALLEY

END TELECINE

32. INT CAR. DAY (B.P.)
(MARSHALL IS ON HIS FAVOURITE THEME, BUT NO ONE IS LISTENING. THEY ARE ALL ENJOYING THE COUNTRYSIDE.)

MARSHALL: We're cluttering up the earth. Ought to be done away with, everybody over sixty.

(Sound dubbed: Car skidding)

MARSHALL'S EYES NEARLY POP OUT OF HIS HEAD, AS HE SWERVES LEFT AND RIGHT)

The Idiot! He nearly killed me!

Activity

Find a person or organisation in your educational setting or local community who would be prepared to commission a short video film.

Research audience, need, resources, limitations, etc. Produce pre-production materials (brief/treatment/script, etc.) to meet the need. Gain feedback from your commissioner on the suitability of what you have prepared.

Production

You will need to establish a certain working routine and discipline. The ***clapperboard*** is a serious piece of equipment. The start of filming needs to be counted down and the end formally announced. Silence amongst workers whilst filming is an absolute requirement. The last thing you want is a take spoiled by someone chatting in the background.

Organise ***rehearsals*** or 'dry runs'. These should be a practice for both actors and technical personnel. Check out lighting, sound levels and possible sources of interruptions. You would not normally want a bell to ring while you are filming, for instance.

One thing you can do to support the smooth running of the production stage is to make a written plan for each time you film. This should detail what ***props and equipment*** you need, and when and where everyone needs to be.

Many student productions rely on the sound level recorded simultaneously with the video. This is acceptable at the level required for this course. It is also useful, however, to record and dub on other sound for editing purposes. If a sound effect is important you may want to exaggerate it or achieve more clarity. ***Sound effects*** can be recorded in house or 'found'. Many public libraries still have access to sound effect recordings released by organisations like the BBC. The internet can also be a source for sound effects: for instance, try www.a1freesoundeffects.com or www.stonewashed.net/sfx

Continuity

You should think about continuity when planning, filming and editing. What is in the shot should maintain consistency of position and appearance so that the world of the film follows the continuity of the real world. For example, if a man in a scene has a pen in his breast pocket, this should not move or disappear without reason in a subsequent shot. If you film a medium shot of a woman picking up a telephone and then take a close-up of the same action, make sure she uses the same hand.

According to www.moviemistakes.com ***Lord of the Rings: The Fellowship of the Ring*** is crammed with continuity errors. For example, Elrond has eyebrows which mysteriously change shape through the film.

Post-production

Editing

Digital editing using editing software on a computer will make your task much easier, but whatever equipment you are using, make sure you can operate it reasonably well before you start editing.

Editing skills involve being able to:

- change the order of your filmed clips
- crop and/or split clips
- use transitions such as dissolves and fades
- add titles and credits
- add recorded music from an audio CD
- add sound effects
- record and add a voice-over
- adjust the volume of added sound
- crop, cut and paste audio clips.

Before you start to edit you should note down the contents of all your clips. On your list each clip should be given a number and any comments about quality or relevance. Then you should do a *paper edit*. This should indicate which clips will be used in which order and what audio should go with each one.

You have some freedom when you are making a product for coursework since you are practising skills and not making a commercial profit. If you did publish or distribute your work in any commercial form you would become liable for royalty payments for anyone else's work you 'borrow' from. You may need to add recorded music from an audio CD. If you do so you should make it clear in your production log that you are aware that you are liable for royalties should your production be commercially distributed. You may be able to produce your own music or download royalty-free music from the internet to get round this point.

If you have time you may want to create a so-called ***assembly edit*** or 'rough cut' which simply establishes the order and content of the video before you produce the final edit.

Evaluation

You need to make an ***evaluation*** of your final product. This should include how you decided on your target audience and how successfully your film interested them. It should also include a description of the genre conventions you used and the narrative techniques employed. Say how successful the filming and editing were, and how they could be improved.

Activity

Produce the opening of a thriller

1 Pre-production

Research thriller openings to identify the conventions of the genre.

Identify those techniques and conventions which you could realistically use in your own production.

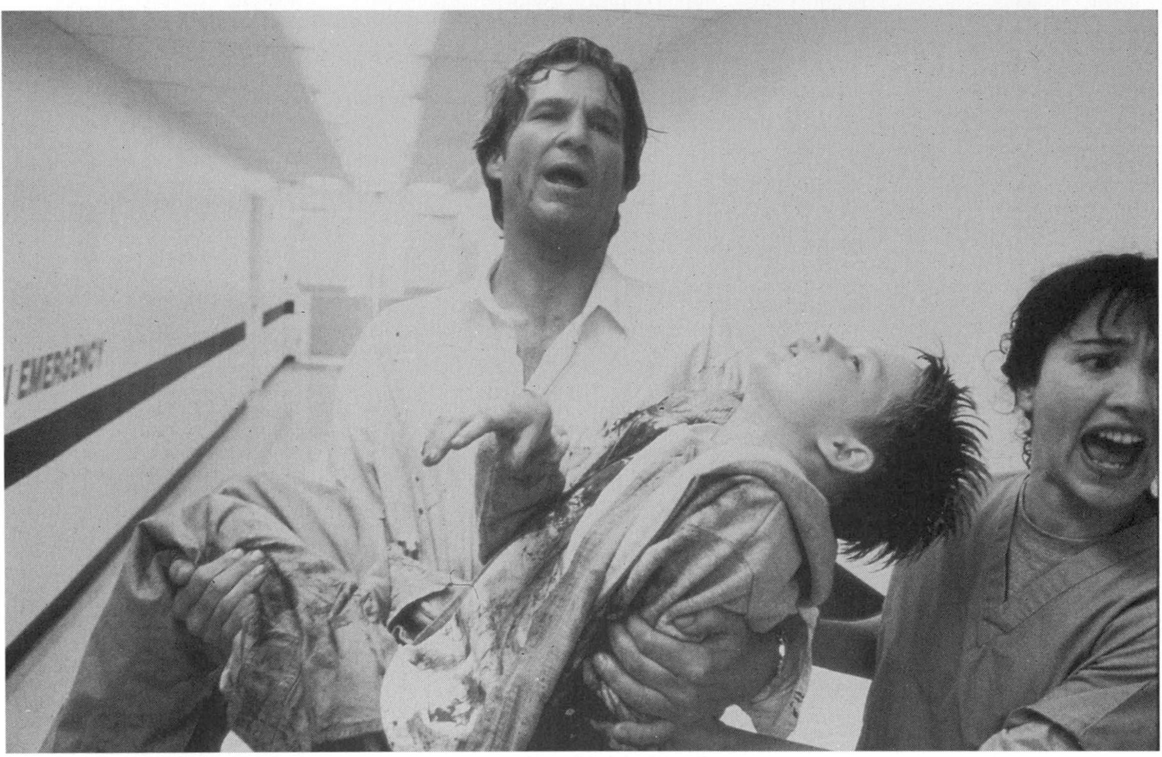

Michael Farraday (Jeff Bridges) rushes the injured boy to hospital near the beginning of *Arlington Road*

For instance, look at the opening of the thriller *Arlington Road* (USA/UK 1998). The film begins with a badly injured boy stumbling along an American suburban street. The sequence has an interesting mixture of shot types, with long shots of the boy from different viewpoints, close-ups and extreme close-ups of the boy, and point of view shots showing the boy's perspective and the view of the man who tries to rescue him. The sequence also uses blurred focus to both imitate the boy's confusion and to keep the viewer in suspense. Tension is heightened by the appearance of drops of blood on the boy's trainers as he walks erratically along the road. There are muffled voice-overs and simple musical effects (xylophone and drums) on the soundtrack which add to the tension.

Research different *types of thriller* and *specify which subcategory* you would like to produce:

- police thriller: e.g. *Fargo* (USA 1995)
- film noir: e.g. *Double Indemnity* (USA 1944)
- science fiction thriller: e.g. *Blade Runner* (USA 1982)
- horror: e.g. *Halloween* (USA 1978)
- heists: e.g. *The Usual Suspects* (USA 1995)
- gangsters: e.g. *The Untouchables* (USA 1987)
- detective: e.g. *The Pledge* (USA 2001)
- spy: e.g. *From Russia With Love* (UK 1963)

Describe your *target audience*: age, gender, cinema/film experience, interests. Research your target audience's expectations by forming a small focus group made up of a cross-section of your target audience. Ask them to talk about what makes a good opening to a thriller. Ask them to give specific examples from films they know well. Record the discussion and summarise the main points you learn from it.

Establish a setting

For the purposes of your production you will want a setting which does not require too much work in terms of design and props. Is there a promising location on or near the site where you are working and which can be 'roped off' for filming? Little-used areas often have a lot of possibilities. Explain in your log why you have selected it. There will be practical reasons as well as aesthetic ones. Check to see if you need permission to film in any of your chosen locations.

Define the purpose of your opening sequence

This requires some knowledge of genre characteristics and narrative techniques.

You might consider:

i) *Hooking the audience*. The attention of the audience is gripped by posing a mystery which often involves a criminal activity.

The opening of *The Usual Suspects*, for instance, has an injured man lying on the deck of a ship with fires burning all around him. Spilled fuel covers the ground. He lights a cigarette and then deliberately sets fire to the fuel, intending to cause a fatal explosion. However, a stranger, who is kept in the shadows, extinguishes the flame and approaches the injured man. It appears they know each other. The stranger shoots the injured man and then reignites the fuel before escaping. A caption tells us that all this happened 'yesterday'.

ii) *Introducing characters*. As well as having a dramatic criminal act plus a mystery, this opening has also introduced two important characters who feature prominently in the narrative, which is essentially a flashback explaining what led to the execution and the explosion on the ship.

Establishing a significant place

Creating a mood or atmosphere by using lighting, colour, costume and objects effectively. (These, together with setting, are termed '*mise en scène*'.)

Write a treatment

This should include a brief description of the genre you are producing and an explanation of the narrative purposes of your opening.

Write a storyboard

The storyboard should describe in pictures and words what each separate camera shot will show and what sounds will be heard.

Write a script

This should be useful for both actors and technical staff such as camera operators.

Choose your actors

Again you should be able to explain your choices with a mixture of practical ('he was the only person who volunteered') and aesthetic ('he had those menacing eyes which would make the audience uneasy and fearful') reasons.

Design costumes

The costumes should suit both the character and the atmosphere of the sequence. In your production log explain the thinking behind your design.

2 Production and post-production

Film your sequence. Make several takes so that you have a choice of material at the editing stage.

Edit your material following the advice given above.

Technical checklist

Here are the skills that examiners are looking for in a video production.

Be able to:

- hold a shot steady;
- frame a shot, including and excluding elements as appropriate;
- use a variety of shot distances as appropriate;
- shoot material that is relevant to the task set;
- select *mise en scène* which are appropriate to the task;
- edit so that the viewer can understand the meaning of the video;
- use a variety of shot transitions and captions appropriately;
- edit to combine sound and images appropriately.

Glossary

Aesthetic

Relating to what is artistic. Pleasing to the sense of beauty. For example you will need to refer to aesthetic choices in your account of production decisions.

Auteur

An auteur is an individual who has the main claim to the authorship of a media product. That is, they have made the most important creative decisions and input. An auteur product is a production which shows such impact of an individual, such as a director, on its style and achievement.

Brief

A document which gives the requirements of a production under headings such as audience, purpose, limitations, etc.

Call sheet

A schedule of instructions and information circulated in advance of each production period. It details when crew, talent and props are needed and where.

Crop

To edit a picture by cutting out part of the shot, or eliminating elements from a shot. Digital manipulation of images makes this easy.

Cutaway

A shot, short in length, which can break or increase the pace of the main sequence. For example, shots of significant items in a person's room or workplace can be edited into conversations or interviews.

Dissolve

A mix or transition where one image gradually disappears and merges with another which replaces it.

Dry run

A practice film shoot. The term derives from the idea that this practice run may include everything required for filming and production except that the tape or film does not record.

Establishing shot

Usually the first shot in a sequence to establish a setting.

Fade

A gradual reduction or increase of a visual image or audio signal.

Filter

Glass or gel placed before or behind a camera lens to change the effect of lighting within the frame.

Frame

This refers either to an individual picture image or the rectangular limits of the shot.

Log

An account of a production from pre-production to final audience feedback.

Pan

The swivelling of a camera on the horizontal axis, i.e. left or right.

Rushes

Film or tape shot during production, i.e. in its raw state before post-production.

Shooting script

A script of dialogue, words and visuals with all the shots required for each scene.

Shot list

A list of each individual shot in the sequence in which they will be recorded on set or location.

Still

A photograph or picture which does not 'move'. May be edited into a film or video.

Tilt

The movement or rotation of a camera in the vertical axis, i.e. up or down.

Timecode

Numbers recorded on tape indicating hour, minute, second.

Tracking shot

A smooth camera movement where the camera moves along a line or track.

Treatment

A summary or synopsis of the content of a production.

Wipe

An editing transition in which the new image appears to push the preceding one off the screen.

Wide angle

A shot that takes in a point of view of 60° or greater.

Zoom

An effect available on the camera which, from the viewer's point of view, appears to move in or away from the object of the shot.

SECTION C **Chapter 16**

Advertising campaigns

INTRODUCTION

This chapter shows you how to plan and produce an advertising campaign for a charity. It has a case study of a professional campaign aimed at introducing new adult literacy packs and suggests how you can apply the same methods to your own work.

Researching advertising

If possible you should find out about the thinking behind an actual advertising campaign. If you have links with a local advertising agency you may be able to meet professionals who can talk you through a campaign. If not, you could find extracts from a series of books called *Advertising Works* (NCT Publications) helpful. The books give detailed analyses of successful advertising campaigns, but they are expensive to buy.

CASE STUDY CASE STUDY CASE STUDY CASE STUDY CASE STUDY CASE STU

Case study: adult literacy

Advertising Works 9 describes the BBC's campaign to introduce a new *adult literacy pack*. It provides an excellent model which you can adapt for your own production.

1 IDENTIFY THE CHALLENGE

In this case it was to persuade parents with literacy needs to apply for a free learning pack. This sounds simple but there were problems. *Audience research* showed that there is a stigma attached to illiteracy and people feel ashamed to admit they have problems. To seek help is potentially shaming and people devise ways of concealing their problems.

Shock tactics in these circumstances would be likely to fail. The advertisers also believed that simply to reason its target audience into responding would not work, as the people concerned had probably spent many years ignoring information about how to tackle their literacy problems.

2 DEVISE THE STRATEGY

The advertisers decided to use *emotional* rather than rational appeals by.

CASE STUDY CASE STUDY CASE STUDY CASE STUDY CASE STUDY CASE STUDY CASE STUDY

- using parents' protective attitude to their children;
- dramatising real-life problems;
- using a direct tone in a plain and unpitying manner.

3 DEVELOP THE CREATIVE SOLUTION

They devised four different situations for mini-plays to achieve empathy with as many people as possible:

- In *Wendy,* a child talks aloud to her doll, finding reasons not to read to it: 'Sorry darling I can't read to you now I'm busy', obviously mimicking her mother.
- In *Jack,* a small boy lies in bed listening to his dad give repeated readings of a story he has learned by heart and asks, 'Daddy, can't you read any other stories?'
- In *Imagine,* the problems of a girl who cannot read are depicted throughout her life. In the penultimate frame a mother holds her baby adoringly and the voice-over says, 'She may have your eyes and mouth but she needn't have the problems you had getting someone to help you read.'

The creative solution depended on parents' feelings and hopes for their children being stronger than parents' own shame at their literacy problems.

4 DECIDE WHICH MEDIA TO USE

The advertisers ruled out print campaigns for obvious reasons and chose television because it is a medium that the target audience feels comfortable with and is ideally suited to emotion-based communication.

Activity

Devise a campaign for a charity using the following advice and the material provided or else similar material from the charity concerned.

- Research the charity itself. If you choose one which has a website you can use the internet to collect useful information such as this from the RSPCA.

ACTION FOR ANIMALS

There are now 328 uniformed RSPCA inspectors and 146 Animal Collection Officers (ACOs) in England and Wales working tirelessly for animals in distress. In 2001 inspectors investigated 123,156 animal cruelty complaints which resulted in 2,449 convictions.

PREVENTING ABUSE

The courts are a last resort for inspectors, who prefer to educate rather than prosecute. They watch the treatment of animals in transit, in markets, pet shops, boarding kennels and farms and offer help and advice about their care.

CRUELTY CASEBOOK

Every 20 seconds someone somewhere in England and Wales dials 0870 55 55 999 – the RSPCA's national cruelty and advice line – for help. In 2001 the RSPCA undertook 8,264 inspections, and removed 184,706 animals from danger or abuse. Inspectors and ACOs are also an emergency service for injured, trapped, or stranded animals and in 2001 they carried out 11,947 rescues.

ANIMAL CARE

The RSPCA rehomed 90,689 animals in 2001 – mostly through the Society's network of 183 branches. Branches are separately registered charities operating subject to RSPCA and branch rules. They work for animal welfare locally and many provide services including subsidized veterinary treatment for those in need, neutering and rehoming schemes. Together, branches are responsible for 40 branch-run clinics, 37 animal centres and ten animal welfare centres.

The RSPCA (National Society) is responsible for four animal hospitals, three specialist wildlife hospitals, one wildlife rehabilitation unit, 13 animal centres and five clinics throughout England and Wales.

ALL ANIMALS

The RSPCA's influence covers the whole range of animal protection. The Society is involved in practical welfare and law enforcement as well as high-profile campaigning and education. It employs veterinary experts and consultants in the care and treatment of farm livestock, wildlife, domestic pets and animals used in research.

PUBLIC EYE

RSPCA advertising campaigns, television exposure, direct mail fundraising, promotional videos, magazines, booklets, leaflets and posters keep the Society at the forefront of public awareness about animal welfare.

- You can find information from the website about particular campaigns which you can use when you design your own version. Here is an example about pig welfare.

CAMPAIGNS – PIG WELFARE

Millions of pigs across the European Union (EU) live in conditions that cause severe stress and suffering. The RSPCA is pushing for change.

Pigs are social, highly intelligent, inquisitive animals. But EU law allows many different systems for keeping pigs – most offer just a barren, crowded environment with no bedding for comfort or recreation.

Most sows in the EU are forced to live on concrete or slatted floors, in stalls too narrow for them to turn around throughout their four-month pregnancies. Sometimes they are tethered to the floor by a short chain. The use of stalls and tethers, both now banned in the UK since 1999, causes severe welfare and health problems. Tethering, but not stalls, will be banned in Europe from 2005.

CONFINING CRATES

The RSPCA wants the use of conventional farrowing crate systems phased out. Modern, farmed sows have at least two litters a year of up to 14 piglets each. Most indoor sows give birth in farrowing crates that aim to protect piglets from crushing but that also stop the sow turning around and nest-building.

Alternative farrowing systems for indoor sows are already used in several EU countries. These may confine sows for just a few days around farrowing, or give them complete freedom throughout.

CONSUMER POWER

If compulsory labelling is introduced, consumers can buy pork products knowing the animals have been reared to certain standards. The RSPCA has its own farm animal welfare food labelling scheme – Freedom Food.

An EU Directive lays down minimum standards for the protection of farmed pigs. Some member states, including the UK, already surpass them in certain areas. But the laws of many EU countries merely implement the minimum requirements.

RSPCA POSITION

The European Commission proposed changes to the Directive early in 2001. The RSPCA called for:

a ban on sow stalls and conventional farrowing crates, except for the first few days
the provision of bedding/rooting material at all stages of production
sufficient space for pigs and a ban on fully slatted floors
a ban on castration and on the routine use of other painful practices, except on veterinary advice
trained and competent pig stock-keepers
clear and informative labelling.

- Study examples of *campaigning* advertising. The RSPCA site has examples such as these:

The text reads:

A voluntary ban on animal testing for cosmetics was introduced in the UK in 1998. But elsewhere, it's a different story. In the rest of Europe it's still perfectly OK to squirt chemicals into a rabbit's eye in the quest for a new hair dye. Around 38,000 animals suffer in tests every year in the EU. And there's no good reason why a single one of them should be harmed – more than 8,000 safe ingredients already exist. Yet in their drive for profits, cosmetic companies continue to carry out these painful experiments.

The European Parliament has decided that the time has come to act. It recently voted in favour of new laws banning the sale of any new cosmetics that have been tested on animals....

If you want to stop animals suffering unnecessarily, please write supporting a sales ban.

- Decide who your *target market* consists of. If you were producing material for the RSPCA campaign above, who would be the most likely sorts of people to send letters of protest? You need to decide whether to aim at a particular age group or at as big an age range as possible. It might be possible to find out whether men or women are more likely to support animal welfare causes. Will there be any difference in attitudes between people who use and don't use hair dye? Will there be any difference between urban dwellers and people who live in the country? Should you target people who have time to write letters?

- Identify the *challenge*.

If you are designing a campaign, your challenge will probably be about one or more of these:

raising funds
changing attitudes
getting people to do something
or making people aware of a problem.

- Research your target market. Find out what makes people more likely to support a particular cause. How do they respond to being shocked? How do they react to pictures of suffering? Are they influenced by facts and figures or is it more a question of being emotionally affected?

You can use examples of campaigning images which have already been used to find out people's reactions to them. You can ask people about when they have actually contributed to charities or taken some action to support a cause and find out what influenced them.

- Devise your *creative solution*.

This means designing your adverts, deciding what form they will take, what images and messages they will communicate.

Think in terms of changing people's attitudes and actions. You should base your creative solution on the results of your target market research.

- Decide which *media* you will use for your campaign. Remember that, though television appeals to mass audiences, it is also the most expensive medium to use. It is advisable to use at least two sorts of media. Choose from:

  television (say which programmes, e.g. if you are aiming at a youthful audience you could advertise during a popular soap opera);
  newspapers (national, regional, local);
  magazines (say which type, e.g. women's, particular hobbies);
  radio (say which types of programme on which radio stations, e.g. early morning pop music on Kiss FM);
  billboards (say where, e.g. busy roundabouts, near nightclubs).

- Plan the *timing* of your campaign.

All campaigns have to be scheduled. Sometimes this means a burst of advertising over a short space of time. This would apply to a campaign such as warning of the effects of drink-driving at Christmas or a response to an urgent crisis. Sometimes it is better to be less intensive but spread the advertising over a longer period. Sometimes advertisers will use a quick TV campaign for maximum effect and then a longer term and cheaper print-based campaign to remind people about the initial message.

- Prepare some *sample advertising materials* to show the charity what your advertising will look like. For example:

  a storyboard of about fifteen to twenty frames for a 30-second TV advert
  a sketch of a full-page magazine advert
  a script for a 60-second radio advert
  a mock-up of a brochure
  a sketch for a billboard poster.

- Produce a series of *print advertisements* for a charity to include advertisements for magazines and/or newspapers, billboards and flyers/brochures.

- Write an *evaluation* of your campaign. Explain your reasoning for making decisions and choices in your planning. Explain the problems you encountered during the production of your materials and how you tried to solve them. Test your final products on a small focus group to see what effects they have.

Print products

Introduction

This chapter takes you through all the steps you need to take to produce newspaper pages. It shows you how to plan the content and find ideas for your stories. It explains how to write the stories in a journalistic format and how to design newspaper pages. There is advice about how to take good photographs and how to produce magazine covers.

Newspaper pages

Decide who you are producing your newspaper pages for. Describe this ***target audience*** in terms of age, gender, geography, lifestyles and interests. When you have decided who you are trying to communicate with, interview a cross-section of such people to find out what they want to read about and make notes or keep recordings of this.

Plan the content

You should decide from the outset the range of material that you want to produce.

Your choices will include:

- feature articles
- photographs
- cartoons
- graphics
- on-page activity (e.g. crosswords)
- comment or opinion
- letters
- gossip
- reviews
- competitions
- advertising.

Finding ideas for feature articles

Feature articles in newspapers are the stories that fill in the background to hard news stories. A hard news story is, for example, a report about the verdict in a trial, while a feature article would be one which explained the background to the court case.

Here are some ideas for feature articles.

- 'How to' articles
  These fall into three categories:
  how to deal with practical problems such as choosing a career or university or managing on a tight budget or keeping fit;
  how to make things;
  how to deal with social or psychological problems such as making and breaking relationships.
- Personal experience
  These could be your own – 'How I survived a disastrous holiday' – or someone else's, such as two contrasting accounts from people who attended a demonstration.
- Consumer surveys
  Find out things such as where to buy the best sandwiches in town, which are the best activity holidays, where is the best 'night out' for a particular age group. These surveys can be based on your own or other people's opinions.
- Achievements
  Think about different types such as sporting, intellectual or overcoming misfortune. Be on the lookout for achievers and let them tell you their stories.
- Changes
  Take notice of things which are changing in your locality. Find out why and interview people about their opinions.
- Moans
  Listen to what your contemporaries are moaning about and find out if something can be done to solve their problems.

Writing the articles

Find out how much space there is for your articles. This means knowing how many words to write, so that you don't waste space or have to pad your work.

Decide what the main purpose of each story is. Write this down in one sentence and keep referring to it so that you stick to the point.

Structure

Pay special attention to the ***opening paragraphs*** – these are important for grabbing the attention of the reader. Good opening paragraphs should make the reader want to know more. They should be short and snappy and get straight to the point. Some editors insist on opening paragraphs having no more than 25 words.

Study newspapers for examples of snappy openings, like these taken from the *Daily Mail*:

> 'Mobile phone giants are to be ordered to end a 'scandalous' call charge rip-off.'

'Britain was battling last night to save the traditional fish-and-chips supper from oblivion.' (A story about fishing quotas in the North Sea.)
'Yoko Ono's battling to stop Sir Paul McCartney putting his name before John Lennon's on some Beatles' song credits.'
'For 27 years John Allen believed he had got away with murdering his wife and two children.'

- Place the events or the information in ***order of importance***. This convention has developed because readers do not always finish a story, they tend to skim read newspapers.
- *Answer the five w's* – who, where, what, why and when.

Here is a standard newspaper story from the ***Daily Mail*** (17/12/02 page 30, reproduced with permission).

Why I lopped off Thatcher's head

A protester 'decapitated' an 8 ft marble statue of Baroness Thatcher because he felt it represented the ills of the world's political system, a court heard yesterday.

Paul Kelleher, 37, took a cricket bat into London's Guildhall in July and struck the £150,000 statue. But it made no impact so he picked up a metal stanchion that was part of a rope barrier.

Using this pole he 'lopped off' the head of the statue, he told Southwark Crown Court.

Kelleher of Isleworth, West London, who is representing himself, denies one charge of damaging property. He told the jury: 'The prosecution will attempt to convince you that my actions amount to criminal damage whereas my defence will centre around artistic expression.'

The trial was adjourned until today.

(Kelleher was sent to prison for this offence in February 2003.)

You can easily identify the five w's:

Who? – Paul Kelleher
What did he do? – chopped off the head of Mrs Thatcher's statue.
Why? – because she represented the ills of the world's political system.
When? – in July.
Where? – in London's Guildhall.
What was the outcome? – he appeared in court.

Style

If you are aiming at a tabloid style of writing you should:

- be concise
- use short words and short sentences
- use adjectives and adverbs sparingly

- use ordinary, everyday language rather than a literary style
- include lots of direct speech
- go for vivid headlines
- use lots of pictures.

Page planning

You should make a ***rough plan*** of your pages. This should indicate how many columns there are, the positioning and size of illustrations, headlines, adverts and copy (the text). It is much less onerous to work this way rather than produce lots of material and then try to make it fit the page.

Your page plan should look something like these.

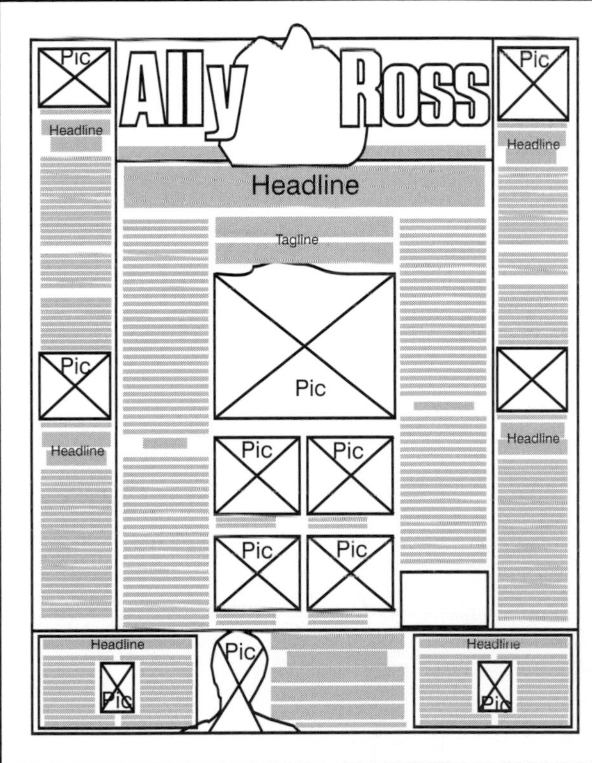

(a) plan

NEWS OF THE WORLD, November 10, 2002 35

Ally Ross

BRITAIN'S No 1 COUCH POTATO

JAMIE: Looking vagrant

TWIST ON OLIVER

WHOLE point of Jamie's Kitchen (working title—If You Can't Stand the P***k, Get Out of the Kitchen) is to take unemployed vagrants and turn them into the next Jamie Oliver.

Which is all very worthy and blah blah blah.

But I can't help thinking it would make much better TV if we took Jamie Oliver and turned him into an unemployed vagrant.

UPMARKET TV station Channel 5 this week asked the question—Was Hitler Gay? Answer—No.

But he did once lift a lot of Brown Shirts.

IN this week of remembrance ITV and Channel 4 both chose to forget, while Channel 5's Hitler Revealed documentary claimed the atmosphere in the first world war trenches was "homoerotic". What contemptible little TV stations.

PYJAMA GIRL: Ulrika

ULRIKA'S QUICKIE

IN a change to our scheduled programme, Ulrika's slot is now filled by gardeners (painters and decorators, wait your turn).

Mr Right—henceforth to be known as Mr Right-Off—is that rare TV beast. A programme so bad, it's only redeeming feature is the producer's name, Tim Quickie.

Which is about the best thing Lance the Boil can hope to get from the assorted potential stalkers left on the ITV dating show.

Beats the hell out of me why ITV don't cut to the chase and declare Jeannie the winner.

Meanwhile, if the show gets any later we may yet see Ulrika Jonsson in pyjamas. A genuine first. And not just for TV.

Give me a break

WITH the glorious exceptions of The Office and Jonathan Ross this week's TV was rubbish, so I've decided to review the adverts.

Why? . . . because you're worth it.

And it's also been clinically proven that eight out of ten TV viewers will spend two years of their life watching commercials, 97 per cent of which will be better than anything that's been on ITV since August, 1981.

Made up statistics? Yes. But this is ad-land we're talking about and I love it.

All time favourites? Steve Davis's epic delivery of "Nescafe's. The one to pot." And Captain Birdseye's unsettling claim that: "Mums will love my crumbly cod wedge."

Liking adverts shouldn't, of course, be confused with thinking they're good and anyone who wants to inflict this madness on the BBC clearly doesn't use Fructis shampoo, which nourishes every inch of your scalp.

Boycott

Those many prime time ads currently prompting a lifelong boycott of their products include: The Nike jogging couple, who'd only be funny if the punchline involved them getting mown down by a charabanc full of Cambodian sweatshop workers. Lacoste's a*se man. The Welch Grape Juice family. And: "Hands up who's got the new Heat?"

Right, no one except the lonely old boiler in accounts then?

Others, however, are minor works of art. With easily the best of the current bunch being the nostril-flaring, elephant-crushing, Bangra-driven, Peugeot 206 masterpiece.

Castlemaine and Guinness also deliver, while on an erotic level manufacturers of shower gel and all bathroom-related gunk should be applauded for their quality turnover in naked female bottoms. But real adver-

ADVERTS ARE BEST THING ON THE BOX

BILLY CONNOLLY: Billy, Billy, Billy. You sold your soul for fool's gold

MYLENE: Everything you want in an ad

SIR ALEX: Looking under the weather

RUBBER DUCK: Nude woman not pictured

LACOSTE MAN: For Graham Norton show

tising gold nearly always involves a celebrity. Almost inevitably, Peter Kay (John Smiths) has the funniest adverts on TV and it's nice also to see Richard E Grant finally reach his true acting potential with Argos.

But preferably the celebs will be slumming it.

And among those currently demeaning themselves for the corporate buck we have Billy Connolly (Lotto), Ian Macshane (L'Oreal anti-sagging cream), Pele (The Impotence Association) and Paul Merton (practically anything, even though English is only his 17th language).

Pity also poor Karl "Jacko off Brush Strokes" Howman, destined to spend the rest of his career cleaning bathrooms and Paul Kaye's descent into Woolworth's hell, which should prompt a reprise of Dennis Pennis's famous Steve Martin question.

"Paul–how come you're not funny any more?"

Wonderful

Best of the lot though is so perfectly awful, yet wonderful that I've either made it up or am watching too much Men and Motors.

Edge forward nervously please a now squint-less Mylene Klass, who reckons Maxivision's laser eye surgery was so good she was back singing again "WITHIN 24 HOURS".

Not actually a selling point. And the entire nation could have a claim here for medical negligence.

But it's everything I want from an advert. Cheap, amateurish and ruthlessly counter-productive.

In fact, it's made me laugh more than nearly anything else on TV this year and–as you can probably tell–helped remind me the new series of Alan Partridge really can't come quick enough.

TO TEA OR NOT TO TEA

Time to get up and make a nice cuppa

On no account must you leave the room

CLEESE: In his prime

KNOCKING FAWLTY

PEOPLE criticise BBC 1's comedy unit but I've just discovered their great new primetime Wednesday show –it's called "Fawlty Towers".

Set in the 1970's, the show's a dramatic return to form for Monty Python's John Cleese, who still looks barely a day over 40.

Well done BBC1 for investing in the comedy future.

RHONA Cameron says she'd "stop being gay for David Beckham." Funny, I think he'd start.

TV'S latest Manchester-based, average-fest is Stan the Man.

First Minder-lite episode promised slightly better things to come.

But if ITV are looking for a compelling drama with John Thomson, then why not just film his real life?

BRILLIANT: Office's Tim

IT'S VERY EYE-BROW

THE Office. Best comedy, best drama and best performance, from brilliant Martin Freeman as Tim, eyebrow twitching conscience of The Office.

Ironically, the show even had a perfect comedy quote to sum up its genius in an otherwise awful TV week. David Brent: "If you want the rainbow, you've got to put up with the rain.

"D'you know which philosopher said that?

"Dolly Parton. And people say she's just a big pair of t*ts."

TV'S "locking the stable door after the horse has bolted" award goes to Richard Madeley, for announcing he turned down Celebrity Big Brother because: "I don't want people to see me go insane on TV."

Sharon could try it with Jam

MAJOR error of judgement at the increasingly weird EastEnders, where Sharon, right, played The Jam's That's Entertainment before Tom's funeral, when the occasion really cried out for Going Underground. Let's just hope that when Sharon snuffs it someone has the good sense to play that other great Jam hit – The Bitterest Phil I Ever Had To . . .

Elsewhere, can anyone explain what happened to Paul's real dad and Anthony's fling with Kat?

IS MELANIE SYKES THE THICKEST WOMAN ON TV?

TO VOTE YES CALL: 09063 612 209

TO VOTE YES CALL: 09063 612 210

Rhona should get the bullet

WHILE Rhona Cameron, right, is hosting quiz shows canned laughter factories will never be short of orders.

The new project? Russian Roulette, "starring" Jono Coleman, Tara Palmer-Tomkinson and Dane Bowers, which could become the best quiz on TV . . . with just the simple introduction of a real revolver. Instead–big deal–the celebs end up flat on their backs on a mattress. Less a punishment, more a way of life for Tara.

(b) actual page

This is a plan for a ***single page***. It is symmetrical and busy, i.e. lots of different items presented in a balanced format.

The figure on the next page shows a plan for a ***double-page spread*** and the actual pages from the *News of the World*.

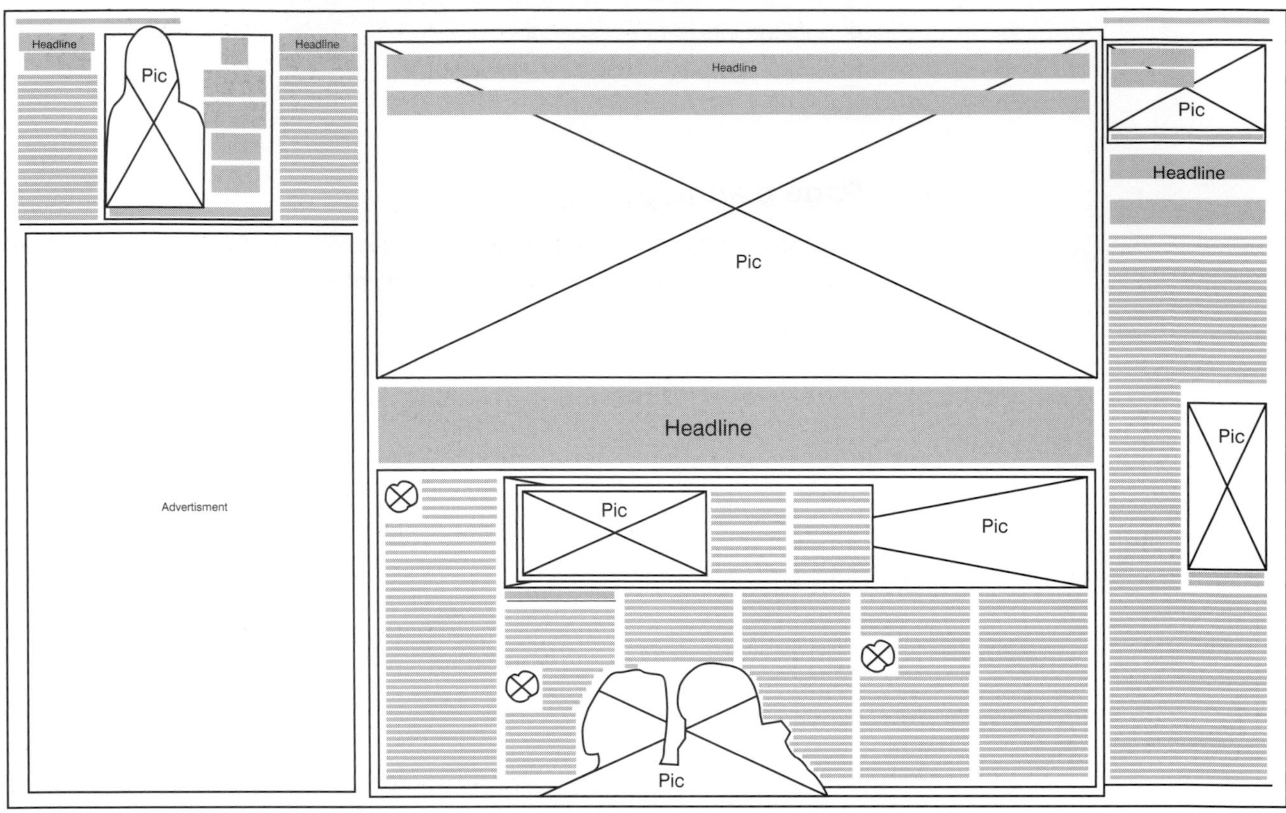

48 NEWS OF THE WORLD, November 10, 2002 2G

SPOOKY NOOKY

GHOSTHUNTERS in a haunted mill really did hear things go bump in the night—a bonking couple.

"We thought it was paranormal activity," said red-faced tour leader Derek Morgan. "I was so excited."

The amorous couple had slipped away from the 40-strong group as they toured the Houldsworth Mill in Stockport, Greater Manchester.

The 40-year-old woman, who was with her 27-year-old boyfriend, said: "It was so embarrassing. Suddenly all these torches flashed and there were 40 people watching."

2nd GLASS HONOURS

BARMY university bosses have been blasted for setting up a course to study BEER drinking.

Students enrolling for Bradford University's Drink and Society course will examine the history of booze across the country.

But Tory peer Lord Trefgarne told the House of Lords that the course was a waste of public money.

Education Minister Baroness Ashton confirmed the course would cost the Higher Education Funding Council about £5,700.

But she said it would also be funded from tuition fees from the 15 students expected to sign up for it.

NEWS OF THE WORLD, November 10, 2002 49

10 soldiers grin out from this photograph. Weeks later three were dead and two seriously wounded. At the going down of the sun and in the morning

We will remember them

HIS finger glides slowly across the grainy picture, trembling as it hovers over each smiling face. And he recites the soldiers' names like a prayer.

BY ALASTAIR McQUEEN

ORDER! ORDER!

Did heroes die in vain?

OUR political masters will line up in a rare show of unity this morning when they honour the glorious dead from two world wars at London's Cenotaph.

Messrs Blair, Duncan Smith and Kennedy should also be wearing white lilies next to their poppies to mourn the slow, inglorious death of the democracy all those heroes fought and died for.

IT'S ANOTHER WREATH, DEAR

Note how in both examples there is a ***lead picture*** and a ***lead story***. You should always try to draw the reader into your pages by making one headline and one picture more prominent than the rest. The picture acts as a 'centre of visual interest'.

Once you have done that, the other elements on the page can be arranged around them. The important thing to aim for is making it easy for the reader to know where to go to next. There should never be a big eye movement from the bottom of one column to the top of the next, for instance.

Typography

Choice of fonts

It is best to restrict the range of fonts. Too many different fonts (styles of print) can make the text look cluttered and confusing.

You should understand the difference between serif and non-serif fonts. Serif fonts have small terminal strokes at the end of the main stroke of a letter. These are missing in sans serif ('without serifs'). Commonly, but not always, newspapers use serif fonts for the main body of text and sans serifs for headlines. This is because the former are supposed to be easier on the eye, but the latter make more impact. A good choice for your paper to begin with would be Times for the body text and Helvetica for your headlines.

Size of the type

The size of the type is important. For the main text something between 9 and 12 point is comfortable for the reader. The choice will partly depend on the width of your columns. You should aim at an average of 6 to 8 words per column. Wide columns with lots of words can make reading very uncomfortable. Narrow columns with few words look silly.

Alignment

Most newsprint is justified. That is the lines of the text are of equal length. An unjustified or ragged right alignment can be used occasionally for variety, but is better suited to magazine rather than newspaper layout.

Taking and using photographs

- Get close to people you are photographing. Most ordinary snapshots are taken from too far away. Try to avoid 'firing squad shots' of people in groups staring straight at the camera.
- Take some close-ups and remember, you don't have to have people looking straight at the camera. More interesting shots can be of people looking slightly away from the camera in a three-quarter view.
- For more natural pictures, try to catch people when they are not aware of being photographed.

- Try to have the subject doing something relevant to the story.
- Give your page variety by including different shapes and sizes of picture.
- Make use of white space around illustrations. They do not have to be surrounded with text.
- Make sure the photograph has something to do with the story it accompanies.
- Try to pick pictures that have an impact, which make the reader take notice.
- Is the quality good enough? Don't use pictures that are out of focus, too light or too dark.
- Don't show people's backs unless there is a purpose to this.
- If you are taking pictures of a group, make a 'left to right', i.e. a list of people's names starting with the one on the left. This has to be done as soon as you have taken the photograph.

3G SL THE SUN, Tuesday, December 17, 2002 7

ONO YOU DON'T!

Yoko to sue as Macca axes Lennon song tag

Sir Paul . . . put name first *Yoko . . . called in lawyers* *Classic credit . . . Lennon*

By DOMINIC MOHAN

JOHN Lennon's furious widow Yoko Ono has called in lawyers after a new eruption in her feud with Sir Paul McCartney.

Yoko, 69, is livid that Macca has axed the famous "Lennon-McCartney" songwriting tag on 19 Beatles tracks on his new album.

Instead, credits on the live CD, Back in the U.S, read "Paul McCartney and John Lennon" – putting Macca first.

Petty

Yoko is so incensed she is investigating possible legal action against multi-millionaire Paul, 60.

Her lawyer Peter Shuka said: "The change is ridiculous, absurd and petty. This was done against her wishes.

"Paul and John made an agreement 40 years ago that they would share credit in this way. To change it now – well, John's not here to argue."

The change is said to be part of an on-going drive by Paul to take more glory for Beatles classics which were written by him. They include Yesterday, Hey Jude and The Long And Winding Road.

His spokesman Geoff Baker insisted: "This is not a divisive thing. It's not Lennon **OR** McCartney.

"Even if Paul did 95 per cent or more on these songs, he's not asking that John's name be taken off. He just doesn't think it should be first."

The row re-opens a long-running rift between Yoko and Paul. Since Lennon's death, Macca has become increasingly concerned about how his name will appear in the history books.

But Yoko recently told Rolling Stone magazine that she had warned Paul that if he changed the credits on some songs, people might think John wrote **ALL** the 200 or so other tracks.

She added: "I said, 'This is like opening a Pandora's box, Paul – don't do it.' I still stand by that statement."

Macca's album, released in America last month, is currently No16 in the US charts. It is thought to be due for release in Britain next year.

Nic's sleek-a-boob

SEXY Nicole Kidman works some black magic as she steps out in a daring low-cut outfit and sleek new hairdo.

Nicole, 35, was at the Big Apple premiere of her latest film The Hours — just days after appearing with curls and demure high collar at the Gangs of New York opening.

Waves goodbye . . star's old look

The *Sun* page 7 on 17/12/02

The figure above shows good use of a variety of close-ups with a lead picture and a lead story in a well-designed page from the *Sun* newspaper.

Checklist

Here is a checklist of what makes a good school/college newspaper:

- Have a balance of news, opinion, advice and entertainment.
- Write in a style and tone that suits the target audience.
- Be topical and local.
- Have some original research.
- Present different points of view.
- Have a variety of features, e.g. quizzes, cartoons, crosswords, letters.
- Have reports on school/college sports.
- Have good quality, original photographs and graphics.
- Write captions on all pictures.
- Have a clear, easy-to-read layout.
- Have eye-catching headlines.
- Check that spelling and punctuation are accurate. Always proofread at least twice, once for 'sense' and again for mistakes.

Newspaper design conventions

Page 11 from *Sun* 21/1/02

3G **Sun lands another big exclusive** THE SUN, Monday, January 21, 2002 11

I WAS GIANT FISH'S LUNCH

But monster spat me out, says diver

Once bitten . . . backpacker Andre has vowed he will never go diving near a giant grouper again

By DAVID MERTENS and FRANK THORNE

A BATTERED backpacker told last night how he ended up as LUNCH for a giant fish.

Andre Ronnlund, 24, said: "I thought I was going to die. I was hit from underneath and suddenly I was inside the mouth of this big fish."

Andre was diving on Australia's Great Barrier Reef when the 7ft grouper grabbed his head. But The Sun told last week how the monster, which weighed almost a ton, decided he tasted a bit fishy and spat him out.

Andre added: "At first I thought it was a shark. I didn't see it coming. I didn't know what hit me.

"I was as helpless as a prawn on the proverbial barbie and I thought, 'This is it.'

Grumpy

"I was stuck in its mouth and it was squeezing pretty hard. I felt the blood running down my neck and I couldn't move. I was in great pain, just waiting to die. Then I blacked out."

After the fish spat out Andre he regained consciousness and swam to the boat he and a pal had been diving from.

Andre, who comes from a small town in the north of Sweden, added: "My neck was bleeding, my cheeks were bruised and I was in shock. I will be diving again but I won't be going near any grouper fish."

The monster grouper has been nicknamed Grumpy by locals, who reckon it is about 80 years old.

Diving instructor Merv Ruggeri said: "Giant groupers have very powerful jaws. Grumpy could have crushed Andre's head like a soft peach and snapped his neck like a twig."

I gotta bite . . . Andre shows bruises on his neck

What a whopper . . . grouper just like Grumpy

Coogan's parents in knife raid

By GUY PATRICK

COMIC Steve Coogan was "sickened" last night after a machete-wielding gang terrorised his parents in their home.

Three men broke into Tony and Kathleen's house, where the star is a regular visitor, by hurling a slab of concrete through the patio doors at 6.15am.

Coogan . . . 'appalled'

They went up to the bedroom at Middleton, Greater Manchester, and woke the pair, forcing Tony, 66, to hand over his car keys. The gang then stole his Volvo V70.

Steve, 35 – spoof TV chat host Alan Partridge – is one of four sons and often speaks affectionately of his parents.

A source close to him said: "He's sickened and appalled. They are a very close-knit family."

Police called the attack "extremely cowardly".

LOTT AT STAKE

One winner has yet to claim half of Saturday's £6.1million Lottery jackpot. Numbers were 7, 18, 34, 37, 39, 42, bonus 21.

SUN SPOT

ANIMAL rescuer Marion Eastwood, 43, took sick calf Bauble into her home – and it **ATE** *£150 of cash and cheques in East Peckham, Kent.*

LAW GIRL ON RUN

PRETTY legal executive Victoria Dudson has gone on the run with a drug baron after he jumped bail during a court case.

Dudson, 22, met John Barber, 35, while she helped work on his defence. She fell pregnant after moving to another firm.

They are believed to be hiding in Spain.

Barber was convicted in his absence by Liverpool Crown Court – and five of his gang were also found guilty.

SUN SPOT

HALF the 7,500 people in Brecon, South Wales, have had nookie behind their partner's back, researchers for a TV sex documentary found.

The page from the *Sun* shown above has a number of design techniques which you could use in your own production.

- The page has an obvious lead story and a centre of visual interest.
- It has been set out in columns. A standard seven-column grid has been used, but has been varied for the main story.
- All pictures have been given captions in a consistent style.
- Headlines are prominent.
- Taglines, e.g. 'But monster spat me out, says diver', act as extra headlines.
- Shorter stories have smaller headlines so that they do not compete with the lead story.
- Highlighting techniques are varied. There is white on black, upper case type, underlining, and background tint.
- There are NIBS – news in brief – here labelled and boxed as 'Sun Spots'.
- One lead paragraph is given extra emphasis with bold print.
- Direct speech is used in stories and in headlines and captions.
- There is an example of a crosshead (mini-headline within a story) used to break up the text.

Activity

Produce a double-page spread for a tabloid newspaper. It should contain at least four original photographs, two main stories and several brief stories.

Evaluation

Use the checklist above as a basis for evaluating your work.

You should outline the aims and purposes of the production with particular reference to target audience and any pre-production research into the audience and/or the topics you wrote about.

Describe all the problems you encountered and how you attempted to solve them.

Point out the strengths and weaknesses of your production.

Set up a focus group representative of your target audience and note its opinions of your final production.

Designing magazine covers

You should study a range of magazine covers and determine what they have in common and how and why they differ.

CASE STUDY CASE

Case study

Here are two magazine covers from publications that aim at slightly different target audiences.

Both *Empire* and *cd:uk* have these features:

1 A main image featuring celebrities. In each case the eye contact with the reader is direct.

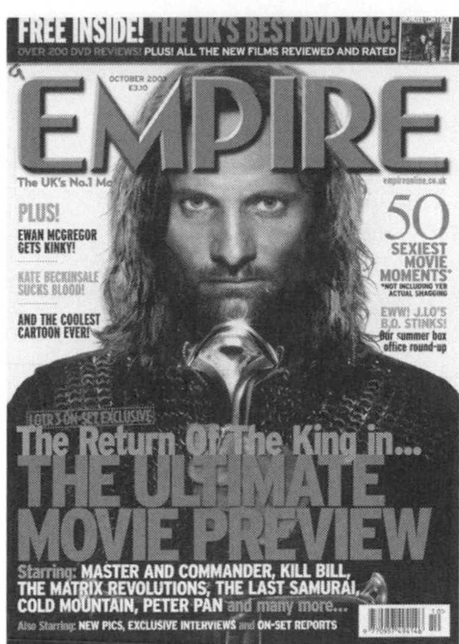

Empire Oct 2003

cd: uk July 2001

2 For readers in doubt about what type of magazine each is, there is information in or next to the title. ***Empire***, which in itself is or was a common title for a cinema, usually has: 'The UK's No.1 movie magazine'. In the example shown (October 2003) part of this is obscured but above the title it says 'Plus! All the new films reviewed and rated'. The cd in the other title is self-explanatory, but it has a circle around the letters to signify a disc.

3 Both magazines have information about date of publication and selling price.

4 Each magazine informs potential readers that sex is a topic covered inside.

Empire '50 SEXIEST MOVIE MOMENTS'
cd:uk: 'I wear a dress at home!' a1 answer your Qs - cripes!

'Cripes' suggests ***cd:uk*** is addressing a younger audience.

5 Next to these lines are inducements to buy. ***Empire*** boasts of 'OVER 200 DVD REVIEWS' , while ***cd:uk*** offers 6 massive posters. This again suggests a younger audience than ***Empire***.

6 Both covers have lists of contents expressed as either questions or exclamations suggesting mystery or excitement on offer. Again there is an emphasis on celebrities.

'EWAN MCGREGOR GETS KINKY!' (***Empire***)

Destiny's Child 'We just can't fancy Robbie!' Discover why on page 14.... (***cd:uk***)

The main difference is in the tone of the language. cd:uk is much more colloquial with phrases such as 'oo-er missus', 'celeb shindigs' and 'Yer name's not down? Yer not comin' in!'

7 The ***cd:uk*** cover has more happening on it with a wide range of font styles, many more celebrity names and more pictures, suggesting vitality perhaps. ***Empire*** uses a more restrained layout imitating the style of a movie poster, trying to suggest quality and maturity.

Activity

Produce a cover for a new magazine.

Decide what sort of magazine it is and what its target market will be.

Think of a suitable title and choose or design font styles which will go with it.

Take original pictures to feature on your cover or modify someone else's images. You should be able to explain in detail why these images will attract potential buyers from your target markets.

Include specific 'reasons to buy' – an exclusive story/interview or a giveaway for instance.

Briefly indicate the kinds of content which will attract readers and make these sound exciting or intriguing with your cover lines.